Coping with Turkey

MW01101351

Coping with Turkey

Simon Cole

Basil Blackwell

Copyright © Simon Cole 1989

First published 1989

Basil Blackwell Ltd
108 Cowley Road, Oxford, OX4 1JF, UK

Basil Blackwell Inc.
432 Park Avenue South, Suite 1503
New York, NY 10016, USA

All rights reserved. Except for the quotation of short passages for
the purposes of criticism and review, no part of this publication
may be reproduced, stored in a retrieval system, or transmitted, in
any form or by any means, electronic, mechanical, photocopying,
recording or otherwise, without the prior permission of the
publisher.

Except in the United States of America, this book is sold subject to
the condition that it shall not, by way of trade or otherwise, be lent,
re-sold, hired out, or otherwise circulated without the publisher's
prior consent in any form of binding or cover other than that in
which it is published and without a similar condition including this
condition being imposed on the subsequent purchaser.

British Library Cataloguing in Publication Data

Cole, Simon
    Coping with Turkey.
    1. Turkey – Visitors' guides
    I. Title
    915.61'0438

    ISBN 0–631–16352–2
    ISBN 0–631–16559–2 Pbk.

Library of Congress Cataloging in Publication Data

Cole, Simon, 1949–
    Coping with Turkey / Simon Cole.
        p. cm.
    Includes index.
    ISBN 0–631–16352–2
    ISBN 0–631–16559–2 (pbk).
    1. Turkey.   I. Title.
DR417.C64 1989
956.1'038 – dc 19   88–31896
                                                                      CIP

Typeset in 10 on 11½ pt Garamond
by Opus, Oxford
Printed in Great Britain by Billing & Sons Ltd, Worcester

Contents

Contents

Acknowledgements

I would like to express my warmest thanks to all the people who have given me assistance in so many ways in the preparation of this book, and especially to: Dr Candan Eralp, Dr Tülay Özsoy, Atanur Oğuz, Mehmet Epsiteti, Ali Coşkun, Doğan Tamer, Engin Sagalier, Patricia Roberts, Muammer Ülker, İnci Salıkgil, Bayram Mülayim, Dr Ali Tekin Çelebioğlu, Mustafa Yörük, Hilda Simpson, Mary Kelly, Patricia Bellotti, Iris Rafferty, Anette Rayner, Ursula Biggers, the family Syer, Oral Tezcan, Naci Ural Oğuz, Sümer Erdem, Professor Ergün Toğrol, Professor Meral Korzay, Namık Kemal İzler, Desmond Whittall, Professor Metin Sözen, Sami Gök, Paul van Wijk, Altan Akat, John Ohta, Leyla Karahan, Adrian Woodhouse, Sheila Austrian, Osman and Karen Kutay, Ian White, John and Wendy Perrott, Ferit Epikmen, Mustafa Mızrak, Necati Kayım, Atilla Midilli, Uğur İnci Çiloğlu, Gogan Sevim, M. Esra Tokar, Guven Terzioğlu, Dr Nurettin Yardımcı, Sensu Yımscı, Besim Tibuk, Matthew Austin, Carolyn Porter, Miss M. Kılıçaslan, Ziya Kılıç, Mrs Nehir Chadwick, Emma Armitage, Fatma Arzık, Paul O'Connor, Robin Culpin and the staff of Salford's Broadwalk Library, Ahmet Ersoy, Ahmet Doğukan, Andrew Hamilton, Andrew Kaye, Anne Collins, Anne Peacock, Barlas Küntay, Biltin Toker, Bruce McGowan, Çelik Gülersoy, Dominick Henry, David Bennett, Tarkan Yavuz, The Ven. Geoffrey Evans, Tony and Rose Barragay, Ümit Niron, V.J. Henderson, Yavuz Büyükdemir, Robert Langley, Philip Thomas, Lavinia White Property Management, Chris Clark, David Tonge, Dr J.R. Evans, E. Düzgünoğlu, Fiona Chapman Purchas, Fiona Sewell, John Lee, Janet Douglas, John Gallaher, John Mallins, Tim Auger, Geoff Howard, Adem and the

Çolpan family, Yüki Kartal, Ken and Brenda Hack-
ett, Angela Naylor, Tahsin Ozmen, Joanna Wilkins.

I would also like to express my especial appreciation to the Prime Ministral Directorate of Press and
Information. When they learned I was working on
this book they invited me to Turkey and made it
possible for me to meet so many people who enabled
me to make the book that much more authoritative.
For any errors and omissions I alone am responsible.

My most sincere thanks go to two companies
whose generous stand-by facilities enabled me to
travel to and from Turkey to check on the detailed
research for this book.

To the Falcon Leisure Group and their Air 2000, I
owe the accuracy of Chapters 13,14 and 18 to 21 in
particular.

To Horizon Holidays and their Orion Airways, I
owe the accuracy of chapters 15 to 17 and 22 to 25 in
particular. Their most courteous, helpful and welcoming staff at airports and on planes made the
business of flying so pleasant.

My special thanks to Semih Balcıoğlu, one of the
country's most respected caricaturists, for his illustra-
tions for the book and for the silhouette on the cover
representing historical and modern Turkey.

Preface

Turkey is attracting a great deal of interest these days, and the reasons are threefold. First, there is now a policy of actively promoting tourism and attracting travellers. Secondly, the economy has been opened up to foreign investment in anticipation of a favourable response to an application to join the EEC. The third reason is that Turkey has been 'discovered'. Word has got around that here is a land of vast open spaces, beautiful scenery, sunny beaches and delightful people waiting to welcome you.

This book is designed to help in understanding the many facets of a country rapidly changing from an eastern and oriental orientation to a twentieth-century European. With such a huge country, and so many cultural differences from our own, the scope of the material that could have been included in this book was enormous. The selection has been entirely mine, with the main criterion being that it promotes comprehension and helps the country come alive for the reader.

I hope it may be useful both to business people considering what Turkey has to offer, and to the tourist and traveller who wishes to get the most from his or her time there. In return for the few hours it takes to read this book I hope you will gain something, not only of what it has taken me many years of travel in the country to learn, but also of the experience of the many visitors and expatriates who have given me so much assistance.

If I have drawn back the veil on a few of Turkey's little secrets, I hope my many Turkish friends will accept that it is done solely in the interest of greater understanding between their country and the English-speaking world.

Getting There

Getting to and into Turkey is extremely easy these days; travellers, tourists and business people arrive in their thousands each week by air, sea, road and rail.

Turkey's overseas Tourism and Information Offices have a very good series of regional guides and information booklets which they will send on request. (See p. 257.)

Partly because the unfavourable exchange rate means they have to operate on a limited budget, and partly because of the enormous interest in the country, it is often very difficult to contact these offices by telephone.

Before you go

Visas

Holders of passports issued by Commonwealth and EEC countries and the United States of America do not need visas for a stay of up to three months. Theoretically this can be extended on application to the Ministry of Foreign Affairs, but nobody ever carries out this very bureaucratic procedure: they simply go out and come in again.

Vaccinations

No vaccination certificates are required, except for visitors from affected areas. The World Health Organization considers there is nothing to be particularly afraid of in Turkey and it groups it with the other Mediterranean areas where too much sun and a change of food and water are likely to prove the greatest hazards. However, anyone planning to go to the more remote parts of central and eastern Anatolia is well advised to have cholera, typhoid and tetanus vaccinations, although the diseases are fairly rare now. Similarly, take malaria pills to the Adana region.

Pets must have a rabies vaccination certificate, translated into Turkish, which has been validated by a Turkish Consulate.

Insurance   Medical treatment is not free and health insurance is highly recommended. Rates are the same as for other European countries, as indeed are the rates for baggage insurance, which is usually included on the same policy.

After reading the section on medical services you may decide that a policy that gets you home by air ambulance in the event of a serious emergency is a wise if expensive precaution. Many expatriates consider it to be vital.

Customs   Visitors arriving as tourists or for business will find the customs formalities as easy as in any Common Market country. It is advisable to ensure that a customs officer records in your passport any particularly valuable items such as radios, cameras and electronic equipment to ensure there are no problems on leaving. Strictly speaking they are in any case supposed to do this to stop you selling these items in Turkey, but with economic liberalization has come an easing of the restrictions.

By air

Scheduled   Regular services by Turkish Airlines (THY), British
flights   Airways and several other major carriers fly direct to Istanbul, Ankara and İzmir from the major European airports. Travellers from the Americas usually change at London or Frankfurt. First-class passengers on THY have the use of the Servisair executive lounge at Heathrow airport.

Charters   Charter flights are quite widely available in the summer and the cost-conscious traveller should shop around the agents (pp. 255–6). Falcon Leisure claim to be the pioneer charterers, and their flights from Manchester and Gatwick to Istanbul, İzmir and Dalaman are considerably cheaper than scheduled fares. Torosair, a new Turkish company with just three planes, operate twice weekly charters from Gatwick to Istanbul which is very good value. They can be contacted via Sunquest and you are likely to have an owner-driver – the operations director is the chief pilot. Horizon Holidays makes inexpensive flight-only arrangements through its Orion Airways.

Many people will be travelling on packages, since the industry really started to get off the ground in 1987. On the whole these tend to be much as described in the brochure, as it is Turkish policy to exercise strict quality control over burgeoning tourism.

Package tours

Should you happen to have your own plane you will be welcomed in Turkey. The machine will be allowed to stay for three months, which can be extended on application to the customs office. Turkish air traffic control advises private pilots to follow international air lanes and navigation rules.

Private planes

Travel time to the centre from Ankara airport is about forty minutes, and from Istanbul airport about thirty minutes. There are plenty of taxis at airports, and regular local and airline buses. At the tourist airports, which tend to be in fairly remote areas, there are taxis with fixed fares to the main resorts and towns. Tour companies lay on buses for their regular transfers.

Travel from airports

Driving takes about five days from the channel ports – and that is keeping to quite a fast schedule. The worst part is the long, straight and rather dangerous stretches through Yugoslavia. Europeans do not need a visa for Yugoslavia; Australians, New Zealanders, Canadians and Americans need a transit visa, good for seven days and free on the border. Everyone needs transit visas for Bulgaria. These should be obtained from a consulate in advance, they cost a contribution to the Bulgarian hard currency fund of £5, and you need one for each direction. Theoretically forty-eight-hour visas are available for an even greater hard currency contribution at the border, but you must expect a long wait. Be careful not to get caught in a radar speed-trap in Bulgaria – it takes a long time

By car

to return to the nearest town to find a bank to change money to pay the fine!

On entering Turkey the particulars of the vehicle are stamped in your passport, and the vehicle can remain in the country for up to three months. It can be taken out and brought back in only once, so the maximum time you can have a foreign-registered car in the country is six months.

A driving licence from an EEC country or an international licence must be shown, and it is advisable, though not strictly required, to have with you the car registration document. Either a Green Card insurance document endorsed in Turkey (European or Asian) must be produced, or third-party insurance can be taken out from one of the agency offices at the border.

Members of the AA, RAC and most of the European motoring organizations automatically get the facilities of the Turkish Touring and Automobile Club (TTOK) on production of their membership card. The AA sends a very informative pack on request and suggests you contact your local Turkish Tourist Information Office, well before leaving home, for an information sheet about the TTOK. Visitors from non-European countries planning to drive in Turkey should consider joining one of the reciprocating motoring organizations, or joining the TTOK on arrival.

By coach   There are regular coach services from Paris, Milan, Geneva, Metz and Munich to Istanbul, with connections from other cities. These are run by the Bosfor and Varan companies, part of the Eurolines consortium. They are an inexpensive, if rather tiring, means of getting there.

By train   Alas, the romantic Orient Express from London, Victoria, to Istanbul – the Stambul train beloved of writers, artists and film-makers – no longer runs. But then it never did, and was always a succession of connecting trains. However, the good news for lovers of train travel is that the extremely luxurious, but thus very expensive, Simplon-Orient Express leaves Victoria for Venice once or twice a week depending on the season. From Venice there is a connection with Sealink's MV *Orient Express* to Istanbul. Alternatively you could change at Venice to the daily Istanbul Express train, which arrives in Istanbul on the morning of the third day; three times a week the service is by luxury wagons-lit.

From Munich and Vienna there are two services to Istanbul daily, by the Bauern-Orient Express and the Balkan Express, which connect up with the Venice train at Belgrade.

By boat

Cruises

For quite a number of people the first taste of Turkey will be with one of the many cruise ships that call at the Mediterranean and Aegean ports. The time ashore is usually well organized, but cruise passengers should not be afraid of striking out on their own for a few hours – even getting away from the touristic areas and seeing a bit of real Turkey.

MV *Orient Express* leaves Venice on Saturday evenings for a three-day cruise to Istanbul, reaching Kuşadasi the following day. Reservations can be made through Sealink in London.

For those not wishing to drive all the way, Turkish Maritime Lines run car ferry services during the May to September period from Venice and Ancona to İzmir. (See p. 257.)

If you like island hopping, you can take ferries from Athens to the Aegean Greek islands and cross into Turkey from Chios to Çeşme or from Samos to Kuşadasi on the limited summer-only service, or every day except Sunday from Cos to Bodrum or Rhodes to Marmaris. Some of the crossings are quite interesting, with cars lashed to the decks of small wooden boats. There is also a regular crossing from Cypriot Famagusta to Mersin on the south-east Mediterranean coast.

Private yachts

On entering Turkish waters, yacht owners must take the ship's registration certificate and ownership papers to the nearest port with customs facilities. Boats can stay for up to three months. On reaching port they must also obtain health clearance, present a passenger list with passports to the port security authorities, clear customs and obtain a transit log from the harbour master's office. Only two crew changes are permitted so as to prevent illegal chartering. Those who have more than two parties of friends visiting them have to go out of Turkish waters and come in again. Certain marinas are licensed for foreign yachts to remain for periods of up to two years.

When in Turkish waters the authorities are very strict that a Turkish courtesy flag is flown from 8 a.m. to sunset. It is important that the flag has the moon and star in the right relationship, since in the wrong position they can become the Turkish flag of pre-republic days. Some flags made in Greece are inaccurate and it is not unknown for a strong request to be made for them to be changed immediately. It is also considered important that the ensign flies higher than the courtesy flag – which presents problems for some owners of two-masters with the ensign on the mizzen mast.

International navigation rules should be observed, and it is inadvisable to zigzag between Greek and Turkish waters. Mooring is forbidden in the entrance to the Dardanelles, the northern part of the Bosphorus, the Gulf of İzmit, the approaches to the port of İzmir and certain other military and sensitive areas. The complete list, which in fact comprises places where you would in any case be unlikely to want to go, will be given to you on arrival. Once the formalities are completed – and although at first they seem to be rather complicated, the authorities tend to be very flexible in practice – you will find you have arrived at the most idyllic of sailing coasts.

What to bring with you

If you really cannot live without bacon or sausages then it is as well to bring some with you. Pigs and pig products are not banned, but they are forbidden in the Islamic religion and they are just not around. Most Turkish people will not be offended if you eat pork in front of them, and may sometimes ask if they can join you.

Most of the common makes of 35 mm colour film are readily available, but it is difficult to find any black-and-white. Whilst other film sizes are around it sometimes takes quite a time to find a place selling them, so it is as well to bring a supply.

Maps are not always readily available, so if you have any it is worthwhile taking them with you. Those travelling by car should make sure they collect their free road-map at the border, which shows the latest additions to the road system.

Instant coffee – Nescafé – can now be bought in every supermarket, but it is expensive. Aficionados claim it is not like the stuff they are used to at home, and the customs limit is 100 g. You will not find Marmite, Vegemite or mincemeat (for Christmas mince pies) on sale, and breakfast cereals are not widely available and are expensive. The sort of tea you may have been used to at home is very expensive indeed. If tea is your drink then be sure to bring with you some of your favourite blend.

Most pharmaceutical products found in Europe are made in Turkey under licence. However, the brand names may be different from any medicines you regularly take and it is as well to bring supplies with you. As an alternative bring the prescription, which can then be matched up in the pharmacy.

Dried baby food is sold in chemist's shops, but the processed varieties cannot be found. Those who know about such things maintain that Turkish-made disposable nappies do not adequately serve their purpose.

Most car makers have agencies, usually in Istanbul, where spares can be obtained. It is as well to get the name and address from your local distributor before taking the car to Turkey, and even then you may well find some gaps in the range of parts available. Obvious things like fan belts and light bulbs should be taken with you. The exceptions are for the Fiat 500, the 1.6 and 2 litre models of Fords Taunus and Cortina, and Renaults 9, 11 and 21, which are made in Turkey under licence. Spares for these are readily available. So they are, too, for all models of Mercedes, who have a Turkish subsidiary, Otomarsan, which was established to service the cars brought back from Germany by returning guest workers, and which is now a major car and commercial vehicle producer. The latest Jaguar and Land Rover models are assembled in Istanbul and the companies may be able to provide a limited range of spares.

Whatever the purpose of your visit, a call at the Tourist Information Office in the main town on arrival is a useful exercise. These government-run offices are marked with the international information symbol, a large dotted I. They should not be confused with commercial enterprises that offer information as an inducement to buying their products.

Brochures of the various sites and regions are sometimes out of stock, especially in the smaller offices, so if you see one that may be of interest later, take it while you have the chance. In the information offices you will usually find staff who take great pride and pleasure in all the diversity of their country, and will be only too happy to tell you all about it.

The Feel of the Country

'The visitor comes from God' and 'my house is your house' – two old Turkish sayings which go a long way towards summing up the reception of visitors. Hospitality to travellers that asks for nothing in return is a tradition carefully guarded. A smile goes a long way, and if your overriding impression of the country is of the welcome meted out by the people, then they themselves will be content.

Turkey is a vast and beautiful country, stretching from Greece and Bulgaria in Europe, to Russia, Iran, Iraq and Syria in Asia. It is a land of contrasts with wide regional variations. You may see a gnarled old farmer leading his cow along the road, equally dutifully followed by his wife; but nowadays, unless you have managed to get right off the beaten track, the little procession is likely to have traffic roaring past it.

Your first impression of the country is much more likely to be how similar to the rest of Europe it is. In dress, manners and attitudes, the people in the cities and the tourist areas have turned away from the east and towards the west. Turkey is hoping to become a full member of the EEC (AET in Turkey) in about ten years. But the cities and the villages are like different worlds in different centuries, being brought together by the great leveller – television.

Present position

From time immemorial Turkey has been the ground on which west meets east, where Islam meets Christianity, and where the differences between these cultures either coexist or conflict. Since the formation of the republic it has, with a considerable measure of success, striven to ensure that relations are harmonious. In fact Turkey is these days carving out a role

for itself as the 'honest broker', a role based on its geographical and cultural position.

Turkey, already an associate member of the EEC, follows Common Market directives rather more scrupulously than some of the full members. It is a founding member of the Council of Europe, the World Bank and the IMF. As a member of the United Nations it participates in the activities of the UN's specialist agencies.

There is a certain sense of pride in Turkey's membership of NATO, a sense of belonging to the

club. It has the longest borders of any member with
Warsaw Pact countries, and the second largest number of troops – as you will see. Largely because of
national service, young uniformed soldiers seem to be
all over the place.

Individuals and the government are extremely
sensitive to anything that appears critical, often
making it very difficult to offer what is intended as
constructive or helpful advice. This sensitivity may
appear sometimes as arrogance, but in reality it comes
from an insecurity which has its origins in the
youthfulness of the republic.

Under the Ottoman Empire a person might have
thought of himself or herself as a Muslim, a subject of
the Sultan or a native of a particular region. The last
thing a person considered himself or herself to be was
a 'Turk', a term used by the elite to refer dispara-
gingly to peasants. In a few short years from 1923,
Mustafa Kemal, almost singlehandedly, caused the
unified republic to be created and engendered a
national pride in the state that has been carried
forward to this day.

**Formation of
the republic**

When he became president, Mustafa Kemal Atatürk immediately instituted a series of reforms. The
state was secularized and a new legal code, based on
the Swiss, was brought in. The fez, the traditional
headgear and symbol of Ottoman power, was
actually banned – technically it still is, and it is
virtually impossible to persuade a Turk to put one on,
even in fun. The foundations were laid of an
infrastructure to enable the country to compete
economically in the markets of Europe. A manifestation of this today is the excellent bus system based on
interchanges in every town.

Arabic script was replaced by a version of the
Roman alphabet, which makes it one of the only
Middle Eastern countries where the average west-
erner can read the the street signs. Mustafa Kemal also
supported a decree making it obligatory for every
family to take a surname. His own was, by acclamation, Atatürk – 'father of the Turks'. You will still see
his picture everywhere.

There have been three setbacks in the republic's development. At the outset only Atatürk's Republican People's Party was permitted to take part in political activity, but after the last war the system became more democratic with the formation of a second party. This, the Democratic Party, had by 1960 become so all-pervading that the fledgling democratic system appeared to be under threat. The army took over the government's executive role, under the provision Atatürk had written into the consitution that gave the army the ultimate responsibility for the protection of both democracy and the constitution itself. Many of the Democratic Party's leaders were tried on charges of violating the constitution, and found guilty. The former prime minister, Adnan Menderes, was hanged in an act of deterrence that has since been regretted. Fresh elections were held the following year under a new constitution that provided for a more clear-cut bicameral parliamentary system.

There was another break in the democratic evolution in 1970, when it was felt the governing party was exceeding the powers granted to it under the constitution. Senior military officers entered the broadcasting stations and made a remarkably brief statement to the nation. The government resigned and elections were held. Democracy was restored under the watchful eyes of the officers.

In the late seventies the two parties, in both the National Assembly and the Senate, were so split they had effectively ceased to govern; they also refused to work together in the lower house to such an extent that they were unable to elect a speaker. The standard of living plummeted for working people as the economy ran out of control, with inflation over 100 per cent. Meanwhile left-wing sympathizers, spurred on, it is thought, by certain foreign governments, were attempting to destabilize the country through the medium of Armenian terrorists. Simultaneously extreme Muslim fundamentalists and neo-Nazi activists were engaging in urban terrorism. In the end it became unsafe to go out in the streets. It was almost coup by acclamation when the army took over the administration in September 1980; it was certainly to the considerable relief of the population at large.

The constitution was revised and the changes approved by a referendum. The main change was the move to the present arrangement of a single-chamber parliament (Grand National Assembly) of 400 members. This was to shorten the legislative process, and to that end also, the annual recess was reduced to three months. The parliament now runs for a fixed term of five years between elections. Charges were laid against those who had committed crimes under the old constitution, and the then political leaders were banned from office: this ban was lifted in 1987 after a referendum.

General Evren, the military leader, resigned his commission and was elected president. Democratic elections held in 1983 brought Turgut Özal, leader of the Motherland Party and a former World Bank economist, to the office of prime minister. He went to the country again in 1988 when his party – Social Democratic with strong Thatcherite overtones – gained a large majority.

There will be enormous sighs of relief throughout the country if 1990 passes without a fourth break in the present pattern of stability.

You are bound to hear the stirring national anthem, if only when the TV goes off. It and the flag are the outward symbols of the republic and are highly respected. Turkish people stand when their anthem is played – you should too.

Attitudes and lifestyles

The contrasts between city and village are paradoxical, and latterly the tourist areas have produced what has become almost a third culture. There is great wealth and, at least by comparison, areas of poverty. But Turkey is not, and never has been, a class society. It has always been a meritocratic society and the present social mobility and improving education system are reinforcing that. There is an elite as in any other society – it tends to be centred on Istanbul – but it is based on merit and education, as well as on conspicuous consumption. And it is differences in attitude and life-style, particularly where women are concerned, that mark these distinctions.

You may see sophistication in the cities, and yet travel only a few miles to a village to find the simple life that has remained unchanged for centuries. Where tourism is taking off there is a new phenomenon: a get-rich-quick attitude that may soon result in tourists feeling hassled.

Turkey's is a very youthful population, with over 50 per cent under twenty years old. Many of them are trying hard to learn English, in keeping with the drive towards westernization. You are likely to be approached by young people, often students, who want to take you under their wing, act as guide and interpreter, and help you see their country. It is likely they are not looking for any reward but are extending the tradition of hospitality; and at the same time taking the opportunity for some English practice.

The Turkish people are by nature optimistic, and honour sometimes takes precedence over truth. A manifestation of this is that you are likely to be told of something as though it were in existence, when in reality it is only at the planning stage. There is also sometimes considerable difference between those things that are 'theoretically' possible and actual practice.

The first impression of a visitor entering the country may well be of a vain, proud, even arrogant people. If any of these impressions remain on closer acquaintance, they are more than compensated for by the Turks' natural warmth and generosity.

Because of the exchange rate – the *lira* has been allowed to fall as inflation has taken off (see p. 20) – by any western standards Turkey is very inexpensive. This means, of course, that there is a considerable difference in spending power between visitors and Turks. Stated bluntly – in relative terms when you are there you are rich. Yet it is very rare indeed to find any bitterness or jealousy. The Turks take the attitude that their visitors may well have material wealth, but they have beautiful countryside, good food and good people.

It is also notable that there is no colour prejudice

whatsoever. This possibly stems from the fact that the present population is the result of successive waves of immigration, although all of that was a very long time ago.

Many people assume, because of the Islamic background, that Turkish people are Arabic. Although certain Arabic cultural traits have been adopted over the years, Turkish and Arabic people do not have common origins.

Should you be going for a holiday you will find sunshine, beautiful scenery and beaches, and enough sites and places of interest to occupy many months. If your visit is for business purposes you will find differences, perhaps sometimes even problems, but it is likely that your overriding impression will be of the determination that the Turkish business community will go into the twenty-first century on an equal footing with any in the world.

Above all, go there with an open mind. Do not expect to find everything as it is at home, and accept what you find on its own terms. That way you, as so many before you, are likely to have an enjoyable and profitable time.

Money Matters

The Turkish people are by nature a cash-preferring society. Tradition and historical usage, coupled with memories of the economic collapse of the late seventies, have left a certain distrust of cashless transactions. Nevertheless, a combination of the liberalization of the economy in recent years, Europeanization, and improved banking methods and communication, has meant that both business and travellers' transactions need be little different from elsewhere in the developed world.

The unit of currency is the Turkish *lira* (TL). Inflation is rife, though the perceived rate is probably considerably higher than the actual rate (see p. 20). The floating exchange rate tends to fall pro rata with inflation so to a visitor prices seem relatively stable.

Currency

Coins   There are coins of 5, 10, 25, 50 and 100 TL, but, even though the last of these have not long been in circulation, they are regarded as something of a nuisance, because inflation devalues them. You may occasionally see references to the *kuruş*, of which theoretically there are one hundred to the lira. With the current exchange rates these are virtually worthless and they have not been in circulation since the late seventies.

Notes   The common notes are 100, 500, 1,000, 5,000, 10,000 and 20,000 TL. Perhaps because many people are unused to dealing with notes of such large denomination, and also because there is a slight similarity in size and colour, the 1,000 and 10,000 TL notes are sometimes confused by visitors. Particular care should be taken on arrival, especially if travelling by taxi. Notes, especially those of 100 TL, are often in very bad condition, and some places refuse to accept those that are almost unrecognizable.

Changing money

There is no limit to the amount of foreign currency that can be brought into the country, but not more than a hundred US dollars worth of Turkish liras can be taken in or out.

Most banks can obtain lira so a small amount may be obtained in advance for immediate use on arrival. This is particularly advisable if it is planned to enter by a land border as the change offices there do not usually offer the best rates, and may not always be open. However, and this is a general rule for a stay in Turkey, no more than the amount required for a couple of days should be exchanged at any one time because of inflation and the falling currency.

The convention for denoting decimals and thousands is the reverse of the British and American custom. In Turkey, the comma indicates a decimal point while a full stop is used to mark thousands. Thus 2.614,5 is two thousand six hundred and fourteen point five.

Eurocheques

Turkey has taken to the Eurocheque system with enthusiasm and most of the commercial banks that offer change facilities (*kambiyo*), and many hotels, will change them. It is certainly the most convenient way of obtaining currency. However, Turkish banks charge a commission of about £1 on each cheque, which makes the system quite expensive, as the issuing bank also charge a percentage when the debit is entered on a statement. Some Turkish banks insist on Eurocheques being written in German marks, Dutch florins or US dollars, which makes for additional cost and exchange variation if a further conversion is done back in British banks. Eurocheques and a card need to be ordered well in advance and travellers whose banks do not issue them often find it useful to open an account specially for the purpose.

Travellers cheques Thomas Cook and American Express travellers cheques are widely recognized and accepted in most banks and in tourist establishments. They can be in any hard currency. Türkiye Garanti Bankası act as refund agent for Thomas Cook, and Türk Ekspress for American Express. In the case of clearing banks that issue their own travellers cheques you may find that sample cheques have not reached branches of the Turkish banks and they may not be readily accepted.

Formalities It is essential to have your passport with you when changing money. Theoretically exchange slips should be retained to prove that purchases have been made with legally exchanged currency, and in case any moneys are to be changed back on leaving the country. However, as the currency markets are being freed from restrictions these slips are not often asked for.

Smaller and more remote towns often have only one bank that does foreign exchange. It is not always clearly marked and foreigners will be directed there by other banks.

Inflation In recent years inflation has proved a serious problem for both the expanding economy and the people. It is variously estimated at between 45 per cent and 85 per cent, and successive attempts to curb it have had little apparent effect. It is likely that the perceived rate is higher than the actual rate if, as many economic commentators maintain, inflation has become the orthodoxy. The lira floats downwards as inflation increases – to someone converting from a stable currency, prices remain roughly constant save for a slight downward drift.

Grey market The former black market is now known as the grey market and has been integrated into the economic system, with the rates quoted in the newspapers alongside the official rates. It is centred in the Tatakale area of the Istanbul bazaar and dealings are in hard currencies and mostly in cash. The effort is hardly worth it for the average traveller, and the differential between the two rates can vary widely and has been known to be negative. Anyone who dabbles in the grey market should be absolutely certain of the integrity of their guide.

Shop purchases made in hard currency notes will sometimes be converted at the grey market rate so it may be worthwhile taking some of your own currency into the country.

Credit and cash cards

Credit cards

The familiar plastic signs of the major credit card companies will be found displayed in shops, hotels and restaurants in large towns and in tourist areas. Iktisat Bankası has just started issuing the first Turkish credit card which is linked to the Visa system. Thus holders of Visa cards are likely to find wider acceptance than many of the others. American Express, Access and Master Charge are accepted in over 2,000 outlets. Although these are becoming more widespread they tend to be concentrated in the cities and tourist areas.

Cash dispensers

NCR automatic teller machines are being introduced into some of the major bank branches. It seems only a matter of time before they will be linked to the European banking system, and it may be worthwhile checking with your bank before leaving home to see if you cashcard will work in Turkey.

Credit transfers

Should you need to have personal funds transferred from abroad to a bank, the money will take four, five or more days to work through the system. It involves the payment of substantial fees and commissions, and is not to be recommended except in an emergency. If such an emergency does arise it is worthwhile arranging to collect the funds in Istanbul, where they have more experience of such transactions. You should also give your own bank the name of a specific branch to which funds are to be transferred, to avoid the transaction getting lost in the system.

In the case of business transactions, international credit transfers work in the same way as in other developed countries.

The banking system The present banking system has its roots in the foundation of the republic. For too long it operated under very rigid controls, and reflected the introspective and closed Turkish economy. However, from 1983 it was restructured on the European and American model and is now spearheading the liberalization of the economy currently taking place.

Central Bank The role of the Central Bank is now similar to that of the Bank of England or the Federal Reserve: it acts as the government's treasurer, financial agent and economic adviser. It has the power to regulate the money market and allocate, buy and sell foreign exchange. It also fixes discount and deposit rates, and sets reserve requirements and liquidity ratios for the commercial banks.

Commercial banks There are more than sixty commercial banks, many of which are state controlled, although it is thought these are likely eventually to move into the private sector. Banks tend to have regional or specialist orientation; thus Ziraat Bankası (Agriculture) has the prime function of mobilizing funds for all-important farming development, while the Vakiflar Bankası holds the pension funds, trusts and foundations which are the basis of what we might call social security. The latter also passes over a sizeable proportion of its profits to conservation projects. Interestingly, the oldest bank, the Ottoman Bank founded in 1863 as the central bank of the Ottoman empire, is an Anglo-French institution owned by bearer shareholders, whose ownership is thought now to be mainly in French hands. The twenty or so foreign banks that have recently started operating in Turkey usually have just one or two branches.

Opening hours Banks open between 8.30 a.m. and 5 p.m. Monday to Friday, and are closed for lunch from 12 noon to 1 p.m. Considerable paperwork is involved in the simplest transaction, with an amazing number of signatures required from both the customer and bank employees. Bank staff tend to be extremely courteous, and you will usually be offered a seat while you wait. Employment in a bank is considered to be a very good job, and the staff often speak English as a second language.

Most Turkish people use banks only to pay bills, and even a house purchase may be paid for with suitcases full of notes. Fixed term deposit accounts with a very high interest rate that may be in excess of inflation are designed to attract funds that would otherwise be deflating under the bed. Turkish people may also hold external accounts in foreign currencies and these are widely used as a hedge against inflation.

Cash accounts and credit

A Turkish person's signature is his or her bond. For this reason cheques are not widely used. If a cheque were to be bounced it would involve a complete loss of prestige and trust, apart from the fact that the person who signed the cheque would be barred from holding a bank account in future.

Some banks now operate consumer loans but the old system of the *sened*, governed by mutual trust and not the law, is preferred. It is used for anything from personal loans to credit from a shop for the purchase of electrical goods. The *sened* is a personal bond or promissory note and the actual document can be purchased from any stationer for a few lira. The lender and the borrower negotiate the fixed sum that will be paid for the loan – this is not interest, which was forbidden under the Ottoman Islamic law – and what will be repaid and when. The borrower then signs a *sened* form, over a stamp, for each repayment.

The lender can sell the *sened* at any time and the loan then becomes due to whoever is holding the document. The *sened* can also be deposited at a bank, which is obliged to give the face value on demand and will then set about recovering the debt. It is considered a sign of mistrust in the borrower if the loan is handed over to a bank.

Promissory notes are also widely used in business; some analysts maintain the market is awash with them. It is not unknown for businesses to resort to Mafia-style strong-arm tactics to recover debts.

Security and safety of money

Because of the exchange rates, foreigners are *de facto* extremely rich by Turkish standards. However, there is no resentment – 'You may have lots of money, but we have the most beautiful country', is an oft-heard remark – and there is relatively little risk in carrying large amounts of cash. In Istanbul it is wise to be careful as it is now a very cosmopolitan city. All hotels are obliged by law to have a safe in which valuables can be locked.

Stocks and shares

The stock exchange reopened in Istanbul in 1985. Its local importance is increasing as the privatization programme proceeds, but it is not yet a major source of investment funding. There is also an exchange in İzmir and it is thought likely this will develop slowly over the next five years. There is a government-led information programme to discourage the long-standing habit of individuals holding large amounts of gold and hard currencies; the hope is that these funds will be directed into commercial investment and possibly through the stock exchanges.

Hitting the big time

Every Turkish person seemingly dreams of being a multimillionaire. Ask them what they would do with all that money and the answer is often that they would buy a ticket to Britain or America! For most people the realization of these dreams is only likely to come through the football pools (*Spor-toto*), which operate on the same system as that found in the UK, or the national lottery (*Piyango*). Increasing numbers of *Piyango* ticket-sellers, paid on commission, can be seen in the streets and calling in on restaurants as the time approaches for the draw, held every ten days. Full tickets cost several pounds or dollars, but half and quarter tickets can be bought. If you think you might be one of the multimillion-lira prize-winners, check in the Turkish newspapers the day after the date of the draw printed on the ticket.

Geography, Climate and some Hazards

Thrace, that part of Turkey in continental Europe, comprises only a thirtieth of Turkey's total area. The Asian remainder is known as Anatolia (Anadolu in Turkish). It was known in classical times as the land where the sun rises, and scholars and historians frequently refer to it as Asia Minor. The country has seven distinct geographical regions.

Turkey has 4,500 miles (7,250 km) of coast and covers an area equal to France and Germany combined. The country is over 1,000 miles (1,600 km) long and 425 miles (685 km) across the widest point, from the Black Sea to the Mediterranean. Its climate, and also its historical strategic importance, are much attributable to the varied topography and in particular to the location of the mountain ranges within it. These run on an east–west axis – the Taurus mountains (Toros Dağları) just behind the Mediterranean shore, and the pontic range (Kuzey Anadolu Dağları) similarly placed in relation to the Black Sea. They become higher towards the east and eventually meet, forming natural boundaries with Iraq, Iran and the Soviet Union. Within these natural barriers lie the Anatolian plateau and its river valleys. Here is concentrated most of the population.

Anatolian Plateau

The centre of Turkey is in the main a gently undulating plain, much covered today with fields of corn bordered by lines of tall poplars and cypresses. Tawny yellow patches of steppe country can be found to the north and east of Konya.

Cappadocia

These give way to the dramatic volcanic landscape of the Kayseri and Göreme region, the old Christian province of Cappadocia. Grapes have been grown here from time immemorial, and now modern methods of viniculture are being applied vineyards have become a dominant feature in the landscape.

Great volcanic cones, some as high as the French Alps, unexpectedly break out of the plains at random. Their higher slopes are covered with pine woods gradually thinning out to icecaps which in some areas remain frozen most of the time.

Ankara   Ankara is set in a natural bowl in the centre, bounded by hills. It has dry hot summers and cold but sunny winters with below average rainfall. Unfortunately the natural contours, coupled with a great deal of industrial activity and a large population that heats its houses with lignite (brown coal) mean that the air is very polluted. Winter smog gives way to summer dust.

Climate   The Anatolian plateau has a climate of extremes; hot and dry in summer, with the rains confined to the spring; cold in winter with sporadic snows. The summer heat is not uncomfortable because of the low humidity and the pleasant cool evenings.

The region is at its most attractive in spring, when the higher plains especially have a particular brilliance. Apple and cherry blossom are found in profusion, growing wild and in cultivated rows – the area is renowned for its fruits. Wild azaleas, iris, poppies and mallows add yet more colour to the vistas. Almond blossom perfumes the evening stillness. It is possible still to find the ruins of ancient and as yet unrecorded cities, wreathed with panoplies of wild flowers.

Later in the season wild peonies, orchids and fritillary lilies come into flower. Turkey has long been the place for the plant collector, and many of our garden plants have their wild origins here.

Eastern   Furthest east the Eastern Highlands rise to 16,000 feet
Anatolia   (4,800 m). Mount Ararat (Ağrı Dağı) the highest mountain, near the borders with both Iran and the USSR, is the presumed place of the landing of Noah's Ark. The tourist authorities have recently triumphed over military strategists and organized tours can now visit the site. In this region too are the sources of the

two great rivers that water the ancient fertile crescent of Mesopotamia, the Tigris (Dicle) and the Euphrates (Fırat nehri).

The climatic extremes are even greater here than those on the plateau. The summer to winter temperature range in eastern Anatolia is from −40 to +40°C.

Climate

The extremely hot and dry summers have a very low humidity. The evenings and nights are cool and can feel very cold, so suitable clothing should be taken. In the winter the area is often inaccessible, with snow several yards deep from October through to April. Whilst layers of warm clothes go without saying, thick hats and gloves should not be omitted from the essential winter clothing list. The towns of Erzurm and Kars, situated on high plains, feel even colder as they are exposed to the winds coming down from the Russian steppes.

At the southern land border with Syria the Taurus mountains give way to the Amanus range. Here you will find spectacular outcrops of rock, sometimes capped with the ruins of crusaders' castles that seem to cling precariously high in the air. The crusaders built the castles to protect their main citadel at Antioch (Antakya). This is an area of isolated mountain villages, reached by stony paths through narrow valleys and rough pasture. Unpleasantly hot in high summer, the valley floors and lower slopes nevertheless support orchards and subsistence farming.

South-east Anatolia

The whole of Anatolia is dotted with isolated lakes. Most of these have a very high salt content and are thus unsuitable for irrigation, and their leisure potential has not be exploited. Thus they remain, as yet, areas of wild and unspoilt beauty. In the east the spectacularly beautiful Lake Van (Van Gölü) covers an area of nearly 1,500 square miles (380,000 hectares) – more than six times the size of Lake Geneva. The lake was formed when an eruption of the now extinct volcano Nemrut Dağı blocked the flow of rivers to the west. The water is very alkaline and swimming in

Lakes

its brilliant blue waters leaves a pleasant silky feeling
on the skin.

Salt Lake (Tuz Gölü), south of Ankara, is a great
expanse of shallow marsh and water surrounded by
near-desert steppe. Its ill-defined banks mean that
care must be exercised when walking near the water,
but it is an ornithologist's delight.

The large and beautiful lakes Egridir Gölü and
Beyşehir Gölü can be seen alongside the road from
İsparta to Beyşehir, which swoops spectacularly
through the mountains and back to the lake shore.

Black Sea region
The Black Sea slopes of the Pontic mountains are
heavily forested; deciduous trees gradually give way
to conifers on the higher slopes. This area is a paradise
for botanists who even now are finding new species of
alpine plants. The temperate coastal strip is the
world's biggest producer of hazelnuts. Here too is
grown the strong tobacco that made Turkish
cigarettes much sought after between the wars. East
of Trabzon the mountains become loftier, more
rugged and more heavily wooded. Around Rize the
terraces of tea gardens seems barely to squeeze in
between the mountains and the sea. The rainfall levels
here are particularly suitable for the plantations.

Coastlands
The Black Sea coast has craggy cliffs and headlands
interspersed with sandy beaches. Legend has it that
these shores were the land of the Amazons whose
queen was supposed to have founded the village of
Sinop. The temperate climate means that the holiday
season runs only from May to September, and the
area does not get as crowded as the other coasts.

Mediterranean and Aegean regions
The Aegean and Mediterranean coasts are a mecca for
tourists. Pine, larch and cedar woods slope down to
sandy beaches or rocky coves. Villages, surrounded
by olive groves and almost inaccessible by land, lie by
the sea in craggy bays and inlets. Reed-edged lagoons
give secret access to the open water.

The Aegean coast has long, hot summers which
begin after a four-week spring in April. Warm
autumns continue through to November, and nearly

all the rainfall is confined to the cool, but not cold, winter months.

On the fertile coastal plains, fields of cotton and maize grow against a backdrop of scrubby outcrops of rock supporting patches of yellow gorse. Donkeys are tethered outside wisteria-covered farmhouses. The central reservation of the wide main *bulvar* of the little towns is usually filled with dusty wallflowers.

Further south, the Mediterranean coast, hotter and more humid in summer, is warm even in winter. The climate east of Antalya is subtropical. Here you will find orange, lemon, peach and apricot groves interspersed with banana plantations.

In the dry season, the carpets of pine needles and undergrowth in the forests get tinder dry. Particular care should be taken with cigarettes, matches and picnic stoves. Large areas of woodland are lost each year through accidental fires.

Forest fires

Swimming in the Aegean is possible from the end of April through to October, whilst on the Mediterranean coast it is only from December to February that it is too cold for a dip.

Swimming

Generally speaking, the country is so large that most wildlife is relatively untouched by current commercial development. However, the loggerhead turtles that every spring since the days of the dinosaur have been nesting on the beaches of this coastline are threatened by tourist development. The Turkish authorities are working with such bodies as the Nature Conservancy Council to try to protect their habitat. The turtles can be seen on remote stretches of beach when they are laying their eggs, and they should not be approached too closely. They have another problem in that they confuse the polythene used to force early crops, and subsequently allowed to blow into the sea, with the jellyfish on which they feed. This has unfortunate consequences for their digestive systems and often proves fatal.

Also threatened are the species of huge crickets and grasshoppers not found anywhere else in the world.

Endangered species

Much of the sand dune habitat in which they live is
disappearing under new hotels.

Whilst ecology is something of a new science in
Turkey, university departments are starting to be set
up. The first rumblings of a 'green' movement are also
starting to emanate from Istanbul. An assortment of
pressure groups, ranging from gays to radicals and
environmentalists, have formed themselves into a
properly registered Green Party, but a great deal of
their energy is devoted to resolving differences within
their own coalition.

Thrace and Marmara region

Thrace is generally drier than central Anatolia, and
less prone to climatic extremes. The centre and south
are very dry; the spring rains drain very quickly away
to the Mediterranean and the Sea of Marmara through
steep-sided valleys cut into the soft limestone. These
days it is an area of intensive meat and cereal farming.
The northern border with Bulgaria is formed naturally by the Istranca mountains which catch most of the
rain brought by the cool north winds across the Black
Sea. The sides of these mountains and the lower slopes
bordering the Black Sea used, as a result, to be
covered with thick forests. Some of these still exist,
the best known being the Belgrade Forest (Beograd
Ormanı) north of Istanbul and used for sport and
leisure purposes from Byzantine times. It has today
the important function of providing a lung for the
rapidly expanding metropolis of greater Istanbul.

Istanbul, the Bosphorus and the area round the Sea
of Marmara combine the best and the worst climatic
extremes. The hot summers are relieved by the north
wind, the *poyraz*; the winter is very changeable, with
periods of snow in most years alternating with cold
rain or warm sunshine. Spring is warm but wet.
Strong waterproof footwear is recommended, especially for Istanbul.

Forecasts are on both TV channels at 8.45 every
evening, and are presented in such a visual way that
they can be understood by non-Turkish speakers.
The forecast is also in English on Channel Two at
9.40 p.m. and in the *Turkish Daily News*.

From the foregoing can be gauged the variety of **Clothing**
different clothing required. As a general rule, the
further east you travel the greater the extremes of heat
and cold you will encounter. West and central
Anatolia have particularly hot summers with cool
evenings, and moderately cold winters. For the
summer on the northern coasts lightweight clothing is
needed, and tropical gear in the south.

In winter the international and tourist hotels and
middle-class houses tend to be extremely well heated,
so be prepared for some very hot nights. Simpler
accommodation, especially away from the main
towns, is often heated by potbellied wood- or
coal-burning stoves which leave hot and cold spots in
the room. Even in the cities it is, fortunately, still
common to find bars and restaurants heated by a
glowing, open charcoal-burning brazier. An easily
removable pullover or cardigan is useful to have to
hand. It is equally useful for the cooler summer
evenings when the stoves, with their stovepipes
snaking across the ceiling, and the polished brass
braziers, will have been removed.

Good shoes or boots are particularly recommended *Footwear*
since the wide expanses of open countryside seem to
inspire walking. For those intending to visit a lot of
mosques, where shoes must always be removed, and
houses in other than urban areas, where it is courtesy
to follow the convention, something that slips off
easily is a good idea.

In the countryside traditional customs still prevail, *Rural dress*
although how much longer they will survive is
another matter. Women are often veiled, are treated
with great respect, and will rarely be seen in public
places and never unaccompanied. The Turks' natural
courtesy, and their easygoing acceptance of foreigners, mean that visitors behaving in a manner likely
to affront will rarely sour the welcome. Nevertheless
it is prudent and courteous for women not to wear
bikinis or shorts in these areas, and men too may find
the welcome more comfortable if they do not wear
shorts and bare their chests.

Dress in the Turkish people in urban areas dress particularly well
towns on the whole, and with great style. Italian fashions are
extremely popular. For business and social relations it
is considered improper if a person has not taken the
trouble to dress appropriately.

If you are invited to dinner in a restaurant you will
find your hosts have dressed smartly for the occasion.
However, at the theatre, opera or concerts semi-
formal wear is the order of the day.

Young people wear slacks, jeans, sweaters and
shirts as anywhere else. Loose-fitting blousons or
windcheaters are very popular.

A collar and tie is preferable for men even on
semi-formal occasions. The tendency is to err
towards the British rather than the American concept
of formal dressing – suits rather than blazer and
flannels. Safari suits are worn for leisure occasions
and are regarded strictly as leisure wear. Dinner
jackets are needed only for a few government and
embassy functions.

For women, suits and dresses that would be
appropriate for the climate and occasion in Europe or
America are equally appropriate here. Regular
travellers to Turkey recommend a lightweight, loose-
fitting, crush-proof coat as part of the wardrobe.
Trousers are suitable for all but very formal occasions, and are very useful for sightseeing and visiting
mosques. The head should also be covered in
mosques, even those that are regularly visited by
tourists or have been converted to museums, since
there is no such thing as the deconsecration of a
building in Islam.

Hats Headgear has always been important for Turkish
men. Where national dress is still worn in the rural
areas, the material from which the head-dress is made
and the way it is worn reflect the status of the wearer.
The fez was made illegal on the formation of the
republic. Paradoxically the fez itself replaced the
turban, whose colour and shape denoted rank within
the Ottoman empire. Atatürk usually wore a flat cap,
which older men in the cities wear to this day.

As in all countries with an Islamic background, *Nakedness* nudism is frowned upon and nakedness is a cause of embarrassment. Nevertheless, as a concession to the tourist industry, there is a nudist beach at the Club Mediterranée Kemer near Antalya. This is a constant source of wonderment to most Turkish people and often referred to by Turkish comedians.

Women alone

For all that Turkey is a secular state, and for all that women have theoretically been emancipated for more than fifty years, it must be remembered that the background to and traditions of the society come from Islam, where the social lives of men and women are completely separate.

Family life and traditions are also still extremely important cultural influences. In the past, women were required to be submissive to men in authority over them; their father, and in his absence their brothers or any male relative to whom this role might be delegated, and then later the husband. The obverse side of this was that the woman's person and chastity would be vigorously protected. This latter relationship remains and it is rare to find an unchaperoned Turkish woman.

It follows that foreign women, who quite naturally carry out their own cultural practice of walking alone in the street, should beware that there is still the possibility that it will prove slightly hazardous. Certainly it was in the past, and bottom pinching and touching were prevalent. With the spread of understanding of western values and life-styles it is now less of a problem than hitherto. Reports vary considerably as to whether men make themselves a nuisance in the street or not.

It seems that the best advice is to look confident and purposeful, avoid looking lost, and, most important of all, try not to make eye contact. Clothing that might be considered provocative should be avoided except in the tourist coastal areas. A woman who accepts a present from a Turkish man, or is taken out, should expect that he will act possessively towards her. A Turkish man will no longer be shocked at a foreign woman's behaving, to Turkish eyes, immodestly – but he may well seek to take advantage of it.

With that proviso it can be said that many women feel safer walking alone in Turkey than they do in European and American cities. Turkish people are by culture law-abiding, a concomitant to the Muslim tradition.

Wild animals The hazards of the outback are easier to quantify and to deal with. One of the commonest animals, the mountain goat, scrambles elegantly away when approached. Wolves, lynx, bears, jackals, foxes and martens are hunted for their fur, and the occasional leopard is to be found in the remoter parts of the south-east. None of these is considered to be a danger to humans so long as they do not take to camping out alone in the wilds. Eagles and vultures are common in the east. If you are fortunate enough to have the opportunity to travel with nomadic people (*yörük*) in the remote parts of Anatolia then many of these species will be, if not seen, at least heard. Storks, whose nests can be seen in the most unlikely places on trees and buildings, make a wonderful sight over the Bosphorus as they migrate to the south in the autumn.

Rabbits and wild boar abound and are hunted for sport in the woods behind the Aegean and Mediterranean coastal plains. Boars will not attack unless provoked, or approached too closely when they are protecting their young. The male with its four tusks can inflict serious damage.

Snakes Snakes are common, especially the harmless Ringed Snake, one of the grass snakes. Several branches of the adder family, all venomous, are found in the south of the country – the Ottoman and Levant vipers have distinctive zigzag markings. The area round Urfa is notorious for its scorpions.

Sheep dogs The animals to steer furthest clear of are Anatolian sheepdogs, especially when they are working. They do not herd the sheep but guard them, particularly from wolves, for which they wear iron-spiked collars for their own protection. There are two species, one of which looks like a wolf itself, the other rather like a husky. They are extremely fast for their size – up to 90 lb (40 kg) in weight and 6 feet (1.8 m) tall when standing on their hind legs. They kill wolves by knocking them off balance with a running blow to the shoulder, then biting their throats. Whilst they are not known for attacking strangers, even foreigners to a village, they are extremely boisterous when just being playful.

Mosquitoes, midges and biting insects can be a serious nuisance. The bites are extremely vicious and as the venom seems to be peculiar to Turkey some visitors will find them extremely uncomfortable. If a bite becomes infected, medical help should be sought: since this is a not uncommon occurrence, doctors have suitable remedies.

Bites and stings

Prevention being better than cure, chemist's shops sell a preparation called Kov which, regularly splashed on the body and clothing, is effective in driving insects off. Mosquito coils which burn like incense can be obtained from hardware stores, as can a cheap electric eradicator which vaporizes an insecticide tablet. Old-fashioned mosquito nets over beds are becoming popular again.

The municipalities are working on a programme to limit the numbers of flying insects – men with gas masks can sometimes be seen spraying hedgerows and verges, using pressurized brass canisters. Needless to say, contact with these sprays should be avoided. In spite of the mosquitoes malaria has been eliminated; Turkey is not considered a danger spot by the World Health Organization.

When walking in open ground ankles and feet are best kept covered, as all sorts of biting insects are found in the grasses.

Other natural hazards

The risk of earthquakes is relatively high, about the same as in the southern parts of Greece and Italy. The

Earthquakes

main fault line runs south of Istanbul and north of
Ankara, parallel to the Pontic mountains where it
turns north. In seismological terms it is considered to
be equal to the San Andreas fault. Another fault runs
parallel to the Büyük Menderes Nehri, east of the
Aegean. The land is still settling and the last major
earthquakes centred on Turkey were in the east in 1976
and in the Aegean in 1983.

The British Overseas Development Administration
has been funding earthquake research in the area, but
at present not enough information exists to predict
future quakes. Cambridge University is also working
on a project to design quake-resistant rural housing in
eastern Turkey, and most modern buildings are
designed, if not built, to resist total collapse in the
event of a major disturbance.

Avalanches   Rainstorms can cause severe avalanches with devas-
tating consequences. Because their cause is so local-
ized they are very unpredictable, but fortunately they
are rare occurrences.

Artificial hazards

Lavatories   Indigenously the lavatories are, to put it delicately, of
the continental or squatter type. However, pedestal
models are now found in most middle-class houses
and all but the cheaper hotels. The small metal pipe
sticking out of the back of the bowl is to convert it to
multi-function equipment and serves the purpose of a
bidet. Trace the pipe to the wall and you will find a
tap – but beware turning it on too far. The narrow
bore of the pipe causes considerable pressure and an
unwary half turn can easily result in clothing wet in
embarrassing places, or a forceful jet of water in a
sensitive spot. If you adopt this method of personal
hygiene, you will quickly become an expert in
judging the local water pressure.

In some places you will find the Greek practice of
providing wastepaper baskets for used toilet paper.
However, in Turkey this is intended only for paper

that has been used for drying after performing the ritual described above.

The standard of cleanliness of the lavatories in public places varies considerably. The government and tourist organizations are trying very hard to get them all brought up to the level expected by their visitors, and there is no doubt this is slowly happening. There was a recent occasion when some expatriates decided to spend a weekend in a remote mountain village in the east. As they climbed, they noted another group some distance behind them carrying an object that glinted white in the sunlight. They were relaxing, exhausted, at their destination when the following party arrived and solemnly placed the porcelain lavatory bowl on top of the usual hole in the ground.

For those who do not find quite this level of hospitality the advice must be: if you see a good one, use it while you have the chance.

Ankara has smog in winter, but a British company is at present laying on natural gas to the city, which should result in a considerable improvement when the system is complete. Istanbul and İzmir also have serious air pollution, but they at least have winds from the sea to clear it away from time to time. The beaches around Istanbul and İzmir suffer from industrial pollution too, and many are no longer safe for swimming. *Pollution*

The pavements in the cities are very uneven and can be particularly treacherous, especially when wet. There are also unguarded cellar steps opening directly off the pavement, with a very dangerous and painful 12 foot (3.5 m) drop. It is an old custom to hold up your thumb in a 'thumbs up' gesture to claim a right of way, and theoretically this can be used on a busy street to stop the traffic to cross the road. It is not recommended you try it these days except if helping an elderly veiled lady across the road, when it is sometimes respected. *Pavements*

Passive smoking   Non-smokers must reconcile themselves in advance to the fact that they are going to inhale a certain amount of nicotine. Smoking is endemic in Turkey: even as you walk down the street the backwash from the person ahead, wreathed in smoke, is impossible to dodge. In the more expensive restaurants it may just be possible to avoid the smoke, but in buses and public places generally the air is usually thick. A non-smoking campaign, with advertisements in newspapers and on television and poster sites, is just getting under way. It has a great deal of ground to cover.

Government, Administration and the People

The average visitor may have little direct contact with the central government and local authorities. If you get away from the beaten track, however, it is quite likely that you will come across village assemblies or a local election campaign. An understanding of the rather complicated system under which they are taking place is necessary to appreciate what is going on. If you get the opportunity to witness a village assembly it should not be missed – it is an excellent example of real grass-roots politics in action.

Prospective business people will soon discover the importance of making contact with all the many levels of administration likely to be concerned with any project. This particularly applies where consents or planning approval are necessary. It is important to be aware of one fundamental difference from the system you may be used to: in Turkey the various levels of local and central administration do not have clearly defined areas of responsibility. Any request or application tends to go up the chain until it reaches someone prepared to take responsibility.

National Government and administration

Since the foundations of the republic were laid in 1923, the series of regimes, both military and civilian, have kept broadly to the principles laid down by Atatürk.

When an elected government took over from the military in 1983, one of its first acts was to revise the constitution so that the system has the separation of powers found in most western countries. Since then two free elections have been held, Turkey is working towards acceptance of its application for full membership of the EEC, and future stability is fervently hoped for by the majority of the population. There are still some restrictions on human rights and press freedom, perhaps no worse than in many developing countries, which are designed to protect the fragile democracy.

The government is now democratic and elected by universal suffrage. It also has the distinction of being the only secular state in the Islamic world.

Parliament and leaders
The legislative body and single-chamber parliament is the Grand National Assembly. It is composed of members, known as deputies (*milletvekili*), elected from parties under a system of proportional representation.

The National Assembly elects a president for a term of seven years. The president's prime function is as head of state, with duties and powers generally very similar to those of the British monarch, but also with powers to enact decrees in certain circumstances without reference to the government, which are not dissimilar to those of the French president.

The prime minister, by convention the leader of the majority party, is appointed by the president. The prime minister then nominates a list of ministers for ratification and appointment by the president. A council of ministers – the equivalent of the British cabinet – is collectively responsible for implementing the government's policy.

Bureaucrats
The administration – the civil service – is given a specific role by the constitution. In theory at least, it is strictly controlled both centrally and at local level. Turkey, but probably no more so than many developing countries, tends to have somewhat inflexible administration as a result and it can appear sometimes that the bureaucracy is more important than the end result. Some expatriate managers complain that there is in-fighting amongst factions of the bureaucracy and that foreign businesses occasionally get caught between them.

The State Planning Office is the branch of the administration most overseas business people will have dealings with. Whilst its title may conjure images of a totalitarian iron curtain regime, it is not quite like that: its main function is as the economic research branch of the administration. However, because of the entrenched power of the bureaucracy, it does fit rather uneasily into the liberal economic scheme of things that is the hallmark of the present government – especially since there is now a tendency to appoint special ministerial economic and political advisers.

The present government is committed to liberalizing *The economy* the economy and freeing it from many of the controls that previously prevented expansion and growth. The lira has been allowed to float, foreign investment is encouraged and subsidies to state enterprises have been gradually cut back.

The 60 per cent of the economy under state control is very gradually being privatized; but slowly, so that the financial infrastructure can be built up first. Despite the fact that many wholesale and retail prices are strictly controlled, inflation has been very high indeed.

The formation, role and conduct of political parties is *Parties* strictly regulated. They can be, and are, proscribed if they engage in activities that are considered by the government of the day not to be conducive to the welfare of the state. Members must be over twenty-one and certain groups, including teachers in higher education, civil servants and students, may not join. Youth branches of political parties are illegal. This is because, in the period leading up to the 1980 military take-over, students were manipulated and used as a front for unrest. Deputies stand for election strictly as members of their party and independent members are unknown. The leaders of two parties, both former prime ministers, were banned from political activity in the early 1980s. After a referendum on the subject in 1987 they are now both involved in politics again.

The activities of trade unions are equally firmly *Trade unions* controlled. After the unrest that preceded the military intervention in 1980, one of the largest unions was banned and its leaders tried under martial law. The role of the unions is now confined to the realization of 'vocational objectives', thus proscribing the political activity that has so often proved disruptive to other European states trying to get their economies in order. The Japanese model has been adopted, whereby only one union is allowed in each company.

Any dispute must in the first instance be referred to arbitration, and in certain industries of national importance strikes are forbidden. If you chance to go into one of the bars frequented by intellectuals and left-wingers, the bones of contention of the proscription of union activities and the lowness of workers' pay will doubtless be outlined at length – usually in faultless English.

Judiciary and the courts
The independence of the judicial system and the courts is clearly stated in the constitution. In recent years this has been put to the test and found to hold in practice. However, there are some types of court that are not common in other democratic states.

The Constitutional Court, rather like the British House of Lords and the American Supreme Court rolled into one, has very wide powers. It can review and annul legislation and has the responsibility of overseeing the democratic working of the system.

The Council of State is the highest administration tribunal. The thirty-one judges are appointed from among those who have achieved distinction and notice. As this includes not only those in law, but in politics, the army, the universities and any facet of public life, it is in fact partly a lay body.

The Military Court of Cassation is the highest military tribunal. It arbitrates, and to some extent controls, the administrative acts of military personnel, especially when these impinge on civilian activities. It is currently widely seen as having an important role as a safeguard against the emergence of another military regime.

There are three basic types of lower court, within which there are many divisions: courts of justice, dealing with both civil and criminal matters, military courts and administrative courts.

On the formation of the republic the Islamic, or Shari'ah, law used by the Ottomans was replaced. New codes based on the Swiss model for civil and the Italian model for criminal laws were introduced. The commercial code is very similar to that found in Germany.

The law and lawyers

There are two types of law. Laws that have been passed by parliament come into force when approved by the president, which can be months or even years later. Decrees under enabling legislation – the equivalent of an order in council in the UK – take immediate effect.

There is not the prohibition on retrospective legislation found in most democracies, a fact that foreign businesses ignore at their peril. At best they can find it rather disconcerting as they cannot presume that the law under which they plan their activities will not be retroactively changed. At worst they can inadvertently fall foul of retrospective changes.

Laws and decrees are given sequential numbers, not titles, and any action taken under a legal framework always carries that number.

There are two branches to the legal profession. Lawyers act as solicitors and advocates without the separation of function found in the British system. As to the other branch, you will see large coloured boards at first floor level in even the smallest town proclaiming '*Noter*' and a number. This indicates there are that number of public notaries working there. Their proliferation does not mean that the Turks are a particularly litigious race: it is simply a reflection of the fact that even the most trivial document needs to be formally witnessed – this is the greater part of the notaries' work.

Local government and administration

The country is divided up into sixty-seven provinces (*vilâyet* or more formally *il*). The provincial governor

Provinces and governors

(*vali*) is appointed by the president on the advice of the Ministry of the Interior, and is the head and chief executive of a corporation elected for four years. Whilst the system could not be described as federal, since the provinces do not make laws, provincial administrations do have a considerable amount of power as regulatory bodies.

Sub-districts Beneath the provincial councils are sub-districts (*bucak*), each with a centrally appointed administrator (*kaymakam*) and an elected mayor (*başkanı*) and council. One of the main functions of this level is liaison between villages and the province – the *nahiye müdür*, a highly regarded figure, is charged with the responsibility.

Village assemblies A group of dwellings with 150 or more inhabitants has a village administration. It is a truly democratic set-up, and one for which the rural population has a great respect. A village assembly of all the residents over the age of twenty-one gathers to elect a headman (*muhtar*) and a council of elders. The local prayer leader (*imam*) and schoolteacher also sit on the assembly by virtue of their office. Village assemblies are responsible for planning matters and so have come to greater prominence latterly as development has come to the rural areas.

It is not uncommon for the village council to enter into commercial arrangements for the common good of the community. In villages in specially designated tourist areas there are several cases of historic public buildings being restored by the village and then leased to an outside operator.

Town councils Of increasing importance, but with similar powers to the rural authorities, are the urban district councils (*belediye*). They are especially involved in the upkeep of streets, the utilities and planning matters. They are also in the course of preparing the land register that may ultimately make easier the establishment of title for property purchases. The mayor (*belediye başkanı*) is elected for a period of four years, and is often a prominent local businessman. He becomes in effect the chief executive, almost in the American mode, and his civic activities become virtually a full-time activity. This post can be a stepping-stone to central government, and party allegiances are all important.

Whereas all the other branches of local government have evolved over many years, the Ankara, Istanbul and İzmir municipal authorities (*büyükşehir*) were formed especially to take account of the rapid population growth in these three cities. They have a very professional administration headed by a chief executive (*genel sekreter*), who are responsible to an elected mayor (*belediye başkanı*) and council. The main activities of these large authorities cover the normal functions of a major metropolitan area: public transport, the utilities, the promotion of tourism and so on. At present they have three particular preoccupations: development of an infrastructure to cope with their rapid expansion, dealing with pollution, and the restoration of the many dilapidated historic buildings in public ownership.

Large municipal authorities

In the last few years there has been a deliberate policy of decentralization, giving, in particular, greater autonomy to the cities. Municipal authorities have been given the freedom to raise capital on the money markets, and the system of property taxes – rates – will be recognizable to people from the UK.

Coexisting within the three large municipal authorities are the urban district councils (*küçükşehir* – literally 'little cities') that were the administration of the original townships that now comprise the cities. Their function has become largely ceremonial, but people making, say, a planning application would ignore them at their peril. It cannot be overstressed that the system is hierarchical and responsibilities are not divided up by function.

The people

With the considerable increase in industrial activity that has accompanied the freeing of the economy, and the move towards full membership of the EEC, have come social changes and a population shift to the

Population growth

towns. Whilst it is still true to say that Turkey is an agricultural economy, and more than 40 per cent of the population is employed in agriculture, there has recently been a massive growth of population in the main cities. Government programmes have also resulted in the development of new industrial centres. More than half the population now lives in urban areas compared with just 16 per cent fifty years ago.

Improved communications, television in particular, have given to the cities a popular image of lands of riches and opportunity. The tendency is to large families, but with mechanization on the farms reducing the need for labour, younger family members have to some extent been driven from the land. Istanbul, Ankara, İzmir and Adana have been the doubtful beneficiaries of huge influxes of population. Heavy industry rapidly followed to take advantage of the pool of available labour.

Development areas To counteract this trend the government has designated these areas as 'developed regions'. New businesses in these regions rarely receive the subsidized loans, tax allowances, cheap provision of land and infrastructure to all the other incentives that are offered to companies in what are known as 'priority development areas'. Generally speaking these benefits, available to both foreign and local companies, are greatest in south-eastern Anatolia, reduced in the centre, and at their lowest in western Anatolia and Thrace.

Schools Improvements in education have also played a part in the recent demographic changes. A better educated youth – and more than half the population is under twenty years of age – tends to be dissatisfied with the simple village life of its forefathers. School is compulsory from the age of seven to twelve. You will often see well-disciplined lines of uniformed pupils waiting for the school to open.

The majority of pupils nowadays go on to secondary schooling, which means a further three years in a middle school (*orta okul*). Those who are considered to be potential university material, or who want to go on to vocational or technical training, then go to the specialist *lycée* for a further three or four years.

Turkey's thirty universities, centred in the cities, attract a youthful student population, whose members are loath to return to the rural areas. Teaching is in English in a number of departments, and some universities – Istanbul's Bosphorus University and the Middle East Technical University in Ankara, for example – are wholly in the English medium. From the annual 700,000 applicants, only some 40,000 are found places. The high demand for university education seems almost a reflection of a national urge for self- and collective improvement. The jibe that Turkey was the sick man of Europe wounded deeply, and there seems a determination that it shall never again be true. Atatürk's morale boosting slogans are still seen all over the campuses: '*Ne mutlu Türküm diyene*' ('How fortunate is a man who can call himself a Turk') and '*Biz bize benzeriz*' (literally, 'We resemble ourselves': its colloquial meaning is 'we are unique').

Universities

University attendance involves considerable sacrifice on the part of the student and the family. Tuition must partly be paid for, and students receive a very small government grant towards their maintenance. Hostel accommodation and food are provided for a nominal sum. Bursaries and scholarships are discreetly given to students from the poorest families. As these mainly come from private foundations it is never known within the university who is in receipt of them, so there is no stigma attached.

There are just two university terms; October to January and March to June. The majority of students take vacation jobs in the summer, particularly in the tourist industry. You will probably discover that the real vocation of the waiter or the receptionist in your hotel who wants to practise English with you lies in mechanics or science.

The universities are trying hard to play a full part in the present economic resurgence and are keen that their expertise is available to commerce. This is

Special projects

particularly noticeable in the tourist industry, in which it is not uncommon for a university to provide a complete package ranging across all its faculties for new projects. So the department of economics may do an initial feasibility study and the computer department set up models and programs. The department of architecture may well prepare designs, especially if it is a conversation project, with the tourism department being responsible for overall supervision.

Other universities
For late developers and for those who fail to get one of the limited university places, there is an Open University (*Anadolu Üniversitesi*) that employs television and radio as the teaching media. It is quite widely used and the qualifications are well regarded. Its students often pay their way through the courses by working in the tourist industry. A year's course fees are roughly equal to one month's wages.

At the other extreme is *Bilkent* – a combination of the words *bilim* (science) and *kent* (city) – a private university set up by an industrial foundation and directed specifically at the brightest students. It is fee paying (and very expensive at that) and teaches in English, and the courses are oriented towards the latest scientific and technological advances. It also attracts a large number of overseas students, especially from the Middle East.

National service
Military service is mandatory for all males. They must do two periods of eight months, with two months' home leave in between, before the age of twenty. The pay is incredibly low, in effect a nominal sum, and food, spartan accommodation, and a cigarette ration are provided. The regime is extremely tough, especially the first few months. Turks accept this stoically as part of their formative and educational process, and you may well find they express great surprise if they learn you have not done a period of service for your country. Undergraduates can defer their military service to fit in with their education programme, and graduates have the choice of serving eight months unpaid in the ranks, or taking an automatic paid

officer commission for sixteen months. Anyone who has been working abroad for two years or more can pay a substantial bounty to gain exemption from the forces, and Turks born overseas and those with dual nationality are now exempt.

The population is growing at a rate of nearly 3 per cent a year and, despite all the increases in economic activity, it is estimated that unemployment overall is somewhere around 14 per cent – higher in the towns than in the rural areas. As there is no centralized social security system an exact figure cannot be calculated. Unemployment benefit and pensions are provided by various schemes for different sectors: as elsewhere, civil servants are particularly well looked after in this respect. A major contribution is also made by charitable foundations and pension funds with their origins in the Islamic tradition. And if you buy something from an English-speaking young man with a suitcase full of goods in an unofficial bazaar it is quite likely you are helping an unemployed graduate.

Unemploy-ment

Except among those who have gone into western-style career-pattern employment, the attitude of the majority of Turkish people towards work is not that found in Europeanized countries. A person who loses a job is likely to shrug it off nonchalantly – in the final analysis someone from the extended family will fulfil their obligation to provide for his or her needs. Furthermore there is often someone in the family who has made a commercial success and can provide temporary work, and will be grateful for the cheap labour in return. By the same token, a person in a job is in all probability providing for other members of the family whilst working.

Employment

Expatriate managers often comment that it is necessary to adopt a carrot-and-stick approach to employees, with more of the latter than the former. This should hardly cause surprise since this is the fundamental attitude to employees found throughout Turkish society.

Ethnic mix   Perhaps the best-known ethnic minority group is that of the Iraqi Kurds, a tribe of people whose historical roots lie in the wild Hakkari region of south-east Turkey, parts of Syria and Iraq, together with North West Iran. Their original language was an amalgam of Turkish and Farsi (Persian), and they have for many years been agitating for an independent homeland. The Kurdish separatist party, which is also socialist, is from time to time in conflict with government troops. Whilst this has no practical effect on the average visitor, anyone travelling east of Van should be aware of it, and it may be a subject of discussion with people you meet. The government takes the line that all people born in the country are Turkish, irrespective of ethnic origin. Kurdish refugees fleeing recently from atrocities in Iraq have been accommodated in camps on the south-east. They are gradually being settled in local towns and villages.

Walking through a Turkish city today you will see examples of all of the ethnic mix that makes up the Turkish people: mustachioed Anatolians, the dark-skinned Georgians from the Black Sea, swarthy gypsies (*çingâne*), and the easygoing Las, blue-eyed fair-haired folk from the coastal region east of Trabzon. These last, fiercely independent people of obscure Caucasian origin, tend to be the butt of Turkish comedians' jokes in the same way that Irish have traditionally been the butt of English comedians or the Poles of Americans.

Cities and Towns

Of the three principal cities, Istanbul, the capital until that was moved to Ankara on the formation of the republic, is by far and away the most important. But Istanbul is just not typical of Turkey, and visitors should not miss the smaller towns, which all have their own particular delights.

Most people go either to one of the three cities or to the tourist towns. This section is intended to provide enough information to get going while you become properly orientated.

Istanbul

Istanbul is divided into three parts, a factor that often confuses new arrivals. The Bosphorus (Boğaziçi) divides the European and Asian parts and most visitors spend their time on the European side. This is itself divided in two by the Golden Horn (Haliç). Do not mistake the smaller Golden Horn for the larger waterway that is the Bosphorus.

The old part of the city, and the site of Byzantium, is the peninsula bounded by the Sea of Marmara and the Golden Horn. This area, the districts from Sultanahmet down to Aksaray, has a Bohemian air these days with an atmosphere reminiscent of the left bank of Paris in the days before it was commercially exploited.

It was on the other side of the Golden Horn that the Europeans built their beautiful embassies, now consulates-general, in the nineteenth century. The British embassy was designed by Sir Charles Barry in the manner of an English country house. The story told of the American building, formerly the pavilion of a Sultan's mistress, is that it was won by the American government at a game of cards.

On this side too, now known as Beyoğlu, is the rapidly expanding international hotel, business and

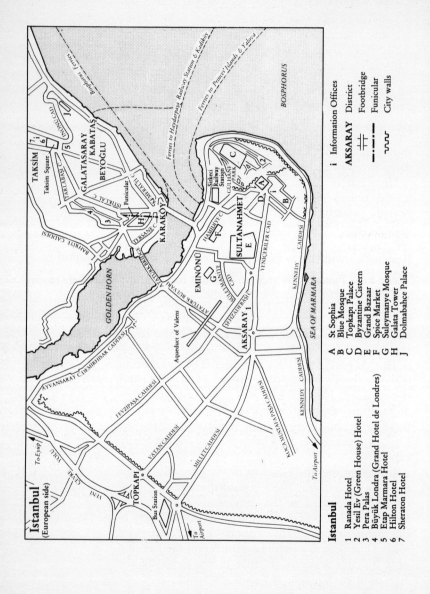

Istanbul
(European side)

1 Ranada Hotel
2 Yesil Ev (Green House) Hotel
3 Pera Palas
4 Büyük Londra (Grand Hotel de Londres)
5 Etap Marmara Hotel
6 Hilton Hotel
7 Sheraton Hotel

A St Sophia
B Blue Mosque
C Topkapi Palace
D Byzantine Cistern
E Grand Bazaar
F Spice Market
G Suleymanye Mosque
H Galata Tower
J Dolmabahce Palace

i Information Offices

AKSARAY District
═╪═ Footbridge
≠ Funicular
⌐⌐⌐ City walls

shopping quarter centred on Taksim Square. Here too is what at night passes for a red light district. The side streets of the pedestrianized İstiklâl Caddesi come alive with ludicrously expensive clubs and bars. You can also find *pavyon* here – the hostess salons that have existed since Ottoman times. They are formally disapproved of, but they have a delightfully old-fashioned air and the women are strictly for company only, even today.

Hilton Entrance
Cumhuriyet Cad.
Taksim
Tel. 133 05 92

Information offices

Divanyolu Cad.
near Aya Sophia
Sultanahmet
Tel. 522 49 03

The Pera Palas Hotel (tel. 151 45 60) on Meşrutiyet Caddesi, between the British and American consulates-general, is surely the last extant example of a colonial resting place. If kings and princes of now forgotten regimes or memsahibs en route for India could return for a day, they would find everything just as they left it.

Where to stay

A flight of marble steps leads to the grand splendour of the atrium. Distant blue-lit domes relieve the heaviness of the ornate gilt ceiling, and *fin-de-siècle* electroliers reflect in brass braziers. The restaurant, through mahogany double doors, is sheer Second Empire: a cornucopia of bas-relief nymphs and fauns and swagged velvet drapes.

Today the hotel is like an elderly lady whose skirts have been gathering dust for nearly 100 years. It takes but little imagination to see in that dust the footprints of Lord Rosebery, Edward VII, Sarah Bernhardt, Agatha Christie, Mata Hari and so many other luminaries of those elegant and pampered pre-war ages who regularly stayed here.

Regrettably, their shades might now complain. These days the service does not match the elegance of the surroundings, and if they were paying the bill they might say it was overpriced. Nevertheless it is well worth a visit, even if just for a drink in the bar, which stays open until 1 a.m.

A little higher up the hill is the Büyük Londra Oteli – the Grand Hotel de Londres (tel. 149 06 70). Rather smaller and family run, it has been carefully restored to its Victorian grandeur. Comfortable and very good value, the rooms at the front have a good view of the Golden Horn. Ernest Hemingway used to stay here.

The Yesil Ev – Green House – hotel (tel. 528 67 64) is a traditional wooden mansion that has been beautifully restored by the Turkish Touring Club. Situated between St Sophia and the Blue Mosque (see p. 55), it is very well placed for the important sites.

The Ramada Hotel (tel. 519 40 50) is another successful restoration project at Aksaray. Originally four blocks of rooms built for the poor, an atrium has been constructed over the crossroads formed by the meeting of the streets on which the blocks stand. The original exteriors now form the central core of the building.

Where to eat and drink

Rejans at Olivo Çıkmazı 15, is an alleyway behind the Büyük Londra Hotel, is an institution. Set up by Russian *emigrés* in the thirties, it has the atmosphere of a Victorian music-hall and excellent, moderately priced food. Booking is advisable (tel. 144 16 10).

On Istiklâl, just before the entrance to Tünel is the Four Seasons (tel. 145 89 41), one of the best-value restaurants in Istanbul. Although run by an English woman – married to a Turk – the food is authentically Turkish.

For a spectacular setting, especially in summer, try the Pierre Loti Restaurant at Karyağdı Sok. 5, Eyüp (tel. 581 26 96). Named after the French traveller and writer, who used to take his constitutional here when he was writing, the restaurant overlooks the Golden Horn.

Under the Galata Bridge are restaurants and bars along the pedestrian walkway, and if you do not fancy sitting down, you can always have some of the fish fried on the little boats tied up on the waterfront. Served with bread and onions, this fish is one of the memorable experiences of Istanbul.

The Topkapı Palace (closed Tuesdays), from which *What to see* the Ottoman Empire was ruled, should not be missed. It is now a superb museum of world repute. Tours of the *harem*, known for centuries as the Grand Seraglio, start at hourly intervals. It can be taken in with St Sophia (closed Mondays), the foremost church in Christendom in the sixth century, and the Basilica Cistern (closed Tuesdays), as they are all closely grouped together in the Sultanahmet quarter.

A visit to the Cistern is well worth while, although the entrance in a small brick building opposite the Olympic Games Headquarters is not clearly marked. Built in the sixth century, this vast brick-vaulted underground cavern was used to store water brought by aqueduct from the Belgrade Forest. The pillars in many different styles supporting the roof, and re-cycled from earlier buildings, are a very early example of architectural salvage.

Across the road, and across the site of the Hippodrome arena, is the very beautiful Blue Mos-que, so called because of the interior tiling. Note the six minarets. The story goes that Sultan Ahmet, who caused it to be built, sent materials and men to build a sixth minaret at Mecca so it should not feel outdone.

A visit to the Dolmabahçe Palace (closed Mondays and Thursdays) is an unforgettable experience. It was built in 1853 in French and Italian baroque style and was the last home of the Sultans. It is also where Atatürk died. Now almost completely restored, it must rank as one of the most sumptuous palaces on public display.

For something not on the usual tourist itinerary, find the Ağa Hamamı Turkish bath in the back streets of Beyoğlu. It was built in 1454 for Fatih Sultan Mehmet and was carefully restored by its present owners in 1987. It can be found at Ağa Hamam Cad. 66 (tel. 149 50 27), about 500 yards from Galatasaray Lisesi (School).

If you feel the need for a break from traffic and pollution, then a trip to the Princes' Islands or Yalova could serve the purpose. There are no motor vehicles on the nine islands, transport for local and visitors alike being by horse-drawn phaeton. As you promenade past waterfront restaurants, or ornate, flower-covered Victorian mansions, the twentieth century might never have happened.

Yalova, on the opposite side of the Marmara Sea, has several restored spa hotels. They range from the excellent but expensive Termal, to the Çınar in its beautiful gardens. Ferries leave regularly from number 5 terminal near Sirkeci station for the one-and-a-half-hour round trip. If you stop at one of the islands you can negotiate a fisherman's boat to take you to some of the others. On leaving the islands you should check that the boat is going the right way, as they operate a circular route.

Other ferries   Across the Marmara Sea, ferries run to Mudanya (for Bursa) on Monday to Thursday at 6 p.m. and on Fridays and Sundays at 9 a.m. They leave from Kadıköy terminal number 7. In the summer only, ferries leave for Çanakkale (for Troy and the site of the Anzac landings) at 9.30 a.m. on Wednesdays.

A boat leaves Istanbul every Wednesday in the summer for the five-day voyage along the Black Sea coast to Trabzon and Rize, calling in at Samsun and three other small ports on the way. The service is monthly in the winter. The weekly car ferry, non-stop to İzmir, takes about eighteen hours and leaves from opposite Sirkeci station. There are additional services in the summer.

It is usually necessary to book several days in advance for all ferry routes – all enquiries to Turkish Maritime Lines. (See p. 257.)

Shopping   Istanbul is a shopper's paradise. The Grand Bazaar (*Çarşı*) has become very touristic; head down from it in the direction of the Golden Horn and you will find yourself in Mahmut Paca. This is what the Grand Bazaar was like before the tourists moved in, and here

you will find Turks doing their shopping, and
hunched and gnarled porters (*hammal*) with enormous loads on their backs.

Go further downhill, nearly to the waterfront, and
you are at Mısır Çarsısı, the spice market, whose
smells are unmistakable as you approach. The pre-
dominant smell is likely to be coriander, which is the
main spice used in kebabs. Nearby is the flower and
cage-bird market.

The Bosphorus apparently supports more fish than
any other waterway in the world. Fresh fish – species
you are never likely to have seen before – is sold on
the waterfront on the Asian side at Kadıköy, at the
Karaköy end of the Galata Bridge, and on the
seafront road along the Marmara Sea.

For smart shopping, the Osmanbey district on the
other side of the Golden Horn is the Knightsbridge
or Park Avenue of Istanbul.

Safety

Istanbul is the only place in Turkey where people
automatically lock up their cars, an unthinkable
practice in country towns. Because of the shifting and
mixed population, care should be exercised in some
districts – especially Beyoğlu – late at night. Mug-
gings are becoming more frequent and pickpockets
are not uncommon. A favourite trick is to stage a
fight in front of you; then as you look on in concern
your wallet is taken.

Ankara

It is said that the only reason for coming to Ankara is
politics. This is perhaps slightly unfair, but the fact
remains that Atatürk's new city was designed for that
purpose. The plan was laid out by a German,
Hermann Jansen, a disciple of Le Corbusier, who also
collaborated on schemes for Prague, Stockholm and
Madrid.

The city is very spread out, which makes walking
from one part to another difficult. The roads have
more of a circular than a grid pattern, which makes
orientation slightly problematic. It is best achieved by
considering the city as having one main thoroughfare,
Atatürk Bulvarı, running right through the centre. At
one end is Ulus, the old town, and at the other are the

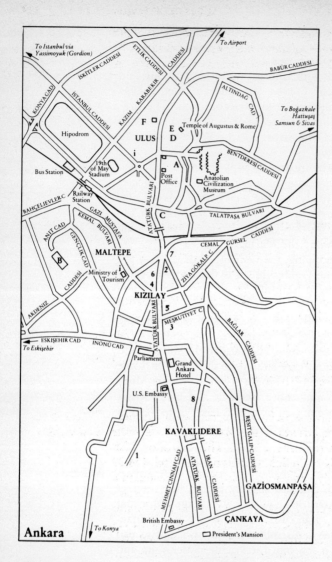

Ankara

1	Hilton Hotel
2	Kent Hotel
3	Ersan Oteli
4	Washington Restaurant
5	Pizzeria Restaurant
6	Piknik Restaurant
7	Beyaz Saray Restaurant
8	Check Point
A	Yeni Haller Produce Market

B	Atatürk Mausoleum
C	Ethnography Museum/Art Gallery
D	Column of Julian
E	Haci Bayram Camii
F	Roman baths
i	Information office
ULUS	District
⌶	Footbridge
꩜	City walls

districts of Kavaklıdere and Çankaya where the embassies and government buildings are situated. In the centre is Kızılay district, the commercial part of the city.

Gazi Mustafa Kemal Bulvarı 33,
Kızılay.
Tel 229 29 30

*Information
offices*

Istanbul Cad. 4,
Ulus.
Tel 311 22 47

The new Hilton, Tahran Cad. 12, Kavaklıdere (tel. 168 28 88), has everything you might expect of a Hilton. The four-star Kent Hotel, Mithatpaşa Cad. 4, Sıhhiye (tel. 135 50 50), has friendly, helpful service and has long been used by business and media people not wanting to use five-star hotels. The Ersan Oteli, Meşrutiyet Cad. 13 (tel. 118 98 75), is good value for money and conveniently located. Just round the corner in Selanik Cad., the Otel Ertan (tel. 118 40 84) is clean, cheap and used by Turkish businessmen and students taking their exams.

Where to stay

One of the most popular restaurants with business people and expatriates is the Washington, Bayındır Sok., Kızılay (tel. 131 22 18). The Yakamoz Fish Restaurant, Köroğlu Sok. Gaziosmanpaşa (tel. 136 09 03), is relatively expensive, as might be expected in a town in the centre of a large landmass. The Piknik, Tuna Cad. Kızılay (tel. 133 81 48), serves kebabs and local cuisine and is popular at lunchtime. It also serves draught beer. The first floor Pizzeria Restaurant (tel. 117 27 34), at the end of Meşrutiyet Cad. 7 just before it meets Atatürk Bulvarı, has framed thirties' posters on the walls, background music that is often opera, and candlelit tables. It is a perfect rendezvouz for assignations.

Check Point, once you have found it upstairs behind a shopping arcade at Seğmenler Çarşısı 96 (tel. 126 67 79), is a bar making a name for itself as a meeting place for English-speaking residents.

*Where to eat
and drink*

What to see   Ankara is not well endowed with sites and beautiful buildings. In fact, it has something of a dearth by Turkish standards. The new town coexists uneasily with the original, divided by a large ramshackle railway marshalling yard. It does have some large parks which come into their own in spring and summer, especially Gençlic Park, where the lake was made from a former swamp on the orders of Atatürk. Some of the newer residential districts in the higher parts of the town are quite attractive.

The Middle East Technical University has a very high reputation and teaching standard, not least because Atatürk encouraged Jewish refugees from German universities to take up residence in Ankara in the thirties.

Start any tour of the city with a visit to the Atatürk Mausoleum on the hillside at Rasattepe, or the Ethnography Museum and the National Art Gallery, side by side at Ulus. They are on opposing hills and provide superb views of the city. There is a *son et lumière* show at the Atatürk Mausoleum from May through to September; you will need to check with the information office for the days on which it is English.

Ulus is the quarter with most of the interesting sites. The Column of Julian was built to commemorate a visit of the Emperor in 362 AD. Not far away is Hacı Bayram Camii, one of Ankara's most important mosques and built on a site that has had significance for different religions for well over 2,000 years. First built by the Kings of Pergamum for the worship of the fertility god Cybele, it was later used for the worship of the Phrygian phallic god Men. The walls you now see were then surrounded by a colonnade. The Byzantines converted it to a church dedicated to the Emperor Augustus. The Muslims built a mosque within the precincts and Hacı Bayram Veli, who founded the Bayraniye Order of Dervishes, is buried there – hence its present name.

A little further up the hill, the remains of the third-century Roman baths have not yet been fully excavated.

In the centre the shops are smart and refined, befitting a capital city, and English is very widely spoken. There is not a large central bazaar but in the older Ulus district can be found Yeni Haller, the new produce market. This is the place where you will see village people from central Anatolia who have brought the goods in from the outlying areas. Behind the market is a restored caravanserai, Vakıf Suluhan Çarşısı. It has a variety of small shops, mainly selling clothes, and an attractive café. *Shopping*

Once known as the pearl of the Aegean, İzmir now, alas, suffers badly from air and water pollution which the authorities are working hard to control. Most of the centre of the city dates from after 1926, when the original cosmopolitan levantine trading post of Smyrna was razed to the ground by a fire. When the spectacular new Marine Drive right round the bay is completed it will rival any Corniche in the world. **İzmir**

Although it has vast suburban sprawl the city centre is very manageable. The two main avenues running parallel to the waterfront are universally known as First and Second Avenue (Birinci and İkinci Kordon). At one end of these is Konak, the plaza where all bus and trolley-bus routes converge, and from where the ferryboats run across the harbour to the residential suburb of Karşiyaka. Until 1922, this suburb was called Cordelio, by local tradition a corruption of 'Coeur de Lion', from the landing there of the English King Richard during the crusades.

Between Turkish Airline Office and Büyük Efes Hotel
Cumhuriyet Meydanı
Tel. 14 21 47 *Information office*

Whilst there are plenty of hotels at the higher and lower ends of the market, İzmir has little in the way of middle-range hotels. *Where to stay*

The four-star Etap İzmir, Cumhuriyet Bulvarı 138 (tel. 14 42 90), is a good business hotel, and the

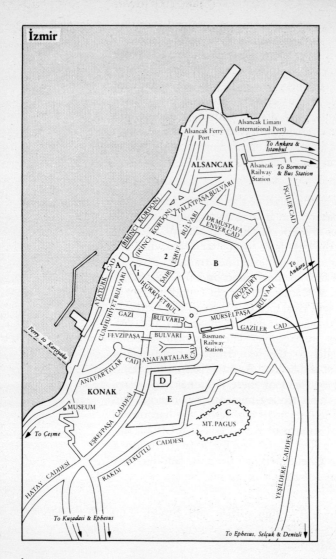

İzmir

1 Büyük Efes Hotel
2 Karaka Oteli
3 Babadon Hotel

A Post Office
B Kultur Park
C Castle

D Agora
E Bazaar

i Information office
KONAK District
╪ Footbridge
∿∿∿ City walls

three-star Karaca Hoteli, Necatibey Bulvarı 1379,
Sok. 55 (tel. 14 44 45), is very good value for money.

Although the Babadan Hotel, Gaziosmanpaşa Bulvar 50 (tel. 13 96 40), has only been given one star it is
friendly and comfortable. The rooms can be noisy
unless you can get one on the top floor at the back.
The Babadan also operates a money-changing service
for non-residents which is extremely useful at
weekends.

Recently opened is a branch of the grey market
(*Kaynak Finans*), now formalized in a smart bank-
like office at Sümerbank pedestrian bridge. If the law
does not change it will continue to offer seven-day-a-
week money-changing, open to midnight, and at
relatively good rates.

İzmir is an open-air, waterfront and boulevard city.
Restaurants with pavement tables abound along
Birinci Kordon between Alsancak and the post office.
Theoretically the road is closed to all traffic in the

Where to eat and drink

evening except horse-drawn phaetons. As in all the coastal towns people tend to take a siesta in the afternoon. As the sun goes down they come out for the *piyasa vakti* – to stroll, talk and watch the sunset, often in family groups.

The boat restaurants moored to the strand make for a good, if relatively expensive, evening's entertainment. At Zeytinlik Cad. 47A behind the railway tracks is Nihat Baba'nın, an old meyhanesi now run as an excellent restaurant. It is used by Turkish businessmen, and, because of its *meyhane* origins (see p. 132), it is very rarely that women are seen there.

At the port end of Birinci Kordon are several *birahane* ('beer houses' – see p. 132) and bars, also with pavement tables, and if you take the ferry to Karsiyeka as you disembark you will be faced by several more, which are downmarket and friendly. Opposite the municipal (*belediye*) offices is the Sembol bar. It stays open very late and is handy for people with late night flights out of İzmir airport. The same young proprietor has opened Sembol 2 in the suburb of Polygon, which serves very good Turkish cooking.

What to see   There is not a lot to see in İzmir itself, but the town makes an excellent base for seeing the Aegean area.

The view from the castle perched on top of Mount Pagus, especially at sunset, is spectacular. Here was once the acropolis of the capital of the Aeolian League that Homer would have known.

The remains of the Roman agora from the time of Marcus Aurelius are on Gaziosmanpaşa Bulvarı. There is a statue of Poseidon seated and a standing figure of Demeter which are reckoned once to have formed the centrepiece of an altar.

Bornova, now a suburb, is where rich foreign merchants built their mansions. Fortunately some of these mansions have been preserved as various departments of Ege University. Others, however, lie forlorn and empty, but there is still a little left of the atmosphere that was the inspiration for Lord Byron's *The Bride of Abydos*. These same merchants are credited with taking the local game of *kledive*, which they called *biriç*, to the London clubs. Anglicized, it became 'bridge'.

Shopping

The bazaar is probably the best in the Middle East. It has none of the hassle of the bazaars in Arabia or North Africa and is still wholly functional without any touristic overtones. Although it gets crowded, especially at weekends, it has a relaxed atmosphere. It covers a vast area and the sections for different trades and products are clearly defined.

The large American presence in İzmir, caused by NATO commitments, regrettably provides a stylistic role model for erstwhile smart İzmirians. This is seen at the most extreme in the American Arcade, where Turkish people flood to buy what they think to be western goods. Pretty well everything sold there has the label 'made in Taiwan'.

Holiday towns

Kuşadası

In spite of its rapid growth, the centre of Kuşadası still has the feel of a small town. It is well endowed with bars and restaurants, but the town sometimes gets rather swamped with foreigners – especially if a cruise ship is alongside, when prices go rocketing. The Friday produce market near the bus station is authentic and worth a visit. The beaches in the town are clean but crowded, and are served by horse bus.

The first English bar has arrived, Trixie's, run by an enterprising British lady. The Harem Restaurant serves good Turkish food and the place for English-speaking expatriates in-the-know is the Baküs Bar, up two flights of stairs near the old town gate that doubles as a police station.

If you visit a certain hotel in Kuşadası it may be your fate to meet the granddaughter of Sultan Mehmet VI, the last Ottoman sultan, who was a young girl at the time of the abolition of the sultanate and Mehmet's flight (see p. 199). This very regal lady speaks eloquently in English of these events.

Bodrum

The place where rich middle-class Turks go to pose

and meet like-minded friends, Bodrum is the equivalent of Brighton or Key West. The harbour, with the backdrop of the restored crusaders' castle, has pleasant waterside cafes and it is possible to swim outside the harbour off the breakwater. There are some superb beaches along the coast which have regular services by dolmuş, taxi and jeep.

Marmaris   Not long ago Marmaris was a delightful little fishing village: now it is devoted to tourism, and the new yacht marina is promised to be completed in 1989. The town divides neatly into two sections which meet at the customs house where the ferries leave for Rhodes. The one half has promenades and tourist hotels stretching for miles, along which there is a train pulled by a tractor in summer. The other half, round the promontory formed by the original village, consists of waterside cafes, all waiting now to see the effect of the new marina being built in front of them. The roads in the town are the worst in the whole of Turkey and need to be seen to be believed. In summer they are rutted, dried mud, which turns to a quagmire in winter.

The Moby Dick restaurant has a French-trained chef and the Mistral bar nearby serves interesting cocktails.

Outside the town are some of the most beautiful beaches and coves imaginable.

Fethiye   A favourite place for yachtsmen, Fethiye has a sheltered harbour and good anchorages. It is a resort used by Turkish people and has a cosmopolitan atmosphere – not only does it have waterside bars and cafés but tea-shops too. Ölüdeniz (literally 'the Dead Sea' but not to be confused with the biblical sea of the same name), a lagoon and beaches about twenty minutes' minibus ride away, is very popular, and at its best in spring and autumn. In summer it gets extremely crowded. It has something of a reputation as a place for Turkish young men to find foreign girlfriends, and vice versa, on a temporary or more permanent basis.

People come to Antalya as a centre for the nearby *Antalya* ruins or for the archaeological museum, which also has a delightful, shaded terrace café. The beaches are away from the town on both sides.

The old town of narrow twisting streets, with its beautiful harbour dating from before the time of Christ, has waterside fish restaurants. On the cliffs above the town are near-tropical gardens.

Whilst the area around has been highly developed for tourism, the centre still manages to have an air of refinement. For minibuses to the surrounding villages, beaches and sites use the Doğu Garajı – the smaller of the two bus stations at the eastern end of the town.

Communications

The telephone system The telephone system is the pride of modern Turkey. It is based on the latest German, British and American technology and is continually being updated and extended; the lines in the rural areas are at present being upgraded.

Turkish people use the telephone all the time for keeping in touch with family in distant parts, and it is rare to find a city phone box without a queue – often comprising nomadic, possibly illiterate, people who have been drawn in to the more prosperous urban areas. Because of this demand it is often easier to get a line overseas than for an internal call.

Be prepared to find the clarity on international calls often better than short-distance calls at home. If you find you get the slight echo that sometimes happens with satellite communications, try speaking more quietly and it may go away.

Directories Telephone directories are comprehensive and accurate, and after a little practice can be used quite easily. The additional letters in the Turkish alphabet, the accented C, S, O, U and the dotted I, come after the regular C, S, O, U and I. The accented g never begins a word. Do remember, however, to check a private number alphabetically under both first name and surname. The latter were only introduced some fifty years ago and are still not as widely used as in other countries.

Enquiries The number for directory enquiries is 011. You have to be able to communicate in pidgin Turkish with a reasonable accent to have much chance of getting the number you want. In any case the enquiry service is very busy during the day, resulting in the engaged tone most of the time. Turkish people and experi-

enced expatriates ring round their friends for a
number before trying 011. Numbers are given in
pairs; thus 4521 becomes *kırk beş, yirmi bir* (forty-
five, twenty-one).

You will usually find a list of the international and   *Dialling codes*
internal city dialling codes beside the phone, but there
are certain differences in the alphabetical listing from
those you will be used to. The US is found under
either *Birleşik Amerika* or ABD, Canada is listed
under K, New Zealand *Yeni Zelanda*, and, with
apologies to the Irish, Scots and the Welsh, the UK is
listed throughout Turkey as *İngiltere*.

Turkish people answer the telephone with 'efendi', or   *Getting the*
in trendy households 'allo' – a reflection of the fact   *person you*
that modern technology is bringing completely alien   *want*
words into the language.

   If the person at the other end does not speak
English, try *'John bey lûtfen'* ('Mr John, please') or
'Mary hanım lûtfen' ('Ms Mary, please'), which is the
conventional way to ask for someone. The response
may well be *'bir dakika'* ('one minute').

   Most modern hotels have digital switchboards.
You will find you have an automatic internal and
overseas dialling in your room, which is billed
electronically. It is necessary to dial different numbers to obtain a line depending on whether you want
to make a local, long-distance or international call.
Charges are at an inflated rate to take account of the
hotel service costs, so if you are being budget
conscious it is as well to go out to a public telephone
to make long-distance calls. Some of the older hotels
still have a manual system, which may make it
difficult to monitor your call charges; again, you may
well feel it is preferable to use the very effective public
telephone system.

   It is worth remembering that if you are desperate to
find someone to interpret, the switchboard operator
in a hotel is likely to be a good English speaker – and
probably a working student.

   Nearly every post office has a call office attached to
it. In the scrum of people paying bills, making

complaints and so on – Turkish people do queue but it's not the orderly standing in line you may have been used to – you need to find the counter marked *telefon*. Write the full number and your name on a piece of paper, and wait. The length of time will depend on whether you have marked your paper *yıldırım* (lightning), *acele* (make haste), or nothing at all, in which case you will get the normal, and very slow service. The faster services cost four and two times the normal service.

Pay-phones   International, long-distance and local calls can also be made from the telephone boxes and booths that are to be found outside post offices, on railway stations and in public squares. Restaurants and hotels do not as a rule have public telephones. Pay-phones are of three types.

Phone Cards   Card-phones are slowly being introduced and becoming more widespread. A yellow plastic card which has a value of 120 units can be purchased at post offices. It is inserted in a slot after lifting the receiver, after which the number of units remaining on the card comes up on the display screen. It is important to wait for this to happen and it can take quite a time.

Tokens   Most public telephones take a token (*jeton*), also purchased at the post office. Tokens theoretically come in three sizes, small (*küçük*), medium (*normal*) and large (*büyük*), but in practice only small and medium are usually available. If you ask for a large token you will be given a medium one.

Lift the receiver, and if the machine is working a little red light comes on. Put the token in the appropriate slot the right way round – there are two lugs on one side of the slot and one on the other – and wait for the light to go out.

Coin boxes   Coin-boxes, although they are being phased out as they cannot keep pace with inflation, are still occasionally seen. Place a 100 TL coin in the slot and wait for the red light to go out.

When the units have come up, or the red light has *Dialling* gone out, check that there is a continuous dialling tone and dial a local number immediately. Otherwise dial 9 for international calls, or 09 for long distance calls within Turkey – and then wait for a different sounding dialling tone. You may have to try this several times until you get the line.

International calls   Then for international calls dial 9 again followed by the country code:

Code		(Approx. hours' difference)
61	Australia	(+8)
1	Canada	(−8)
45	Denmark	(0)
33	France	(−1)
49	Germany	(−1)
44	Great Britain	(−2)
31	Netherlands	(−1)
64	New Zealand	(+10)
81	Japan	(+7)
1	USA	(−8)

Follow the country code with the STD (city) code without 0, and then the number. You will hear the normal ringing or engaged tones for the country you are calling.

Internal long-distance calls   Or for long-distance calls dial the city code, which you will find displayed in the booth, followed by the number. When the phone is ringing you will hear a long tone followed by a pause of equal length. The engaged sound is alternate short and long tones. If there is no reply after ten rings the system automatically disconnects and the line goes dead.

All types of call are most expensive between 8 a.m. *Payment* and 8 p.m.; the cheap rate comes into operation after 8 p.m. and at weekends. Payment at the call office is made when you have finished at the counter where you booked the call.

A small *jeton* gives a two-minute local call. When the red light goes out and you hear two pips it is time to put in another *jeton*.

International transfer charge or collect calls can theoretically be made from public call offices, but as they cannot be made within Turkey it is often difficult to get the operator to understand what you want. You ask for *ödemeli* and write down the information as for a normal call office connection. The local operator has to get through via the international operator, so be prepared for a long wait. You cannot transfer the charge from a phone box, nor for internal calls.

International telephone credit cards are not accepted in Turkey.

International dialling from pay-phones is extremely easy, relatively inexpensive, and for those on holiday an easy means of keeping in touch with home. The authorities take mobile equipment to seasonal tourist areas to meet the additional demand. If you are likely to need to use the telephone with any frequency, and in case of emergency, you are well advised to get into the habit of carrying a couple of tokens in your change, since it is not possible to buy them at all the places where you find a telephone.

Car phones Car telephones operate in the major cities. At the moment they are at the stage of being a very expensive status symbol.

Facsimile transmission and telex Fax, using ordinary telephone lines, is quite widely used by both local and foreign businesses. It is noticeably superseding telex, which has limited numbers of lines outside the major cities. There are fax bureaux at a few of the main post offices, and embassies, consulates-general and the appropriate chambers of commerce often assist with communication facilities for bona fide business people.

International hotels provide all the usual communication, secretarial and translation facilities found elsewhere in the world.

There are public telex offices at the main post offices in Istanbul, Ankara, İzmir and some other towns that have a large business community. There can be delays in telexes being sent if the operator cannot get an outgoing line. It is not unknown in smaller offices, if the operator's English is not too good, for the sender to be asked to type out the message on the telex machine. Telegrams can be sent from all post offices and are accepted in English. However, it is worth remembering that telegrams to the UK are delivered with the next day's post.

Reuters' monitor and financial news services are on-line in the major cities.

The postal service

Post offices are marked by large yellow PTT signs. The main post office in Istanbul, at Sirkeci near the station on the Sultanahmet side of the Golden Horn, is open twenty-four hours a day; that in Ankara, at Ulus, opens from 9 a.m. to 7 p.m.; quite a few offices stay open to 11.30 p.m. and smaller ones close at 6 p.m. They all close on Sundays. Some offices close for lunch between noon and 1 p.m.

Stamps

Postage rates are very cheap and it is quite usual for the post office clerk to frank your letter rather than stick on a stamp (*pul*). You should double check to be sure you have been charged the airmail (*uçakla*) rate, or it could go surface. Stamps can also be bought at hotels, some newsagents and souvenir shops which also sell stamped letter-cards, useful for short notes overseas.

Posting a letter

Post boxes in the walls of post offices have different slits for overseas (*yurtdışı*), inland (*yurtiçi*) and local (*şehiriçi*) mail. Beware – the freestanding, square, yellow boxes on street corners are all too easily mistaken for litter bins and vice versa. In the more remote areas the postman picks up the mail as he makes deliveries.

Time to and from most overseas countries is four to five days, but a higher than average proportion of letters addressed to Turkey does go astray. There are two deliveries a day in the towns, morning and afternoon.

Addresses Post-codes (zip codes) have recently been introduced. If they are used the mail does certainly get there more quickly. It also helps to adopt the convention of putting the number after the street, followed by the flat or floor number. Where the road is small and likely to be unknown the main road from which it runs is written first. Thus

Cumhuriyet Cad.
Küçük Sok. 10/3
35210 Alsancak
İzmir

translates as Flat 3 (or the third floor), 10, Small Alley, off the bigger Republic Street, post-code 35210 in the Alsancak district of İzmir. *Cad.* is the abbreviation for *Caddesi* (street) and *Sok.* for *Sokak* (alley). There are also *Bulvarı* and *Pasaj*, which are self-evident.

If you write to friends, do not expect to get a reply – Turks are not very good correspondents. This is particularly true of social mail but can apply equally to business.

Poste *Postrestant* – it's one word in Turkish – facilities are
Restante available at the main post office in each town. This department, surprisingly, often closes earlier than the other sections. You will need your passport or some other acceptable form of identification before letters will be released, and they should be addressed 'Poste Restante, *Merkez Postanesi* (Central Post Office)' before the name of the town. American Express also operate a post-holding service at the Turk Ekspres offices in Ankara and Istanbul.

Express and There is an express postal service to Europe and the
courier US, and between thirty-six of the larger towns.
delivery Express packets up to 2 kg (about 4½ lb) can be sent only from those post offices which have an APS (*Acele Posta Servisi*) sign.

Courier services operate in the main cities. Özgür

Nakliyat (World Courier: tel. Istanbul 143 25 74, Ankara 118 08 08) deliver to Europe in twenty-four hours and the US in thirty-six. The world-wide DHL organization can be found on Istanbul 172 89 20 and Ankara 141 26 33.

Parcels must be taken to a counter marked *Paket* in the post office. Anything going overseas must be left open for customs inspection, and the most incredibly complicated form filled in. If you have occasion to go through this procedure you will undoubtedly come to the conclusion that post office workers are some of the least helpful people in the country. They are marginally less surly to foreigners than they are to Turkish people.

Parcel post

Journals

The newspapers from Britain, France and Germany can usually be found in city shops the following day, as can the *Herald Tribune* and *USA Today*. In Istanbul that day's *Financial Times* is on sale in the Hilton Hotel each evening, and the other papers can often be found from about 5 p.m. in the two newsagents on Divanyolu Cad., the main street in Sultanahmet district.

Foreign newspapers

The English-language *Turkish Daily News* is available in all but the smallest towns. It covers the important international news stories together with the background to events in Turkey. You should be aware that it takes a fairly passionate anti-government line.

Also published locally is the weekly *Dateline Turkey* which diplomatic and business personnel consider essential reading. They also rely on the daily *Economic Bulletin*, the weekly journal *Investments and Biddings*, and the political weekly *Briefing*, all published by the Economic Press Agency (EBA). *Anka Review*, an economic and financial weekly published by the semi-official Ankara News Agency (ANKA), is useful for keeping abreast of the government's line. The Government Information Office produces the weekly *Newspot*, which is a good

Local English-language publications

background digest of political events in the country; the office also produces a quarterly *Turkish Review* which has well-informed articles by Turkish writers on political, economic and social matters. *New Middle East* and *Middle East Banking* are Turkish equivalents to *The Economist* or *Time*.

Turkish newspapers *Cumhuriyet* (Republic) is the main serious news-paper. Its politics are slightly left of centre, though it supports the government on major issues. *Jercüman* (Interpreter) is the equivalent to the right of centre. *Hürriyet* (Freedom) is slightly more populist, whilst *Güneş* (Sun) and *Sabah* (Morning) are the popular downmarket papers – the latter notorious for its page three girls.

Radio and television

radio A small radio which picks up the short-wave bands is a good way of keeping in touch with what is going on at home and in the world. The BBC World Service is reckoned to be an important source of impartial information to many politicians and heads of state. It can be found on 9.401, 12.095, 6.180, 18.080 or 15.070 MHz depending on the time of day. Reception in Ankara is very limited in the evening and improves the further south, and thus closer to the transmitter on Cyprus, you travel.

London Calling, the programme schedule and magazine, is available from BBC External Services, POB 76, Bush House, London WC2B 4PH (tel. 01 240 3456), who also publish a frequency guide.

Voice, the equivalent publication of Voice of America, can be got from VOA, Washington, 20547 (tel. 202 485 7700). The station can be found on 3.980, 5.965 and 11.925 MHz.

Turkish Radio's stereo Third Programme, a mainly classical music station (Western and Turkish), broadcasts news bulletins in English, French and German at 12 p.m., 3 p.m. and 7 p.m. It can be found on frequencies between 88 and 99.2 MHz; you may need to get local help to find the correct position on the dial.

Television Channel 2, gradually being extended from *Television*
its present coverage of Istanbul, Ankara, İzmir and
Adana, carries the news and weather forecast in
English at 9.30 each evening after the national news.
It covers the main local items together with one or
two of the main stories from Britain, America or
Europe.

The use of surnames and forms of address is different **Forms of**
from that in the English-speaking world. Even on **address**
first acquaintance, people are addressed by their first
name, followed by *bey* for man and *hanım* for a
woman. These forms are nearly always used, as it is
very informal indeed to adopt our convention of
using the first name only. Thus friends are addressed
as, for example, *Engin bey* and *Leyla hanım*.

In correspondence, *bay* and *bayan* are used in
exactly the same way as our Mr and Mrs/Miss/Ms, or
more usually the alternative *sayın* (literally meaning
'esteemed') is used in both cases. A formal letter
could begın *Sayın Bay veya Bayan* (Dear Sir or
Madam).

There is no difference in the form of address to
married or single women.

Efendim means 'I beg your pardon', when you
wish to have something repeated. *Efendi* is an
old-fashioned form of address literally meaning
'master' and it is perhaps best thought of as 'sir'. It is
now used on its own for either sex, and you will hear
it in a restaurant to call over a waiter in a polite way.
A less formal way to attract the attention of a waiter is
arkadaş (friend), and the really matey way – and the
form usually used for taxi drivers – is *abi* (big
brother).

The Turkish people tend much more to formality
and politeness than you may be used to, especially on
first meeting; and they are far more respectful to
people older than themselves.

Transport

As with so much else in Turkey, public transport is very much cheaper than that found in the rest of Europe. You can cross the country by bus, or traverse it from end to end, for a few pounds or dollars. For a few more, if you are prepared to miss everything that comes in between, you can do it by plane. Public transport is also extremely efficient and well run.

Cross-country transport

Flying The monopoly of Turkish Airlines (THY) on internal flights has been broken, and new companies are slowly being formed. In the summer a few military airports near tourist areas are opened up for civilian traffic. Security at all airports is very tight – even for domestic flights you should arrive in plenty of time for check-in. THY do not make seat reservations for domestic flights so there is something of a scramble for seats. It is also a security requirement that you identify your luggage on a baggage trolley as you board the plane. Failure to do so means that the luggage is not loaded. There is a no smoking rule on internal flights.

Bookings for THY are best made at the local airline office in the town or possibly at the nearest international hotel. It should be remembered that flights get very booked up in summer. Telephone reservations are accepted, and can be held until up to four hours before take-off. In the case of the smaller companies it is necessary to call the airline office at the airport, and the Istanbul numbers are: Istanbul Airlines (561 34 66) to Ankara, Trabzon, and İzmir; Talia (573 37 93) to

İzmir and Antalya; and Sönmez Airlines (573 2920) to Bursa.

Airport flight indicator boards are quite often out of action. Never rely on them, and if you see people in the departure lounge moving towards the boarding gate, check in case the information about your flight has got round by word of mouth.

Plane hire Private charter companies are a new phenomenon and are used by business people and for sightseeing. Information and bookings are from major hotels and some travel agents. As new private enterprises in a hitherto state-controlled sector, they are having some difficulty in getting their activities widely known.

One of the new companies, NESU, runs a helicopter charter service between Istanbul's Hilton Hotel and the airport, for sightseeing and short business trips. As the hotel was built before the property boom it has the advantage over its competitors, in that a chopper can land on its extensive lawns.

Intercity buses The bus stations and interchanges (*otogar*), found near the centre of every town, are a legacy of Atatürk's reforms. They are now the hub of a bus network that, taking advantage of the rapidly improving road system, should be the envy of many more developed countries.

Bus companies are privately owned, extremely competitive, and vary in comfort, safety and service. The best companies are very good indeed and a look at the state of the buses will quickly establish which these are; as a general rule they will usually be slightly more expensive. Prices are fixed by the government at a rate per kilometre depending on the standard and the quality of service, and it does pay to shop around. A tachometer is mandatory and the police make spot checks on adherence to speed limits. The safety advice from embassies is to use only the best companies, but many people have travelled all over the country using whichever service happened to be convenient and without the slightest problem. The choice must be

yours – and it is quite a choice, as you will see when
you get to the bus station.

Bus stations and reservations   Advance reservations
are sometimes necessary on the very popular services
and during the two Bayram holidays (see p. 270). For
the bigger companies you may be able to find an
agent in the town who can make reservations;
otherwise you must go to the ticket booth of the
appropriate company at the bus station.

There is a chaotic, carnival atmosphere at bus
stations, as people arrive and leave with effusive
leave-takings or greetings of friends. What with all
the people – and to go on a journey without friends to
see you off is considered very strange – and the
luggage being piled in and on the buses, it is difficult
for the novice to find out just what is going on.
Destinations, times and fares are chalked on boards
outside the various company offices, and from these
you can get an indication as to which ones go where.
If you look a bit lost, or even if you are just carrying a
bag or looking foreign, a tout will soon take you in
hand and help you fix up your ticket. (They get
commission, so it is not necessary to tip them. If you
feel you want to give them a present they will not be
averse.) Once you are in the right place and have
made your choice, ticketing is extremely simple.

On the bus   Many of the buses are air-conditioned
and most have an attendant. In the summer you will
be offered bottles of chilled water, damp flannels and
strong, pungent, lemon cologne for which you should
hold out your hands as though taking communion.
One of the abiding smells of Turkey, forever linked
with bus travel, is of this cologne.

On the modern buses the windows do not open, so
in the hottest weather it is prudent to get a seat behind
the roof vent, especially since most drivers seem loath
actually to switch on the air-conditioning. Foreigners
are often placed at the front as a courtesy, but this is a
doubtful privilege on routes through steep mountain
passes. There are frequent stops for meals and breaks,

and journeys, although not particularly quick, are not
too arduous on the better quality buses.

Minibuses   In the countryside, any small town or
village not served by a regular bus will have a minibus
service. Minibuses wait at fixed stops and leave when
they are full. In rural areas you are likely to be
wedged in between farmers and their families, complete with their chickens and goats – and they nearly
always seem to have a couple of potted plants too!
These buses will stop pretty well anywhere if they are
hailed; the driver will in any case know most of his
regular passengers. Do not be too surprised when, if
you say you want to go somewhere, the driver,
without stopping, turns round to join in the general
meeting to discuss the best place to drop you off –
minibus drivers do seem to have some sort of radar
guidance to enable them to steer round pot-holes and
traffic.
    The most isolated communities are reached once a
day by the post bus, which also takes passengers.

Dolmuş   Small towns and the suburbs are also served
by *dolmuş* (literally meaning 'stuffed'). These are
shared taxis operating on set routes which, like the
minibuses, leave when they are full – usually very full,
whence the name. They are cars with a yellow band
round them, or sometimes minibuses are used on
busy routes. The fares are fixed by the local authority; you pay for the distance you travel and indicate
to the driver when you want to get out. The actual
routes are a mystery known only to the driver and
getting somewhere can often be a question of trial and
error.

Cars   Many visitors, especially from Germany, bring their
own vehicles. In the summer large numbers of
dormobiles and recreational vehicles can be seen on
the roads.

Car hire   The international car-rental firms are to be
found in the main towns and tourist centres, and they
accept the usual credit cards. They have similar

standards and service to those you would expect to find anywhere, and you can often leave the car at a different town at no extra charge. However, the vehicles of some of the smaller, and cheaper, independent car-hire firms need to be checked over carefully before you take them out, as they will invariably have been driven very hard indeed.

To hire a car you should in theory produce an international driving licence, but a national one is accepted more often than not. Insurance is provided by the hire company – be sure to check that the third-party cover is substantial.

Roads   The road system is improving all the time, and most of the major towns are connected by reasonable, asphalted, arterial roads. Twentieth-century industrialization and technology came to Turkey late and the infrastructure has a lot of catching up to do. The crash programme of road building means that the roads exist – but a lot of the earlier workmanship was not of the highest quality. As a result some of the routes are likely to be good in parts but have sections that are pot-holed and rutted. Those that are marked on a map or have a sign reading *stabilize* (stabilized) are of loose gravel chippings ready for asphalting. Tourist areas, both scenic and historic, have been given priority in the road building programme, and it should not be too long before a good road links all the resorts on the Aegean and Mediterranean coasts. Reference should be made to the latest free road map, obtainable from the Tourist Offices, which is updated annually.

The E5 axis road, which runs from the Bulgarian border via Istanbul and Ankara to Tarsus and Adana on the south coast, and then on to Syria, will eventually be a complete two-lane highway. The section from Istanbul to Ankara is not yet complete and it is fast and rather dangerous, with the worst parts where the improved road drops down to unfinished sections, usually with no let-up in the speed of the traffic. It has twenty-four-hour service areas at regular intervals.

The section from Edirne to Istanbul, known as

Londra Asfaltı (the London Tarmac) is used by many trucks of all nationalities, as this is the highway from Europe to the Middle East. It is notorious for serious accidents and great care should be exercised. If you arrive in Turkey from Bulgaria late in the day it is a great temptation to drive on to Istanbul that night – but to do so is very unwise.

Branching off the E5 are the E24 to Iraq and the E23 to Iran, both asphalted and in course of improvement. In winter the Tahir Pass on the E23 and the Gülek Boğazı Pass on the E5 between Ankara and Adana can on occasion be closed. Meltwater from the surrounding mountains sometimes carries away parts of the E24 in spring.

Driving

Driving is on the right. The symbols on the road signs are more or less those found in the rest of Europe, as Turkey is conforming to EEC standards. The important written signs are: *dur* (stop); *dikkat* (caution); *girilmez* (no entry); *tehlike* (danger); and *tek istikamet* or *tek yön* (one way only). Also look out for the delightful sign indicating a slippery road – it's an umbrella surmounting a skid-mark.

There is a system of on-the-spot fines for traffic offences, but foreigners are rarely stopped unless the transgression is very serious indeed.

Seat belts, or motor-cycle crash helmets, should be worn by law and you are likely to be stopped and cautioned for not wearing them; nevertheless, few people put them on. The speed limits are 50 kph (31 mph) in towns and 99 kph (60 mph) on the rest of the road system. They are not often adhered to!

Traffic lights follow the sequence found in Britain; red is followed by red and amber together, then green; amber on its own comes before the red light. At night and weekends some lights show: flashing yellow, which means proceed with caution; flashing red, which means pass only if you can see the road is clear; and flashing green, which means pass but be aware that the crossing is not light-controlled. At roundabouts controlled by traffic lights you may find you are stopped part-way round by a red light. Some traffic lights have an arrow silhouetted on the red and green lights. This indicates the direction to which that light refers when lit, and can be confusing until you are used to it.

Pedestrian crossing   Pedestrian crossings are marked by black and white markings on the road and a sign with a man silhouetted on a blue background. If, as a driver, you stop at one to give way to pedestrians you will provoke a cacophony of outraged hooting from the cars behind you. As a walker you are safer finding a traffic-free spot to cross the road – and certainly never place any reliance on traffic giving way on crossings.

Night driving   Off the main highways the good roads are very good, traffic is relatively light, and it is a pleasure to drive. However, the accident rate is disproportionately high for the number of cars on the roads, and most foreigners rarely if ever drive at night. This is because it is not uncommon to find broken-down vehicles, especially trucks, on the side of the road without lights, which adds to the difficulties of occasional pot-holes, stray sheep, unlit tractors racing home at dusk and petrol tankers trying to make their last deliveries before all the petrol stations close at 10 o'clock.

Having said all that, the British representative of a firm distributing English-language books to schools has, for the past two years, driven alone all over Turkey by day and night. She – yes, and on a single-status (unmarried) posting – reports nothing but courtesy from the Turkish people both on the roads and off.

Driving and car tests   The Turkish driving test, until recently merely a formality but now very strict, has separate eyesight, theory and practical sections. Turks generally drive very well, with a sort of exuberant anarchy. Traffic lights and road signs are often disregarded if there is no one about, and on crowded roads the rule is to find a space and move into it. Turks tend to be as courteous to foreigners on the roads as they are elsewhere.

Theoretically vehicles are tested every two years for roadworthiness. This has recently been extended from six months in an attempt to catch up with the backlog and bring all cars into the net; until this happens there will continue to be a lot of ramshackle vehicles on the roads.

Seeing the sites   Thousands of foreign visitors drive successfully and without incident all over Turkey every year. It is undoubtedly the best way to see the countryside and especially the more remote archaeological sites, which are signposted with yellow finger-boards. Towns are marked by blue signs which also show the population (*nüfus*) and the height above sea level in metres (*rakım*); villages are marked by white signs with black lettering. If you see a place marked by a yellow sign with blue lettering it is a village with tourist development.

If you have a breakdown or accident, turn to p. 92.

Asking for directions Turkish people are not the world's best at reading maps. Give them the sun, the stars and some landmarks and they are happy, but a plan often causes confusion and sometimes embarrassment. A Turk does not like to say no to a request from a traveller and will always try to help: honour may on occasion come before truth. Directions are therefore given regardless. Unless particularly westernized Turks do not use reference books or guidebooks, seeing them as a sign of failure and weakness. A method some visitors adopt is to ask directions from three (some insist it must be five) people and take the majority view. The important thing is not to rush, not to get upset about directions, and to realize that you will probably meet many pleasant and interesting people as you take a circuitous route.

Fuel Petrol (*benzin*) and diesel (*dizel* or *motorin*) pumps are not as widely available as in other parts of Europe and you may find only two-star petrol in the remoter areas. It is always advisable to keep the tank fairly full. Fuel is very cheap, not only because of the exchange rate but also because this is government policy.

Bicycles

Quite a number of people, especially from Germany, choose to cycle round Turkey, taking advantage of the cheap hotels and plentiful campsites. There are no particular difficulties, but motorized Turks do adopt a rather macho attitude towards those travelling under their own steam. Despite the limitations of the road surfaces, not to mention the mountains, it is a delightful way to see the country. Very few Turkish people ride bicycles.

Although the rail network runs over 5,000 miles *Trains*
(8,000 km) it rarely seems necessary to use it, since
the buses are so good and the trains are rather old and
slow. The one exception is the line from Istanbul to
Ankara, where the *Mavi Tren* (Blue Train) runs daily
from Haydarapaşa Station on the Asian side. Advance
reservations are always necessary (tel. 337 9911), as
they are for the night express which has a choice of
couchette or sleepers.

An investment programme to improve the rolling
stock is in hand, and no doubt it will eventually be
better. The service between Istanbul and İzmir has
been one of the first beneficiaries, and a sleeper train
runs each night.

Rather than take the train all the way round the Sea of *Ferries*
Marmara from Istanbul to İzmir, there is a ferry and
train service with a connection via Bandırma.

In fact, except for their toilets and the problem
finding out where they are going, the ferries are one
of the pleasantest forms of long-distance travel in
Turkey. The network is based on Istanbul and is run
by the nationalized Turkish Maritime Lines: if ever
there was a classic example of the dead hand of state
control, this is it. The organization is redolent of the
introspection found before the current liberalization
programme – as far as they are concerned, you can
take their services or leave them. Turkish people
themselves have difficulty in obtaining timetable
information, and for a foreigner it is virtually
impossible. The network is about the only organization that has not taken advantage of the tourist boom
and marketed its services in foreign languages. It is
very rare even to find an employee who speaks
English, and that nowadays is unusual for Turkey.

As for the toilets on their boats, they must be the
dirtiest and most disgusting anywhere in the world.

The twenty-four-hour clock is used throughout – in *Timetables*
fact if you ask someone the time they are more than
likely to tell you it is, say, twenty-one thirty, rather
than nine-thirty p.m.

Departure times are indicated by '*dan*' or '*den*' (they mean exactly the same thing) after the name of the town; thus 'İzmir '*den* 10.30' and Istanbul '*dan* 17.30' are departures from İzmir at 10.30 a.m. and Istanbul at 5.30 p.m.

Without doubt the best information about transport schedules and timetables is to be found in '*Spot on Istanbul*' and '*Spot on Turkish Travel*' (see p. 265).

Urban Transport Within cities and towns, transport is by bus, trolley bus, dolmuş, taxi (*taksi*), car and ferry.

Bus and trolley Tickets for these must be bought from booths at the main stopping points, and placed in a box beside the driver as you get in. You will sometimes find old men and cripples at bus stops selling tickets at very slightly inflated prices – and it is charitable to use their services.

Routes and plans It is impossible to find plans of the bus routes, save for that of Istanbul published in *Spot on Istanbul* (see p. 625). However, tourist offices usually provide a town map – in smaller places a photocopy of a hand-drawn map – on which they will carefully draw the main stops. These are a great aid to getting around since very few streets have name signs.

Bus passes In the main cities you can get a monthly bus pass, for which you need to take two passport-type pictures to the local bus office. They take a lot of journeys to be worthwhile, and they are not valid on minibuses and those not owned by the municipality.

Minibus Privately run minibuses operate competitively on regular routes; their destination is shown by a plastic sign in the front window. At busy periods they have a boy hanging out of the half-open door shouting where they are going. His job is also to cram in the last six passengers just when you had observed to the two people sitting on your lap that this one should win the record for numbers in a minibus. If you ask the boy the way and your pronunciation vaguely approximates anywhere *en route* you will

find yourself grabbed by the shoulder and shoved in.
Fares are not expensive.

Dolmuş The *dolmuş* in the town are the same as
those in the rural area, except they stop more
frequently. They usually take the form of large fifties'
American cars, again with the yellow band, and they
have a plastic sign in the windscreen stating the
ultimate destination. The point where they wait to fill
up is often marked in the town by a sign with a black
D on a blue background. Indicate that you want to
get out and the driver will pull up at the next point
(unmarked and known only to him and the regulars)
where, by convention, he stops. The *dolmuş* provides
a cheap, if somewhat squashed, form of transport and
a good chance to get speaking to the locals. The only
way to discover the routes is by trial and error. If you
ask locals, it is unlikely they will know unless they
happen to go that way themselves – but, for the
reasons given earlier, they will not fail to give
directions. Bon voyage!

Taxi Taxi (*taksi*) fares are very cheap compared with the
rest of Europe. Taxis can be recognized by the
chequered yellow and black band round the car, and
many of them are painted yellow all over. It is now
becoming common, especially in the cities and tourist
areas, to telephone for taxis. Hotels usually have the
number of a firm they use. Until recently it was the
practice to haggle and negotiate the fare in advance,
save on a few routes, such as to and from the airport,
for which prices were fixed by the municipality.
Meters have recently been introduced and are now
common in most municipalities. Following from the
practice of fixed fares, tipping is not commonplace
nor expected. It is prudent when getting into the car
to check that the driver has switched on the meter
display. In some tourist spots drivers of metered taxis
illegally try to haggle a fixed price before setting off –
they should be beaten down if they absolutely refuse
to turn on the meter.

   Taxi drivers in Turkey, especially away from the
tourist areas, tend to be helpful and courteous – even

though they will rarely know the street you want to
go to.

Car   *Hired limousine* Chauffeured limousine services
are available in the main towns. They can be found
through travel bureaux, the international hotels and
advertisements in the English-language newspapers.
They are usually Mercedes or Cadillacs, but what is
believed to be the only Rolls Royce in Turkey can be
hired from Inter Limousine in Istanbul (tel. 168 69
90).

Parking Parking in towns is a problem. However, it
is rare for cars with foreign plates to get a ticket, so
why not just join in the general mêlée! There are
many 'No parking' (*Park Yapılmaz*) areas, which
seem an invitation to Turks to park. In fact there are
all sorts of local arrangements, and some cars have
permits to park on the pavements. This makes
walking a little hazardous, especially if you are
passing just as the workers from a nearby office are all
leaving together and driving home along the pavement.
    The most outrageously parked cars are towed away
by the municipality from time to time.

Boat   Ferries are an important part of the municipal
transport systems in Istanbul and İzmir. In the tourist
regions you will find motor boats for transport to
remote bays and beaches. These tend to operate on
the *dolmuş* principle of leaving when full. They also
operate day trips to sites of special interest, and can be
hired exclusively for special trips at a negotiated price.

Fortunately all is not mechanized – yet. In the more
remote areas you may just be offered a lift on the back
of a donkey or pony, in a horse and phaeton or even
in an ox cart. Perhaps you should take it while you
have the chance, for those modes of transport are
disappearing fast.

Medical and Emergency Services

Turkey is an active participant in the work of the World Health Organization, which has an office in Ankara. The government has a policy of working to the WHO's standards, especially those of the Food and Agriculture Organization (FAO).

The emergency services – and the authorities would be the first to admit it – have been lagging behind in the advances towards Europeanization. This means that the visitor should take certain elementary precautions.

Medical emergencies

Make sure you are fully covered by insurance. Emergency medical treatment is free for all irrespective of country of origin or means; thereafter you must, in certain cases, pay for your own medicines and prescriptions. There are charges for certain treatments: in the case of a foreigner, whether covered by insurance or not, these charges would be dealt with later. There is no question of the American practice applying, whereby your means are checked before you can be dealt with in an emergency.

Telephone 077. Istanbul has an ambulance service run by the Ministry of Health which is hoped to be a model for other cities. It has been set up by a very dynamic director, a lady who has tried to take the best elements of other European ambulance services, and is constrained only by the resources available. Most of the vehicles are new and have the latest resuscitation equipment, and crews are being trained in emergency procedures.

Ambulance

Other cities' ambulance services are not so good as yet, and the best policy in the case of serious accident is to get to hospital by whatever means as quickly as possible.

Turkish people are anxious to help visitors in an emergency just as in everything else. However, many people do not have even an elementary knowledge of first aid and they can on occasion compound injuries by moving people when they would be better left where they are until skilled help arrives. Anyone having the misfortune to find themselves in this situation should remember the words *bir dakika* (literally meaning 'one minute' but used for 'hang on') and *dikkat et* ('be careful').

There are private ambulance services in the main towns and they vary in the quality of service they offer. Telephone numbers are listed in Friday's *Turkish Daily News* and the weekly *Dateline Turkey*, together with those of the major hospitals and other emergency numbers.

Car crash Most car crashes occur on the very fast E5 trunk road – and some are extremely spectacular. Because of this, special provisions have been made and the emergency services should theoretically be quickly on the scene.

In the event of an accident, whether anyone is injured or not, the police must be notified as a report has to be made. Once the injured have been taken to hospital (see above), you can think about the car.

If you are a member of a motoring organization that has a reciprocating arrangement, the Turkish Touring Club (TTOK) will see to it that you get the same facilities as you would at home. They can arrange transport of the vehicle and repairs, and get payment from your own organization later.

Turkish mechanics are some of the most ingenious found anywhere; they seem to be able to repair anything using bits of old tin can and wire, and do not charge the earth for it. In fact, if you feel you are going to have a breakdown it's well worth heading straight for Turkey!

If the car is a write-off or stolen, do not forget it is stamped in your passport and you will not be allowed to leave the country without the car or a cancelled stamp. You must arrange for a written-off car to be taken to the nearest customs compound, where the stamp will be cancelled. Any cars not collected in three months are disposed of. In the case of a stolen car you need a certificate from the governor (*vali*) of the province in which it happened – a procedure that involves a large number of forms.

Hospitals

The quality of hospital services varies, as it does in any country, from region to region and from speciality to speciality. Turkish people are not on the whole content with the medical services, and there is a great deal of criticism in the press. This is in part due to the high expectations of people returning from foreign countries, especially from Germany, who want the best of what they have seen there. As yet the resources are not available. However, as a guest and foreigner you will get the best of everything, and may never see the worst side of the facilities.

The standard of nursing will fairly certainly not be as high as that you might find at home. Nurses are trained as they go along and are not very well paid. In any case, except in specialist hospitals in the main cities, it is usual to take somebody along to act as your personal nurse. This person will deal with food and laundry, and will also be responsible for watching to see that any drips or medical equipment continue to function properly.

If you go into hospital for an operation the surgeon will give you a list of drugs, syringes and so on that must be bought in advance from a pharmacy.

International hospitals Generally speaking, the expertise is greater in the university and teaching hospitals in the main cities, than it is in the smaller towns. Theoretically the best is in the foreign hospitals in Istanbul, Ankara and İzmir, but this is not necessarily the case as there is so much variation between specialities. You must make your own judgement. If you are able, consult with others who are likely to know.

Organs There is one little convention that you may find strange, and the squeamish may find rather disturbing. If you have an organ removed in an operation you will be presented with it, in a plastic

bag, shortly after you come round from the anaesthe-
tic. You should give a fairly substantial tip to the
person who presents you with the bag, as a good luck
token against further illnesses.

Doctors Local doctors can be recognized by the large boards
outside their surgeries announcing their speciality:
operator, for example, means the doctor is a surgeon.
There is an English-speaking doctor in most communities, as most doctors do part of their training in a
foreign language. The difficulty, especially in a small
town, is to find someone with both the right
speciality and the right language. You may have to
find someone to act as an interpreter.

Dentists You can spot a dentist by the sign *diş operatörü* (tooth
operator). The standards vary as anywhere else, but
are reckoned in general to be fairly high. In the main
cities English-speaking dentists advertise in the
English-language newspapers. The best way to find
the right dentist for non-emergency treatment is by
recommendation. Treatment, which is relatively inexpensive, has to be paid for.

Pharmacies In all the cities and most of the main towns there is at
and least one chemist's shop or pharmacy (*eczane*) which
prescriptions is open twenty-four hours a day. A notice in the
window of all the pharmacies tells you which it is,
and may have directions on how to get there and a
phone number. Trying ringing if you are really stuck,
as many pharmacists speak English.

Most of the drugs found in the western world are
available in Turkey – many of them are made there
under licence. However, you are advised to take a
supply with you of anything you need, as the brand
and trade names are often different and some locally
made products may not be of the same standard. It is a
good idea to keep the prescription of anything you
need (you will find it on the side of the box or on a
piece of paper inside), and if you are in difficulty a
pharmacist will be able to match it up to a local
product.

Contraception and worse Condoms and contraceptive pills are freely available in pharmacies. However, if you are taking a regular brand of pill the above comments apply. The 'morning after' pill is not available.

Abortion is legal up to twelve weeks and the final decision, by law, is that of the mother. If the father wants the baby aborted against the mother's wishes it will not be done. And if it seems strange to you that this legislation should be necessary, remember the traditional role of women and see p. 173–4.

Other emergency services

The Police

There are four types of police.

Polis These are the national force in green uniforms that you will first come across at the border as you enter the country. They have roughly the same duties as the police anywhere – and are as bureaucratic as you might expect. If you have something stolen, the form-filling at the police station takes an age.

The emergency telephone number is 055. It is unlikely the operator will speak English, and if you are desperately having a go in pidgin Turkish, do remember the stress is on the ends of words.

Trafik polisi The *Trafik polisi* are just that. They try to keep the traffic flowing in very overcrowded cities and can impose on-the-spot fines, for which they issue a receipt. They can be recognized by the words *Trafik Polisi* on the front of their cars.

Turistik polis These will be found only in areas where there is the greatest concentration of tourists. They are given English, French and German lessons and speak these languages with a wide variety of proficiency. Seemingly selected as much for their diplomacy as their policing, they do not have the aggressive and forbidding manner that characterizes members of the other branches.

Jandarma Soldiers who wear the red armband marked '*jandarma*' are military police – soldiers who carry out a policing function. Many of them are conscripts, and they can probably tell you exactly how many days they have left to serve. They are more approachable than the ordinary police and usually try to be as helpful as the rest of the population are. They are given guard duties, and often function in a detective role. Those of them that have white lanyards, pistols in white holsters and '*As İz*' written on their helmets are *Askeri İnzibat*. Their job is to keep off-duty soldiers under control.

Belediye zabitasi These blue-uniformed officials are a leftover of the old Islamic commercial police. They are trading standards officers, and they also attempt to prevent illegal trading. They have quite wide powers over retailers and if you should feel cheated at any time they may be able to help.

If you have a problem with faulty goods and they have a TSE (Türk Standartları Enstitüsü) label on them, complain to the TSE office in Ankara.

Night watchmen Every walled city used to have its night watchman, but sadly they have all gone save one: Kayseri's night watchman has, since the time the town was named Caeserea, blown his tin whistle on every street corner to tell people that all is well.

Fire brigade The fire service is part professionals and part volunteers. The emergency telephone number is 000. The most common cause of fires is badly maintained LPG (liquefied petroleum gas) equipment and you should keep a wary eye on it, especially if staying in cheaper hotels. Fire regulations, escape routes and emergency procedures are not yet as well developed as those in other tourist countries, although they are being worked on.

Hotels and Accommodation

The range of accommodation in Turkey is wide, and there is quite a difference between that in the towns and that found in the villages and the countryside. Much of it is very good – the tradition of hospitality to travellers makes sure of that – and all of it is cheaper than the equivalent standard elsewhere in Europe.

The Ministry of Tourism is in the process of inspecting public accommodation. Eventually it will all be registered and licensed in various categories. A great deal of the work has already been done and those hotels not licensed by the ministry have usually been granted a certificate by the municipality. In an attempt to keep hotels up to scratch, it is compulsory for them to have a book for suggestions and complaints prominently displayed; these, in theory, are regularly looked at by inspectors. Tourist offices publish lists of licensed hotels, but they do tend to be a little out of date and some of the information may be wrong. In a few cases the relationship of the hotelier to the compiler of the list is the criterion for inclusion.

When the potential for tourism was first recognized and the first tourist hotels were built, they were not really up to western standards. They have become a little dilapidated since. There is currently a boom in hotel building, to service not only the tourist industry but also increasing business interest in the country. Theoretically this is under the control of the Ministry of Tourism, and building standards and the quality of fittings should be of an acceptable level. They are certainly better than they were.

Hotels

Hotel categories Hotels are divided into five classes, an important fact since the range of prices allowed to be charged within each class is fixed by the government. The system of symbols by which they are designated on brochures and signs is a little confusing, and a wrong interpretation can lead to wrong expectations.

International standard The premier class, designated by 'HL' or five stars and referred to as *lüks sınıf* (luxury class), is of hotels of ubiquitous international standard. Their prices are fixed and marked in US dollars and, although expensive in Turkish terms, are better value than in the remainder of Europe. Here you will find most of the staff speak English and probably at least one other language.

Hilton was the first of the chains to come to Turkey, with its hotel on a large site overlooking the Bosphorus in Istanbul. It was quickly followed by Sheraton and the two hotels, together with the Etap Marmara, now dominate the skyline of the Taksim district, sticking incongruously out of nineteenth-century and earlier architecture. Hilton have added a conference centre and sports facilities in Istanbul, have opened a hotel in Ankara, and are building a third in İzmir, to open in 1991. They also have a smaller tourist hotel in Mersin. Sheraton have recently refurbished the interior at Istanbul so that the standard is as good as that found anywhere in the world. They too have moved into Ankara, and to Antalya.

There are also two Turkish groups with luxury hotels. Etap, now part of the Pullman Group, is on a par with any of the international companies. The other group, whose hotels can be recognized by the prefix *Büyük* (which in this context means 'grand', although the more normal meaning is 'big'), is a government-run organization, although it is thought to be fairly high on the list for privatization. Overall their hotels are not as good as the others in the HL class but, as Turks and foreigners alike are frequently heard to observe, what do you expect from a hotel run by civil servants?

Star ratings Below the international class, hotels are graded from one to four in a rather complicated system that can cause some confusion. The star markings are clear enough, since they work in descending order from ★★★★ through to ★. However, hotels with four stars are designated 'H1' or '*1 sınıf*' (first class) and should not be confused with luxury class; thereafter they descend to 'H4' or '*4 sınıf*' (fourth class) which is, of course, one star. Below this there are establishments designated with just 'H', which usually indicates a cheap local transit hotel licensed by the local authority. (See p. 108–9.)

Value for money

There is sometimes very little to choose between hotels in the various classes save the price, which is fixed in US dollars in the case of international (HL) and four star (H1) hotels, and German marks thereafter. It can happen that the hotel has made improvements and, as redesignation takes some time, is still trading at the old prices. Conversely, of course, hotels may have slipped from grace but have not yet received a visit from a ministry inspector.

The answer must always be: if you do not like the hotel or you feel it is bad value, then move somewhere else. There are plenty of good hotels to choose from, especially if you look off the main streets, forget the star markings and make your own checks. In any case it is as well to check the room in advance, as the standard of the reception area is not always a good indicator.

Most towns are extremely noisy – and it starts at dawn. A room at the back, considered less desirable and often cheaper, may well be the one that allows you a few extra hours' peaceful sleep.

By law the hotel charges must be displayed in reception and again in the rooms. A service charge of 10 or 15 per cent is usually added to bills in hotels with a star rating. Tipping on top of this is not usual except as appreciation for some personal and exceptional service. Value Added Tax (KDV) at 12 per cent is extra in five-star hotels and down to about three-star; below this level the price is usually quoted inclusive, and in these establishments it is often quite easy to negotiate prices.

Women and   Hotels at the cheaper end of the market are intended
couples   for men only. This is not to say that women alone or in groups will have problems, but they may feel more comfortable if they ask to be directed to an *aile hoteli* (family hotel) where single men are not admitted. These days unmarried couples – who will be identified by the passports required to be produced in all hotels – do not often have problems in sharing a room. This is a concession to the odd cultural ways of foreigners; if one or both of the couple were Turkish they would more than likely be refused admission. These cultural differences have in the past been the cause of some unpleasant incidents in more remote areas, and it is as well to be aware of possible difficulties.

Lifts and   In all except international hotels, lifts have no inner
elevators   door. Particular care should be taken to keep children away from the moving wall. When opening the door do it quickly, since the lift is likely to move off again as someone else calls it. Floors are marked ground (*zemin* or Z), first, second and so on, in the British as opposed to the American form of numbering.

Gambling   'Casinos' (*gazino*) are found in luxury class hotels and in some tourist spots. They have been barred to Turkish people. In fact the label 'casino' is something of a misnomer, since table games are illegal except in four places (to which Turkish people have never been admitted), and there they consist solely of one-armed bandits. Anyone who gambles in public can be sent to prison for between one and two months.

Turks, nevertheless, are inveterate gamblers. The Istanbul Hilton had to remove a neon sign with a moving ball in a routlette wheel as waiting chauffeurs were found to be betting on it.

Visitors on package tours do not have as much choice, **Package deals**
but the tour companies and the Turkish government
are very keen that the Spanish situation – unfinished
hotels, polluted beaches and so on – should not
happen in Turkey. The government theoretically
exercises strict controls over waste-disposal systems,
and all building work in the tourist areas must stop at
the end of April. The effect of this latter law is that
during April there is a frenzied scramble to get
building work finished, and work in progress tends to
be more of a nuisance than ever.

The best value packages tend to be those that
include *pansiyons* (see below), where the accommodation is simple and friendly.

As in any developing industry, teething problems
inevitably happen. Only time can tell if they will
become serious.

Apart from hotels there are motels, guest houses **Other**
(*pansiyons*), *auberges*, holiday villages and mocamps, **accommoda-**
campsites and short-stay apartments. **tion**

Hot water in these is often provided by a system of
solar panels on the roof. In many establishments this
does not have an alternative fuel booster, and the
water can only be lukewarm on overcast days in April
and October.

Motels are classed in two groups, M1 and M2. As *Motels*
they are a relatively new phenomenon and built to
western European and American models and standards, they are on the whole comfortable and good
value. One group to look out for in particular is
Turban Motels. These have been developed under the
auspices of the Tourism Bank (hence the name),
which exercises strict quality controls. Motels are
located on the major highways and in some tourist
areas.

Guest houses are designated 'P' for *pansiyon*, from *Pansiyons*
the French *pension*. In fact they tend to be more like
small hotels with basic facilities and the minimum of
frills. They are often attached to restaurants and bars
on the coast, and usually offer extremely good value

for clean if somewhat spartan accommodation. Theoretically they are divided into three classes, which again has the effect of controlling how much they may charge, but in practice a free market pretty well exists and a little bit of haggling can result in some bargains.

Auberges   *Auberges*, designated 'O', are hostels in mountain locations associated with climbing or skiing. They tend to have a minimum of facilities and are being used less frequently as hotels are built to service the developing interest in mountain sports. Similar accommodation at spas is labelled 'K'.

Spas and thermal resorts went out of fashion and fell into disuse earlier this century, but their hot and curative water kept on flowing. With the resurgence of interest in historical sites came a realization that spas too might have something to offer. They range from beautiful, restored marble buildings with channelled water and baths, to bowls of natural limestone fed from springs. In total they are claimed to cure just about every known ailment – some are even reckoned to have cosmetic properties – and the Tourist Board publishes a list of the chemical analyses of the various waters and the claims made for them.

Holiday   Holiday villages in various forms are found all over
villages and   the coastal and tourist areas. They are often sign-
mocamps   posted 'TK', from the Turkish translation *tatil köyu*, and are classed A and B according to the facilities they offer. There is a wide variety of styles, from Butlin-like camps with log cabin chalets to self-catering operations with central facilities suitable for conference use. At many holiday villages it is possible just to turn up and stay for one or two nights without advance booking.

The BP company runs seven mocamps under the Kervansaray label: these are part campsite and part holiday village. They are all near historical sites, the standard is deliberately high and many of them have sports facilities.

There are campsites, open from April through to October, in all the popular tourist areas. They are signposted *Kamping* or *Mokamp* and many have extremely good facilities and beautiful settings. Tents, motor homes and caravans are usually all mixed in together and most sites have electricity points and communal cooking facilities. There is nearly always a restaurant attached to the camp, and communal and family barbecues are a popular pastime. Some of the more attractive camps are on beaches and in isolated spots in the country, and they make a good base from which to see the countryside. It is often possible to rent tent- or chalet-type accommodation if you turn up on spec.

Campsites

Individuals find it very difficult to find flats and apartments, especially for short stays. Landlords invariably want six months' rent in advance, and usually more. However, one company, First Apartments, has opened a block of studios in Ankara which can be rented for upwards of a week. They are of luxury standard and have kitchens, although they can be taken fully serviced, and they offer very good value for money. Net Holdings, a Turkish company which specializes in turning historic buildings to alternative commercial uses, is currently converting a row of buildings in Istanbul put up by the Ottoman Sultans as dormitories for naval officers. They will become an apartment hotel managed by Ramada Hotels.

Short-stay appartments

Without doubt the best way to get to understand Turkey is to stay with a family. It is not unusual for foreign visitors to be invited into homes; indeed the tradition of hospitality to *misafir* (travellers) almost conveys a sense of obligation for such an invitation. In the cities nowadays, and in middle-class homes, little difference will be found in the way of life from that found in the west. However, in other areas older customs still prevail and you should, for example, remove your shoes on entering a house. Some families live, eat and sleep in one room, kept spotlessly clean, and with the bedding stowed neatly away each

Family hospitality

morning, because the beds double up as seating. You will probably sit cross-legged on the floor to eat food placed in the centre on a large tin tray. Traditionally the men eat first, served by the wife and daughters; if western visitors are of both sexes the women seem to be treated as honorary men, in a perfectly natural-seeming concession to their own cultural traditions.

If you have been invited to stay the night in a family home of any type, you will find that the whole of the routine of the household revolves around your comfort.

Ancient *housing rights*   *Gecekondu* (loosely translated as 'night dwelling') houses are self-built by the poor. An ancient rule is that if someone lays claim to a vacant piece of municipally owned land at dusk, and can build a dwelling with the roof on before sunrise, it gives squatter's rights to the land. Gradually the family

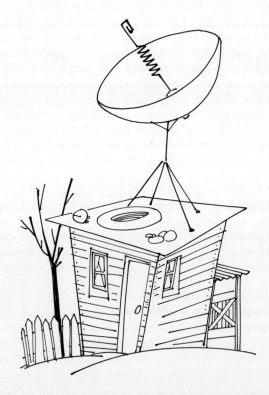

makes the shack into a more permanent house with brick walls and a tiled roof: inside these houses look like any other, often with stereos and televisions.

Vast areas on the outskirts of the expanding cities have been covered with these houses, to the consternation of the planning authorities. Legislation has now been passed that no more *gecekondu* rights may be established. Those already in occupation are being given the right to buy the title to the property at a price that to us seems incredibly cheap, but which for many people takes a lot of raising. Some municipalities enforce this more rigidly than others and from time to time you may see bulldozers moving into new squatters' dwellings. The system has theoretically been replaced by a system of cheap loans for housing.

On a Shoestring

In relative terms, because Turkey is much less expensive than the rest of Europe, any budget-conscious traveller will virtually be 'on a shoestring'. You can spend as you normally would, and live to a standard that elsewhere might be beyond your means; or you can stretch a small amount of money an awfully long way.

In Istanbul's Sultanahmet district is the Lâle ('Tulip', the symbol of Istanbul) Restaurant and Bar. The 'World Famous Pudding Shop', as the sign outside proclaims, used to mark the start of the 'hippie trail'. Once lifts to Afghanistan and India were arranged here, and stories swapped with outward-bound Antipodeans about conditions in Goa and Nepal. A notice-board held scribbled notes, and mail with Thai and Malaysian stamps, as venturers to the far-flung parts of the trail contacted their compatriots.

The notice-board is still there; it even has a few uncollected messages with curled brown edges. There are cloths on the tables now, and the floor has been tiled. The closure of Iran and Afghanistan means that seekers of nirvana must take another route, but the cosmopolitan atmosphere remains. The lingua franca is still English, and Turks wanting language practice mix with travellers and visitors who are going to the nearby tourist sites, or are just there to savour the good-value food and the atmosphere.

When you are there try the Asure pudding. The recipe is reputed to have been handed down from Noah and to be what he did with the leftovers when the Ark grounded on Mount Ararat. It is very good if you like *compote* of dried fruit and nuts – and who are we to dispute its provenance?

Just round the corner is the Bodrum ('Cellar') Bar.

It is cramped, smoky, noisy, and a super and friendly rendezvous.

Travel

The variety of flight-only charter deals available means that flying in should not be dismissed. Turkish Maritime Lines' ferries from Venice and Ancona give student discounts of 15 per cent on single and 25 per cent on return journeys. There are also extremely valuable reductions for journalists on all forms of transport to and within Turkey.

The cheapest means of getting to Turkey is undoubtedly by bus or coach (see p. 6). Whilst there are no formal discounts, haggling is theoretically possible as the coaches are run by private companies. If you say you are a student, you may get 10 or 15 per cent off.

Many students and young people arrive in Istanbul by rail on an under-26 Inter-Rail or Transalpino ticket. The last part from the border can be infuriatingly slow and uncomfortable, especially at the end of a long journey. It is a good idea, and costs just a couple of pounds or a few dollars, to get out and switch to a local bus at Edirne.

Inter-Rail is only valid for Europe, so it stops at Istanbul. Transalpino, with its discounted tickets to specific destinations, covers the whole of Turkey.

Discounts

Those who are eligible for a student card should make sure they have with them an ISTC international card. This will enable them to get 10 per cent discount on Turkish Airlines domestic flights, 20 per cent discounts on the railways, and an enormous 50 per cent on the already cheap entrance to museums, cinemas and concerts, and on Turkish Maritime Lines' ferries. This last discount makes travel on the ferries one of the best travel bargains in the world, and the trip from Istanbul along the Black Sea to Hopa, almost on the USSR border, is well worth investigation. Advance bookings are necessary and should be made at Turkish Maritime Lines' offices on the Karaköy side of the Golden Horn – plenty of time should be allowed to find the right desk and the right person.

Hitching Although in the west and the tourist areas the thumbing gesture is recognized, the usual Turkish way of hitching is to flag down approaching vehicles with the palm down in a 'come here' gesture. It probably happens this way because to hitch a short-distance lift is normal in the rural areas.

Long distance, it's a different proposition altogether, and few people hitch far because the buses are so cheap. It is mostly trucks that stop and the drivers usually expect some payment, often not far short of the bus fare. Though the whole thing soon ceases to be economically worth while you may well have an interesting journey, including the pleasure of sharing water-melon by a roadside fountain with some interesting characters.

Women should not hitch-hike alone – to do so is taken as an invitation to trouble. Hitch in pairs if you are absolutely determined, but still never get into a vehicle with more than one man (although if there are children around it is likely you will have no problems). Remember that in the eyes of your hosts you are behaving in a very provocative manner by hitching.

Accommoda-tion, washing and clothes

Cheap hotels Really cheap hotels (and they will be around a pound Sterling or a couple of US dollars a night) come in two types.

There are those that are intended as cheap hotels for itinerant Turks – road workers, nomadic people visiting the towns, and people on the way to begin military service. These can vary in standards of cleanliness, and though there may be a few single rooms of the broom-cupboard variety, the majority will have between two and six beds. In these hotels the idea is that you are renting a bed-space rather than a room, and they must be regarded more as dormitor-ies. It would be inadvisable for women to book in alone, but these days mixed parties will often be put

in a room together. This type of hotel should not necessarily be avoided, as in most cases you will find a typical Turkish welcome and hospitality – coupled with curiosity, since ordinary Turks consider all foreigners to be rich and therefore not needing to stay in such places.

The other type is that intended primarily for budget foreign travellers, and Turkish and overseas students. These hotels are roughly the equivalent of youth hostels, which do not exist in Turkey in the form we know them. There are a few places where a YHA card will result in a discount, but they are not significant.

Most travellers go first to Istanbul. The owners of the old Sultan Hostel, Yerebatan Cad. 35 (tel. 520 75 76) just behind the pudding shop, have now opened two more and can usually find a bed somewhere day or night – if you can wake them up. It is a good value starting point for new arrivals.

The universities are very keen on cultural exchanges, not least because, just as Turkey seems cheap to you, so your country is correspondingly expensive to Turkish people and foreign travel is very difficult. You may make contact with people from a student union who are keen to enlist your help in making contacts.

Rooms

Although not easy to find, it is possible to rent rooms – bed-sits – in family houses. The best way is to put an advertisement in *Hürriyet* and make sure there is a Turkish speaker to answer the phone on the day it goes in.

Getting clean   If you are really roughing it, then for a few hundred lira a visit to the *hamam* is not only relaxing but you get cleaned up at the same time. You will also invariably be made welcome at the ablutions outside the mosque; but try to avoid them at prayer time or on Fridays, when people are washing for religious purposes.

Clothes for the mosque   Travelling on a shoestring, you may not have a well-pressed suit in your rucksack! As the tendency in Turkey is to dress extremely well some difficulties can occur, especially when visiting mosques. In spite of the fact that allowance is always made for the strange ways of foreigners, as a courtesy you should wear your *best* jeans, certainly not shorts, and women's heads, arms and shoulders should be covered. Some mosques on tourist routes will offer you a long robe if your dress is not suitable – a few hundred lira in the offering box is called for in this case.

Entertainment and eating

Music   In the summer there is a great deal of music in parks and in the street. Throughout the year, festivals (see pp. 271–6) make for entertainment at little cost. In Ankara the State Symphony Orchestra repeats the previous evening's concert at 11 a.m. on Saturdays, with very cheap seat prices.

Cheap food   Unless you go to smart upmarket or tourist restaurants you will be hard pressed to spend a lot on food. However, a few tips may be useful. Eat lots of bread – it comes with all meals, is locally baked and wholesome and can be dipped in the sauces that are part of many dishes. Do as Turkish people do and order *meze* (starters) first. Often this is enough, as they are very filling, and it is easy to order too much of these and main courses.

Always send back any unordered dishes. In the tourist places a few unscrupulous restaurateurs will ask you to try something and then send it to your table if you say you like it – and these always seem to be the most expensive dishes.

If you really are in dire straits, Turkish people will never see you go hungry; but a few people abuse Turkish hospitality, taking it for granted, and they spoil it for the rest of us.

Casual work

Theoretically casual work is out of the question for foreigners, and until recently it was so in practice too. However, as the move towards the EEC gathers pace the authorities are taking a much more relaxed attitude. Girls in particular can sometimes pick up work in bars and restaurants in the tourist areas, and work teaching English is becoming easier to get while there. Occasionally the police have a purge on foreigners working illegally in particular districts, but prosecutions rarely follow and the employer is usually reprimanded.

Things to avoid

Drugs

You have been warned: the penalties are extremely severe for anybody caught in possession of drugs – there is a *minimum* sentence of sixteen months in gaol. Turkey had an undeserved reputation as a drug-takers' paradise in the sixties and the authorities are determined to stamp it out. The film *Midnight Express* goes some way to describing life in a Turkish gaol and embassies can do very little in these cases. The law has a concept of 'guilt by association', and everyone in the company of a person caught in possession is liable to prosecution.

The number of Turkish drug addicts is very small indeed. This is because of the strength of the family and the cultural aversion to artificial stimulants, stemming from their prohibition in the Koran and reinforced by television campaigns two or three times a year.

Fighting Disputes rarely come to blows, since Turkish people are slow to lose their temper, and most things can be settled verbally. If it should come to a fight, though, a Turk will be out to win by whatever means. If you see a fight you may note that complete strangers usually pull the protagonists apart, from embarrassment and fear of what the outcome might be.

It is very unlikely that a foreign man, even if drunk and in the lowest of bars, will get into this sort of dispute, owing to the respect all foreigners are accorded. In the even more unlikely event of a foreign woman getting into a dispute with a Turkish man, she should beware doing or saying anything that might insult his manhood, as this does cause immediate retaliation.

Onward travel The traditional overland route has been scuppered by the situation in Iran and Afghanistan. It is theoretically possible to cross the latter, but, of people from English-speaking countries, only Australians and New Zealanders are being granted visas for Iran – and they can wait up to three months for a stamp or a refusal.

Visas for Iraq and Syria are easier to obtain. Sadly, before going overland these days you are well advised to ring your embassy or consulate-general to check the current situation. Gaziantep is the staging post for bus connections to Aleppo, Lattakia, Damascus and Baghdad. Those staying in Syria, even if they have a visa, are required to change the equivalent of about £60 or $95 US at the border. There are also buses to Saudi Arabia but very few visas are issued, and then only for work or visiting relations.

It is possible to cross the border into the Soviet Union by rail from Kars. A USSR visa is needed, and you have to pre-book accommodation through the Soviet organization Intourist. If you know your schedule and when you are likely to be in eastern Turkey, it is worth considering. The road between Turkey and the Soviet Union, closed by Stalin in

1937, has been opened as part of *glasnost*. At present, crossing is limited to families split by the border, but it is thought that it will eventually become the main European trade route into the south-western part of the Soviet Union. Check the current position as it may soon provide some interesting hitching possibilities. Buses could also run eventually.

Hitching on the Levant coast is easy and relatively safe, but for most travellers it's a case of gritting the teeth, paying the fares and missing all the cultural experiences you have to fly over.

Food

Turkish food has elements of the culinary traditions of the wide variety of cultures that formed the Ottoman empire; the origins of the recipes stretch from the Danube to the Persian Gulf, from the Balkans as far south as the Sudan. The fact that the country is completely self-sufficient in food is reflected in the wide range of fresh dishes served. The Turks claim, with some justification, that theirs is the third cuisine after Chinese and French.

The distinctive flavour of the food comes from the practice of cooking meat and vegetables together. Separate sauces are rarely seen, except that yogurt is poured over some dishes. Olive oil is much used, and cold vegetable dishes cooked in oil with a little sugar are typical. Some sort of salad is customarily served with most meals.

Aubergine (*patlıcan*), potatoes (*patates*) and spinach (*ıspanak*) are among the more commonly found vegetables. Fish and fresh meats, of which lamb is the most common, are usually grilled if they are to be eaten on their own.

Apricots (*kayısı*), cherries (*kiraz*), water-melon (*karpuz*) and strawberries (*çilek*) are amongst the fruits found in season – and the wide variation in the climate means this is most of the year round.

Eating habits The word *yemek* means food, a meal, a course of a meal and to eat – the distinctions we make are just not used. Food is not eaten very hot, and lukewarm dishes are the norm. This is fortunate because meals are taken slowly, with conversation given equal importance to the food.

Meal times are less rigid than you might be used to: people are more likely to eat when they are hungry than because it is time to eat. Turkish people do not have fixed courses, but traditionally share individual dishes. In the home you just get to the stage of thinking you cannot manage anything else when another dish is brought to the table. In restaurants it is the practice to order more as you go along.

Since there is little difference in the cost of preparing food at home and eating out in one of the cheaper restaurants, eating *in* is an occasion for some Turkish families. As anywhere else dinner can be a social occasion, but in Turkey the simplest meal can also be a celebration, especially if large numbers of family are present.

Turkish people do not generally eat with the fingers as is the custom in Arab countries. In middle-class homes and restaurants the knife and fork are used in a way that is a combination of British and American conventions. Amongst many other people a spoon and fork are used in whatever way is appropriate to the food being eaten. However, there is not the significance attached to the way you eat that there is in Britain. Whatever your normal practice it will be accepted, and no special attempt should be made to conform to the local customs – except in the (widespread) use of the toothpick. The convention is to pick the teeth with the right hand, using the left hand as a shield. If you do not cover your mouth when picking your teeth it is rightly considered offensive.

Table manners

You will find a *lokanta* or *restoran* on every street corner, and a few more besides. Restaurants tend to specialize much more than you may be used to and often concentrate on one or two dishes only. The menu tends to be fairly small, as usually only the freely available seasonal foodstuffs are on offer.

General restaurants fall into two types. The first have a chiller displaying hors d'oeuvres (*meze*) ready for serving, and meat, fish and possibly vegetables waiting to be cooked. When you have indicated your choice it is prepared to order, and customers are quite welcome to wander in to the kitchen to inspect the progress.

General establish- ments

In the second, used by working Turks and incredibly cheap, cooked dishes are displayed in a warming cabinet. The portions served tend to be on the small side and several dishes are usually chosen. It should be remembered that the food in these establishments is cooked in the early morning and the quality thus deteriorates during the course of the day.

You have to get into the habit of deciding what you fancy eating in two stages. Firstly decide roughly the kind of food you would like to eat and choose the restaurant. In so doing it is quite permissible to go in and out of several restaurants and look at the food in

the cold cabinet. Once settled in a restaurant, point to
the exact food you want in the cold cabinet or in the
kitchen. It is quite usual for customers to be taken
into the kitchen to help them decide what to eat –
Turkish people do it all the time.

The more important routes have a wide variety of
shacks, huts and permanent buildings catering for the
traveller. Remember that Turkish people are very
clean by nature and you are likely to come to little
harm from buying a kebab from a hand-turned spit
under a leafy shelter. The food here, again, is
amazingly cheap.
Roadside restaurants

   Look out in summer for the piles of green
water-melons and the different varieties of yellow
melon for sale beside the road. The farmer, complete
with the panniered donkey which has transported the
melons there, will usually cut one up for you to eat on
the spot. He will also be extremely curious about you
and probably make you a gift of more than you have
asked for, and you are likely to part with promises of
enduring friendship, having swapped telephone numbers.

In the towns there are kiosks selling all sorts of snack
foods, catering to the Turks' habit of eating when
hungry. The late Earl of Sandwich has a lot to answer
for – one of the more popular items is *sosis sandviç*.
These toasted sandwiches are cooked on a griddle
while you wait. Round bagels sold by street vendors,
who have glass cases on wheels, are *simit* – they are
very cheap, bread-like and filling. Sometimes the
vendor uses a stick to flick the *simit* in the direction of
the purchaser. Watch those that have fallen on the
floor being surreptitiously put back on display.
Bufe and street vendors

Speciality establish-ments

Pide, oval, flat bread-like bases with a range of
toppings, are cooked in an open-fronted oven to
order. They are pushed in with long spatulas, and cut
Pide

into slices before serving. You can ask for *yarım* (half) or *küçük (small) portions for children*. *Pide solunu*, found mainly in the western half of the country, serve the equivalent of pizza with a wide choice of ingredients. *Lahmacun pide* has minced meat and onions with tomato on top, whilst a particular Black Sea favourite, *Karadeniz peynirlisi*, combines cheese and sausage.

Börekçi   In *börekçi* only *börek* are cooked – meat or cheese sandwiched in a flaky, slightly oily, pastry, to eat there or take away. They are extremely filling and in a *borekci* it is rare to find anything else on sale save soft drinks.

Kebap salunu   *Kebap solonu* serve the *şiş* (cooked on skewers) and *doner* (cooked on an upright spit) kebabs. These days they will be familiar to most people. Sometimes they also sell *çöp kebap*, which are something of an acquired taste: *çöp* means rubbish – you will see it written on the side of bins – but in this context it refers to offal. The ingredients are mixed with herbs and spices and cooked on small spits, usually over charcoal.

Pastahane   Turkish people love sticky sweet things. In pastry shops (*pastahane*) people sit or stand to eat and talk. They are a particular favourite of students at the end of the university day. You will find traditional sweets and pastries, amongst them *hanım göbeği* (lady's navel), *dilber dudağı* (Lips of the beloved) and *bülbül yuvasi* (nightingale's nest) which is like shredded wheat formed into a nest shape and filled with pistachio nuts. All of these are soaked in syrup. Everything in a *pastahane* can also be bought to take away; purchases are carefully boxed and wrapped.

Vegetarians beware: *tavuk göğsü* and *kazan dibi* are both milk puddings flavoured with very finely minced chicken breast. *Kazan dibi* is the scrapings from the bottom of the pan when *tavuk göğsü* is poured off; it looks and tastes rather like crème caramel.

The *pastahane* is also the place to buy *lokum*

(Turkish delight), which comes in a wide variety of textures and flavours and covered with all sorts of nuts. Sugared almonds, also a Turkish speciality, are found here too.

The large international hotels tend to serve ubiquitous international cuisine. However, their Turkish specialities are to be recommended as an introduction to local cooking. The Revan Restaurant on the top of Istanbul's Sheraton Hotel takes great care in the presentation and authenticity of its Turkish regional cuisine. For those people nervous of trying new culinary experiences this restaurant is a particularly good starting point. The restaurant attached to the nearby Divan Hotel is good, and popular with expatriates.

Cosmopolitan restaurants

Fast-food establishments are springing up in the main cities and tourist resorts. One large American (not Scottish) hamburger chain is proving alarmingly popular with young Turks.

In Istanbul, Ankara and İzmir there are some very good, and in relative terms very expensive, restaurants catering for expatriate and Turkish business people. They advertise regularly in the English-language newspapers.

Staff

Nobody seems to know why it should be, but the best cooks in Turkey come from Mengen near Bolu, about halfway between Ankara and Istanbul. Ask a chef if he is Bolu trained and he will be flattered. Nowadays there is a catering school there, but the phenomenon of Bolu chefs goes back well into Ottoman times, and the annual chefs' festival there attracts thousands of entries.

Chefs

Cooks have a very definite hierarchy in the kitchen – a legacy of Ottoman days – and it is only in domestic kitchens that any women will be found.

Atatürk gave a dinner party in the Dolmabahçe Palace to King Edward VIII and Mrs Simpson (later Duke and Duchess of Windsor) when the new republic was

Waiters

just starting to achieve economic success. The gold service was in use, and a waiter came up behind the president and the King with a large tray of hors d'oeuvres – which he promptly dropped. 'I could teach everything to this nation,' said Atatürk, 'but I could never teach them to be good servants.'

The management of the burgeoning tourist industry is having the same problems. Until the formation of the republic it was Armenians and Greeks who worked in hotels and restaurants. There are now quite a few catering training schools and the standard of service is gradually improving.

It is not that waiters are rude – Turks are never deliberately rude to their guests – nor is it slow, since staff in hotels and restaurants tend to rush around all over the place. It is just that the service is delightfully and peculiarly Turkish. Dishes may not come in the order you wanted or expected, some may be forgotten or alternatives served, and you may possibly be kept waiting. If you accept that, do not expect anything different, and above all do not try to change in on the spot, all will be well.

There is one custom that some people find particularly irritating. The moment you have put the last forkful in you mouth the plate is whipped away from under your nose, giving no time to ruminate or even put the fork down again. There is a simple explanation for the haste. It is an affront to Turkish hospitality for a guest to sit before an empty plate.

Meals and dishes

Breakfast The traditional breakfast is bread, olives, white cheese, butter and jam or honey. Some people take crackers and jars of instant coffee when they go to the more remote parts so that they do not have to make too adventurous a start to the day. British lovers of bacon and eggs will have to do without the former, except in a very few establishments in the tourist areas and in the international hotels. In the more ordinary restaurants *omlet* comes fried in its own tin pan and, eaten with bread, makes quite a good breakfast.

Menemen is also a good stand-by for breakfast. It is an Aegean regional dish and consists of eggs, tomatoes and peppers cooked like an omelette.

Top class hotels usually serve a buffet breakfast with a selection of local and international foods.

To call it 'hors d'oeuvre' does not do justice to *meze*, since it pretty well makes a meal by itself. Essentially it comprises lots of little dishes, amongst which you may find the following.

Meze

Beyin salata   This is sheep's brain salad. In fact the whole organ is usually served on a bed of lettuce, and it is not for the squeamish.

Çoban salata   Literally meaning 'shepherd's salad', this is a mix of tomatoes, cucumber, olives, parsley and peppers.

Hydari   This is thick yogurt with, garlic, olive oil and mint, and has a very sharp taste.

Midye dolma   These are mussels stuffed with rice, onions and garlic and served on half the shell. Vendors often come round selling them, especially near the coast. The main mussel beds are at İzmir and at the Black Sea end of the Bosphorus, and the shellfish is very popular. However, like all trawl-feeders it can be a source of hepatitis B.

   Midye 'mussels' also come grilled on sticks, fried in batter and in mixed seafood salad.

Tarama salata   This is smoked fish roe (usually from a red mullet, but it could be caviar) mixed to a smooth paste with yogurt, garlic and olive oil. You will only find it in the more expensive restaurants.

It is said that aubergines can be cooked in a hundred different ways. The original and traditional method is to throw the tuber into the embers of a wood fire and leave to cook for about an hour. It can then be eaten out of its blackened skin or the contents scooped out and mixed with olive oil to make *patlıcan salat*. In the

The ubiquitous aubergine

best restaurants even where they do not have a wood fire it should still have a slightly smoky taste.

The equally The Turks have really taken to chips – they appear
ubiquitous everywhere disguised as *ponfrits*. Attempts at
chip nouvelle cuisine will have a couple of soggy specimens decorously draped round the plate; ask for frogs' legs and they come with chips; and a restaurateur who failed to have them regularly on the menu would soon go out of business. Traditionalists, and conservationists, may be pleased to know that they are even sold in bags made from recycled newspaper at corner *bufe*; and in restaurants a plate of chips is almost invariably smothered in tomato ketchup.

Rice İç *pilâv* is rice cooked with little pieces of liver, tomato, pine nut, onion and spices. *Bulgur pilâvı*, a staple food in the villages, is in fact boiled wheat which has been dried in the sun, and then cooked with meat or chicken broth.

Fish Whilst fish is extremely cheap in the markets, it is relatively expensive in restaurants. This is probably some quirk of governmental price control, since even in a restaurant you choose your fish, it is weighed, and you pay by the kilo.

Uskumru dolması is stuffed mackerel. The stuffing is made of carrot, pine nuts, spices and cinnamon. *Kılıç şiş* is cubed swordfish, marinated in lemon juice and olive oil, then seasoned with paprika and grilled.

Cheeses In the villages and rural areas can be found superb cheeses, the variety of which is claimed by aficionados to rival France's. However, these are rarely sold far from where they are made, and each area tends to have its own specialities. In the towns, save in Istanbul's Çiçek Pasajı and the delicatessens listed in *Spot on Istanbul*, you will usually find only pasteurized cheeses, made by the Pınar milk conglomerate, and *beyaz peynir* – an unripened, white, sheep's milk cheese which resembles salted cottage cheese and whose fat content depends on where it was made.

Tulum peynir is salty, dry and crumbly goat's milk cheese which is made in a goatskin bag. The salt content, texture and flavour vary from region to region, some of the tastiest coming from mountain goats near the eastern town of Erzincan.

Kaşa peynir is a mature, hard cheese from Thrace with a strong flavour. It is matured for several months and it originated from Bulgaria.

Kelle peynir comes from the Aegean town of Ayvalık and is an unsalted sheep's milk cheese matured in olive oil. It has a very distinctive flavour.

Perhaps the nicest of all the unusual cheeses is *oltu peynir*, from the Surt area in the Black Sea hills. This one is made in a sheepskin and is flavoured with wild garlic, parsley and many of the other herbs that grow on the higher slopes.

Dondurma (ice cream) is home made and so the variety and quality varies from place to place. Usually it is very good. In the tourist areas the vendors dress in Ottoman costumes and make quite a performance of digging ice cream out of wooden barrels and placing it in cones.

Ice cream

In Ottoman times, with a harem to be serviced, special aphrodisiacal recipes and dishes were very popular. The most common of these was, and indeed still is, *Koç yumurtası*. Found in quite a few restaurants, it translates literally as 'ram's eggs' – we might call them sweetbreads. To be effective they should be grilled over charcoal. The cheeks of the *lüfer* or blue fish have a similar effect, we are told, especially if cooked with thyme, as this too has special properties.

Aphrodisiacs

In the spice bazaars you can find *padişah kuvvet macunu*. The traders are rather coy about the current popularity of this product – loosely translated, it means 'strength paste'.

Drink

Soft drinks

Tea Tea is the main drink in Turkey and tea boys, with their trays swinging on a tripodal handle, are to be seen everywhere as they dart into offices and shops. It is served milkless in small bulbous glasses with sugar lumps on the saucer. Tea drinking is something of a ritual and the small glasses are frequently refilled.

Local *rize* tea is more bitter than you may be used to, and the method of infusion is different. The water is boiled in a kettle on top of which the teapot stands, acting as a lid. Quite a large amount of tea is put in the pot and the water and poured on. The pot is left to brew while being kept warm on top of the kettle, which is itself left on a low flame. When it is poured a little of the tea is put in the glass, and then diluted with hot water from the kettle.

In a tea garden you can ask for a *semaver* (samovar), from which everyone helps themselves through the tap at the bottom.

You will be brought tea when you sit to inspect the merchandise in a shop, or when discussing business in an office. To refuse it is slightly offensive and if you find yourself completely unable to take any more, ask for *su* (water).

Other 'teas' Eucalyptus 'tea' is very refreshing and good for colds. However, you will also be offered apple and lemon teas which are instant, chemical and a perfect example of how television marketing can change a local custom.

'A nice cup of tea' In spite of the profusion of tea, those British people who might be hoping to find a cup just like the ones they have always been used to are in for a disappointment.

Even in international hotels only Turkish tea is

available, which is more bitter than Indian. It is quite palatable with milk – but if you ask for milk with tea you will be looked at with absolute incredulity. It is just possible to get some milk, but it will invariably be brought hot. If you succeed in getting a jug of cold milk and put some in your tea, you will be surrounded by a crowd of disbelieving waiters.

Tea dances Afternoon teas are becoming popular in the major hotels. They usually have a small orchestra and sometimes dancing, and have a delightful old-fashioned air of sophistication and style.

Coffee

Thick, powdery, sweet Turkish coffee *(kahve)* is imported and thus expensive. It is drunk from small, round, porcelain cups and you will be asked how you would like it, as each cup is made individually. *Az şekerli* is with a little sugar and *orta* is medium. You can also ask for it *sade* (no sugar) or *şekerli*, which is very sweet indeed.

For instant coffee ask for *nescafe*, pretty well universally available these days (but see p. 9).

Milk Drinks

Salep is a small glass of hot milk into which has been mixed ground root of *orchis mascula* (tapioca to you and me) with cinnamon powder sprinkled on the top. It is drunk as a late-night or bedtime drink.

Hot, sweetened milk is drunk at breakfast time in a few households and you may be able to find it in restaurants. Flavoured milk drinks are also popular in winter, especially chocolate.

Yogurt

Turkey lays claim to the invention of yogurt; from there it spread throughout the Middle East. Kanlica on the Asian side of the Bosphorus, and Silivri in Thrace, are the main areas where it is produced. In villages you may find yogurt from various milks sold in the earthenware pots in which it is made.

Ayran, the mix of yogurt, water and salt sold by vendors at bus stations and wherever there are crowds of people is very refreshing once the taste has been acquired. *Cacık*, found in restaurants, is *ayran* with little bits of cucumber and is eaten or drunk with a spoon.

Water   Tap water, heavily chlorinated and not especially pleasant, is safe to drink everywhere. There are a few public fountains that are for washing only and these are marked *içilmez*. In the main cities the water pressure can get very low in the summer months.

Bottled water is on sale everywhere and many Turkish and expatriate families have canisters of fresh water routinely delivered to the door. A regular weekend excursion for some families is a visit to a local spring with the car loaded with plastic barrels.

Sadly, with the advent of packaged and marketed chemically made drinks, it is becoming increasingly rare to meet a Turk who is an expert in water sources. It is only older people now who are connoisseurs of spring waters in the manner of a wine-taster; they can tell the exact source from one mouthful. Various *maden suyu* (mineral waters) have different curative properties. If you want to be altruistic in your water purchases *Afyonkarahisar*, from the province of Afyon, is bottled by *kızılay* – the Turkish Red Crescent, equivalent to the Red Cross.

Fizzy drinks   Coke and Pepsi Colas are widely available and, thanks to TV advertising, are considered smart. Whichever one you ask for you will be served the one in stock, since little distinction is made between them. Usually people just ask for *kola*.

Yedigün (seven days) is Turkish Seven-Up, *gazoz* is fizzy lemonade or ginger beer – you never know quite which you are going to get – and *fruko* is orange soda.

Fresh fruit   There should really be no need to resort to manufac-
juices   tured, chemical drinks since a wonderful range of squeezed fruits is always on sale in soda fountains and kiosks. Orange is in season much of the year; other fruits appear as they come into season.

These establishments also sell diluted squash drinks, which should not be confused with the real thing.

In spite of the importance of Islam to Turkish culture, **Alcoholic**
there is no taboo on drinking alcohol in the main **drinks**
towns and tourist areas. In the smaller towns, and as
you travel further east, the sale and drinking of
alcohol tends to become more discreet.

In the holy month of Ramadan ('Ramazan' in
Turkish) some towns – Fethiye, for example – ban the
sale of alcohol during the daylight hours except in
tourist hotels. In some places thick curtains are hung
at the windows of bars and beer-houses. The resulting
clandestine atmosphere alone almost makes them
worth a visit. The general rule is to be sensitive and
discreet, especially during Ramadan, but the majority
of travellers will hardly notice any difference between
Turkey and other European countries in this respect.

The greater part of alcoholic drink production and
distribution is carried out by the giant state
monopoly Tekel. It distils all of the hard liquor, and
is the sole importer of foreign spirits.

The national drink, *rakı* was known as *arak* when the   *Rakı*
Turks came to Anatolia. It is made of raisins
flavoured with aniseed. Very like the French *pastis*, it
is 50 per cent proof. Turkish people drink it in bars or
with food, either straight or more usually mixed with
water, which makes the clear liquid turn cloudy.

The two most popular local bears, Efes and Tuborg   *Beers*
(Yugoslav and German lagers respectively), are made
in Turkey under a licensing arrangement. They both
come in bottles, in cans and on draught, and Efes in
particular is not unlike Australian beer. They are both
best when drunk cold, and are usually served chilled.
Tekel beer is found in the cheaper bars, and is more
like British bitter.

The local wines are very underrated these days. In   *Wines*
Ottoman times Turkey was a major wine exporter,
but now, although it is the world's fifth largest grape
producer, only 3 per cent of that is used in the wine
making. There are thirty-four grape varieties, but in
the cities it is unlikely you will see more than three or
four different types of wine on sale. However,

travelling round the countryside is a different story
and you will come across small, local producers and
make some excellent finds. Wine is mainly drunk as it
is produced, and there are not really any vintage
wines. To order white wine ask for *sek*, which means
'dry', as indeed most Turkish white wine is.

Şarab, the Turkish word for wine, comes from
Persian and translates as 'bad water' – a result of the
ban on artificial stimulants in the Koran. Generally
speaking Turkish people do not appreciate wine very
much.

There are three main producers, Doluca, Kavakli-
dere and the state-run Tekel. The table shows a few of
the more common wines.

Producer	Wine	From	Comments
Red			
Doluca	Doluca	Thrace	The most common wine in the cities, it is a palatable table wine.
Tekel	Güzel Marmara	Round the Sea of Marmara	Well-balanced table wine.
Local grower	Örnek	Denizli	Very acceptable. Like a slightly tart claret.
Tekel	Buzbag	Elâziğ	A hearty burgundy type wine with a distinctive flavour and bouquet.
Kavaklı-dere	Çankaya	Central and south-east Anatolia	This is a superb wine, matured in wood.
Diren	Karmen	Tokat	Not as widely available as it should be. Typical of region. Full bodied, balanced, dark and preferred by connoisseurs.
Bordo	Zelve	Cappad-ocia	Pale and clear. Smoky flavour with a strong nose.

Producer	Wine	From	Comments
White			
Tekel	Barbaros	Tekirdag	Greenish yellow, very like Portuguese wines and with a thin bouquet.
Al-Ar	Doruk	Mürefte	Stable, balanced, mature flavour.
Doluca	Riesling	Thrace	Made from Riesling grapes and comparable to the German version.
Diren	Vadi	Tokat	Demi-sec with a rich bouquet.
Tekel	Narbağ	Tokat	Very similar to German Liebfraumilch.
Tekel	Misbağ	İzmir	A good after-lunch wine. Tastes fruitily of the raisin grapes it is made from.

Producer	Wine	From	Comments
Sparkling			
Al-Ar	Harem	Thrace	White or pink, light and refreshing.
Kavaklıdere	Inci Damlasi	Tokat	Means 'pearl drop'. Produced by the champagne method. Light and smooth.

Producer	Wine	From	Comments
Rosé			
Mutuk	Dona Villa	Thrace	Light and pink with a slight bouquet.
Akmanlar	Külüp	Central Anatolia	A light and bright pink wine.

Spirits These days all the well-known spirits are readily available, although they are subject to a hefty import tax and are quite expensive.

Tekel produces a very palatable local gin (*cin*) and vodka (*votka*), although whisky and brandy drinkers will probably not be so happy with the locally produced hooch. When drinking the local brandy (*kanyak*), specify *beş yıldız* (five stars) – it is indistinguishable from the real thing by non-connoisseurs.

Liqueurs Tekel again: they produce a liqueur from most fruits and some of them are really quite palatable. They are extremely cheap in the shops and a good buy to take home.

Drinking habits **Ice** Ice (*buz*) is widely available wherever drinks are served. If you are avoiding the water then quite clearly you should not put ice in your drinks. Ice machines are being installed in some establishments in tourist areas. However, ice is usually delivered in blocks by truck from the local ice factory (*buz fabrikası*). It may be broken up on the floor before being put in the freezer and you must make your own judgement as to how hygienic the ice you are offered might be.

Nuts and nibbles Order *fındık* in any bar and you will get a dish of dried nuts, usually including hazelnuts, peanuts with salted skins and pistachios. They might also have a variety of different melon seeds, dried and salted; you eat them whole or pick out the tiny kernel.

Smarter bars serve fresh fruit (*meyva*) which comes to the table peeled and sliced on a dish for communal eating.

Cheers When drinking it is greatly appreciated if you use the local salutation, raise your glass and say *şerefe* or, believe it or not *çin çin*. Salutations can occur at any time while you are drinking: someone knocks on the table with his glass and raises it, and everyone else is expected to follow suit.

Paying It is usual to sit down to drink, and the normal system is for a bill to be presented to the table or the party when they are ready to leave. There is thus no question of buying a round of drinks and the bill is usually divided up as it is paid – although someone might say that they had ordered some particular drinks and pay for them accordingly.

İşkembeci At the end of a particularly alcoholic evening, why not do as the Turkish people do and repair to an *işkembeci*? They stay open until the early hours of the morning and serve tripe and offal dishes, and tripe soup in particular. *Iskembe çorba* (tripe soup) is reckoned to be a good antidote to a hangover – it is delicious and it does work. You ladle garlic oil and vinegar condiment (made of vinegar, oil and crushed garlic) into it to taste and sprinkle on a little cayenne pepper.

Where to get a drink

For Turkish tea houses see p. 172–3. Soft drinks are available everywhere, although it is as well to think twice about buying glasses of lemonade from street vendors unless you have a strong stomach. Whilst you can usually eat in most drinking establishments, the reverse is not true.

Off-licences

The sale of alcoholic drinks in shops is strictly controlled, and whilst most of them close earlier, 11 p.m. is the latest they may serve you – so make sure your party is not going to run out. Under an old statute bottles must be wrapped up, so that your shame in carrying alcohol in the streets cannot be seen.

International and tourist hotels

The so-called better quality hotels have bars and waiter service in the lounges similar to those anywhere else in the world. They close some time between 12 a.m. and 2 a.m. depending on the amount of custom, and there are no legal time restrictions on residents. In the tourist resorts some of the hotels have a strange system of payment by beads. No money is taken at the bar and you purchase tokens at the reception which you hand over for your drinks.

In the hotel restaurants all types of drink are served.

Restaurants   Bottled water, usually chilled, is served pretty well in every restaurant, and the establishment may or may not have soft drinks in stock. Only a few restaurants are licensed to sell alcohol, although for you as a guest and a foreigner they may well send out for whatever you want.

Bars   The bar scene is changing rapidly as westernization is creeping inland from the tourist areas. Old style bars (*birahane*) can be found in most towns if you look hard. They are very basic, serving beer in pint glasses, and it is usual to sit or stand at tables where you will be served. For some completely inexplicable reason the large litre beer mugs, which are used only for tourists, are known as *arjantin*.

Meyhane are disappearing fast. Originally wine shops, they developed into taverna-style bars where people eat *meze*, sing, dance and drink wine or rakı. They are still found in very poor areas and there are several in the Kocamustafapaşa area of old Istanbul, near the railway station of the same name. If you find one it is well worth a visit just to experience the conviviality – but women are likely to feel rather out of place.

The smart places now are the Pub, the American Bar, and the Cocktail Bar. Pubs are upmarket *birahane* with upmarket prices, whilst theoretically in American Bars you sit on high stools at the counter – not often done in Turkey. Cocktail Bars are found in resorts. Often they have a pianist or a trio playing, sometimes the seating is on traditional low-level divans, and in many cases they are a nice blend of old and new Turkey.

Time please   Closing times are fixed by the local council and can vary from 11 p.m. in rural areas to very late indeed on the coast in the summer. Away from the resorts the fixed closing time is strictly enforced.

Shopping

Shopping is yet another of the delights of Turkey, not only because of the relative cheapness, but because of the variety of goods, foodstuffs and services available.

General information

Prices and taxes

Most purchases have KDV (Value Added Tax) at 12 per cent added to the price. On food, books and some other items it is 8 per cent. There is an ongoing advertising campaign urging people to get a receipt for anything they buy, in an attempt to prevent evasion. Most prices are marked *KDV dahildir* (VAT included) with the actual amount of the tax underneath. There is also a legal requirement that the wholesale price is shown – this is part of the attempt to control inflation.

There is an arrangement, operated only by some shops, whereby tourists can recover VAT paid on expensive items as they leave the country. Get the shop to issue a VAT refund receipt, which you can present at the customs to be converted into cash as you leave the country. Alternatively the shop can arrange it all for you and theoretically it will send a cheque when the formalities are completed – not the recommended system.

Opening times

Shops are normally open 9 a.m.–7 p.m. Monday to Saturday, with lunch-time closing some time between 12 and 2. They are closed all day Sunday and on public holidays. Some shops, however, and grocers in particular, tend to open between 7 a.m. and 7 p.m. In the rural areas shops generally open earlier, and on the southern coasts they often adopt siesta style closing from 12.30 to 4 p.m.

Bazaars are open from 9 a.m. or earlier to 6 p.m., Monday to Friday, and from 9 a.m. or earlier to 12 p.m. on Saturday.

Opening hours are controlled by the municipalities and there are regional variations.

Street hawkers On Sundays and public holidays all the shops and official markets are closed. This is the day when the street hawkers really come into their own, although they can be seen mingling with the crowds most of the time. They set up their pitch on the pavement or in shop doorways with their wares on sacking bags with rope handles. The more organized may have licensed barrows; the opportunists will just have their arms full of goods. Watch for the moment when the municipal inspector with his peaked cap comes along. Suddenly all the bags are bundled up, butlers' trays are folded, and they all melt into the background – to return to exactly the same spot the moment the inspector has passed by.

Pretty well anything can be bought from street traders, just depending on supply and demand. In winter you will find umbrellas, hats and gloves and in summer T-shirts and battery powered fans. For toiletries, padlocks and biros their prices are unbeatable!

Supermarkets Department stores are never seen: the bazaar performs that function. However, the supermarket is creeping in, under the name *super*, pronounced as in the French. Everything has a set price and is marked as in the rest of Europe, and you will end up in a familiar queue at the cash register.

Small shops Small shops specialize in much the same way as is found in Britain and America, with the exception that a chemist's shop (*eczane*) stocks only medicinal products – for toiletries and perfumes it is necessary to find a *parfümeri* (or street hawker).

It is quite usual for you to be invited to take a seat while you are making your choice, and to be offered tea or coffee, although regrettably this custom is becoming less common these days in the larger cities.

In the villages and towns it can take a long time to make progress down a street as you are invited to come in and drink tea, or to sit on a stool outside under the shade of an awning in the summer. A tea boy will be hailed and he will bring it in a tripod tray – the shopkeeper will give him a token for settlement at the end of the week. The hospitality being offered is that traditionally due to a traveller: making a sale is of secondary importance.

Purchases are carefully wrapped and tied with string in a way that seems delightfully civilized, even old-fashioned, to the shopper from societies that have 'progressed' further.

If you ask for something not in stock, shopkeepers will often send out for it, or guide you to somewhere where you can find it even if it means taking you to one of their competitors – they know he will do the same for them one day.

Sales

An *ucuzluk* sign in a shop window means that goods are supposedly marked down, as in sales in western Europe. However, this is usually accompanied from day one with the word *gün* (last day). There is no guarantee that goods were ever sold at the price from which they are marked down, and whilst there is limited consumer protection legislation in Turkey, it does not as yet cover this area.

Bazaars

It is shopping in the bazaars and markets that is the real pleasure. There you will find all the excitement of the orient, without too much of the hassle. Turkish bazaars must rank amongst the cheapest, with the greatest variety of goods and produce, and probably the most fun, in the world. They are also extremely safe – it is rare to find pickpockets and thieves in the crowds. Beyond taking the normal sensible precautions of any traveller abroad, you should feel safe to wander at will. The first-time traveller in Asia can meander and get lost – and feel the frisson of a real explorer – yet have the expectation of coming to no harm.

All bazaars and markets are divided into speciality quarters, manufacturing as well as retailing. The

quarters or the streets are named after the trade that
traditionally worked there. The bazaar is a complete
community where, in addition to shops and kiosks,
you will see workshops and store-rooms, fountains
and toilets, banks, tea houses, restaurants and, of
course, mosques – in fact, everything needed for
artisans and merchants to ply their trades.

Bargaining   Customers in shops seldom haggle these days, but in
the bazaar a sort of vicious circle has crept in.
Household items, likely to be of interest only to
Turkish people tend to have fixed prices. But where
there are foreigners the traders have got the idea that
we think it is romantic to bargain – and we seem to
think it is expected of us. In fact it was never very
important in Turkey's trading tradition, more of a
social ritual, and you will rarely reduce the price more
than about 15 per cent.

In tourist shops in tourist areas you may find prices
that are well in excess of what Turkish people would
pay, or of what you would pay if you went outside
that area. To get the bottom line raise your eyes
heavenwards, put your tongue behind your top teeth
to make a tut sound, and start to walk away. The
important thing is not to make an offer unless you are
prepared to stick by it; it is considered extremely bad
form to back out if the seller agrees to a price you
have suggested.

Beware the guide who offers his services in the
bazaar. In the tourist areas they tend to swoop on
anyone looking the slightest bit lost, and their
commission will be added to the price you pay.

Bazaar 54   An especially enterprising company, Net Holdings,
has set up the Bazaar 54 shops that are to be found
anywhere there are tourists. Cleverly named after the
street number of their first shop in Istanbul – Turkish
people read it as *Bazaar elli dört* in the same way that
you read it as 'fifty-four' – they stock just about every
craft-made Turkish product. To some extent they
take the fun out of the local shopping, although they
are quite amenable to haggling. They are very
convenient for people on a short stop-over. Their

advantage to the shopper is that they will take any valid form of payment, including personal cheques, and they guarantee the quality and authenticity of everything they sell. Carpets are sold with a certificate of origin, and they can also arrange the transport of bulky items.

The extravagant displays of fruit (*meyva*), vegetables (*sebze*) and flowers (*çiçek*) in the shops and markets are a joy to behold. Traders seem to have great sensitivity to the colours and shapes found in nature.

Fruit, vegetables and flowers

Not many years ago, all Turkey's agricultural produce was organically grown as a matter of course, but nowadays this is not the case. With intensive farming and market gardening have come chemical aids, so be sure to wash fruit and vegetables. A green movement is becoming an appreciable force as a pressure group, and has formed itself into a political party, although it is predominantly a loose federation of those with liberal inclinations. In the cities there are rumblings about healthy eating – and the Ministry of Health exercises strict controls, identical to EEC regulations, over food additives.

Most people nowadays will be familiar with the *patlıcan*, the aubergine that is (almost) as ubiquitous in the Turkish diet as the potato is in the British. However, nowhere else in the world will it be found so perfectly pear-shaped, so irridescently purple, and so delicious. Alongside it are peppers and cucumbers, *kabak* (a sort of small ridged marrow, eaten stuffed), tomatoes, onions – the list seems endless.

You will also find strawberries and cherries from April onwards. Then it is the peach and apricot season; later oranges come into the markets, followed by apples and pears. From late August the markets are flooded with walnuts and hazelnuts, figs and all kinds of dried fruit. As the season for melon (*kavun*) and water-melon (*karpuz*) closes, they are almost given away.

Turkish people love flowers. They are always an acceptable present and all flower shops do a delivery service. At a commercial or social reception, floral displays on tall wooden stands are often sent, with the name of the hosts and of the sender inscribed on a sash. These displays are also customarily sent by neighbouring enterprises and clients when a new business opens, and are placed on the pavement outside. Visitors often mistake times of business expansion for an outbreak of plague, as a result: to western eyes the offerings look just like wreaths.

Carpets   Many people will want to take home a Turkish carpet, and the salesmen in the carpet shops, who in the main work on a commission-only basis, seem to think you have come to Turkey solely for that purpose. However, it is all good humoured; you will be offered tea and there will be no hard feelings if you let them display all their carpets with the full sales routine, then leave without buying.

Old carpets   Everywhere you will find both old and new carpets on sale. Before buying an antique carpet it is really necessary to become something of an expert, and the unwary can make bad mistakes (and see pp. 140 and 143 for export regulations. You are unlikely to see anything on sale that is more than 150 years old. A visit to one of the carpet museums may help in this direction – Istanbul's *Türk ve İslam Eserleri Müzesi* (Museum of Turkish and Islamic Arts) has one of the most comprehensive collections in the world and is regularly consulted by experts.

Value for money   Even carpets bought in the tourist areas and the city bazaars are relatively good value compared with prices in the rest of Europe; but if you want a real bargain go to the small towns and villages in rural Anatolia, where you can see the carpets being made. In reality the carpets you see in town are likely, although still hand-made, to have been woven by cheap labour in urban factories.

Choosing   The value of a carpet depends not only on how and where it is made, but on the materials and the dyes used, the number of knots per square centimetre, and the pattern. But in the final analysis the things that count are the carpet's value to you, and what you are prepared to pay.

Cotton, wool and silk   Cheaper carpets are made of wool woven on to a cotton base, and a look at the tassel at the end will tell you the material used. The more normal quality, wool woven on to a wool base, is more expensive. Silk carpets, usually priced by the square metre, can be very expensive indeed.

Knots   The main difference between Turkish and other hand-made carpets is in the knotting. Turkish carpets have a double knot, which makes them proportionally stronger and longer lasting. Look at the closeness of the weave on the back: the tighter the weave and the smaller the knots, the more durable and valuable the carpet.

Dyes   Good quality carpets are coloured with natural vegetable dyes. To a large extent you will be in the hands of the salesman, since it takes a real expert to know the various colourings. What you can do is rub a damp handkerchief over the pile: if it is colour fast it will leave no traces. Look at the pile closest to the backing and see if the surface has faded. Check the carpet in natural light – showrooms are lit rather like television studios. There should be some variation in the colours as natural dyes are not completely consistent.

Designs   The patterns all have regional origins and, again, you need to be something of an expert to know one from another. It is a case of personal preference coupled with the skill of the salesman. There are some good locally produced books which will tell you a little of the differences between the various designs.

Kilim

As typically Turkish but much less expensive are *Kilim*. These are woven rugs without a cut pile, and their origin lies in the mats carried by nomads as they travelled around Anatolia.

Export regulations Those old carpets that come under the rather imprecise definition of 'museum quality' are considered antiquities and cannot be exported. They can cause problems as you are leaving the country, since the customs officer is likely to know less about antique carpets even than you do. If you buy an old carpet the best thing is to get the shopkeeper, or a local museum, if it really is likely to be contentious, to give you a letter saying that it is not of 'museum quality'.

Carpet bags and slippers If you fancy yourself as a politician, real carpet bags can be found in the bazaars. Or you may prefer to take home some carpet slippers – they last for years.

Leather After carpets the second most popular buy is leather, in particular jackets, bags and shoes. Apart from the quality of the work, prospective purchasers should look at the type of leather that has been used. The tanning industry grew up in the area between Bergama and İzmir where there are large deposits of alum and where the acorns of the gnarled, old, valonia oak trees are particularly rich in tannin – both needed to make leather.

Most of the leather garments you will see displayed are made from the soft leather that comes from sheep, but calf hide and even camel can also be found. The quality of the leather itself, and of the work, varies considerably. If you are not an expert, shop around while at the same time learning what to look for from the salesman.

It is likely that you will find the prices for shoes about half what you pay at home for comparable quality. However, the leather is much softer and therefore not so strong. Beware the stiff back put on to compensate – a new pair worn for a lot sightseeing can produce a very nasty blister!

Clothes Clothes made both of wool and cotton, are a good buy. Ranges of casual shirts, suits, trousers, dresses, blouses, skirts and jeans of all shapes, sizes and colours can be found in the shops and bazaars. The cheaper cotton clothes shrink when washed, and the stitching on some garments is weak and may soon need redoing.

In the touristic areas, cheesecloth cotton shirts are very cheap – consider whether it is worth taking away many leisure shirts, as you can buy them there. It is more than likely that men can also find a workshop where shirts, trousers and safari suits are made to measure. There is not such a variety of women's clothes away from the cities: they are restricted to shirts and skirts, and women may find it difficult to get stylish trousers and slacks. In the east, however, you will find extremely attractive locally embroidered shirts and jerkins, and in the more remote areas the local tailor will make up a pair of baggy unisex *salvar* (Turkish trousers).

In the cities, Istanbul in particular, there is always a good range of men's and women's fashion clothes. You will find copies of the latest French and Italian fashions at a fraction of the price.

The table shows some middle-range sizes, from *Sizes* which smaller and larger sizes can be calculated.

Item	British	American	Turkish
Women			
Dresses	10	8	30
and suits	12	10	32
	14	12	34
Shoes	4	5½	37
	5	6½	38
	6	7½	39
Men			
Suits	38″ (97 cm)	38	48
	40″ (102 cm)	40	50
	42″ (107 cm)	42	52
Shirts	16″ (41 cm)	16	41
	17″ (44.5 cm)	17	43
	18″ (46 cm)	18	45
Shoes	8	8	41
	8½	8½	42
	9	9	43

Crafts There are all sorts of regional products made from local minerals, shaped by the successors to centuries-old craft industries. Beautiful, intricately carved white pipes made of *lületaşi*, the volcanic silicate rock we know as meerschaum, come from the villages of Koxlubey and Sepeteci near Eskişehir. This rock is much cheaper here than anywhere else in the world – blocks used to be exported for carving overseas, but this is now prohibited, as a measure to keep the employment in the country.

Silver is mined in the nearby village of Kütahya – Turkey is the world's second largest producer. There is a hallmark which a reputable dealer will point out to you, but a lot of costume jewellery is made from nickel silver and various alloys. Filigree work in silver, from eastern Turkey round Diyarbakir, is very attractive.

Gold, precious and semiprecious stones are also found in the brightly lit jewellers' market that is usually part of any town's bazaar. The daily gold price will be marked up somewhere on a board, so you can have pieces weighed and calculate what you are paying for the workmanship.

Onyx is made into ubiquitous ashtrays and sold in souvenir shops, but also formed into attractive chess pieces and backgammon sets. Marquetry and inlay work is also widely sold, but check anything you buy carefully as the inlay may not be what it seems.

In the heyday of the Ottoman empire, underglazed polychrome tiles and pottery were manufactured from the hard, white clay found near İznik and Kütahya. You will find many reproductions of the intricate, brightly coloured designs on sale. There are also plenty of pots, plates, cups and bowls made to simple designs; they are fired at low temperatures, so are rather fragile to take home.

Cautions and customs

Antiquities Great care should be exercised when even considering buying antiques. Apart from the fact that there are severe penalties for taking antiquities out of the country, there are many fakes. At the more popular archaeological sites you will find children selling reproduction coins and lamps they claim just to have dug up, and in the antique shops in the more touristic bazaars there may be more reproductions – often highly sophisticated imitations – than authentic pieces. A good buy are old hubble-bubble water pipes, old beaten brass plates and *hamam* (bath) slippers inlaid with mother of pearl.

You should be particularly careful when buying copper vessels for use. The bazaars are full of them, ranging from the newly made to those of several hundred years old. Copper is poisonous and the interior should be tinned – there will always be a workshop nearby where it can be done cheaply.

Copper

The regulations concerning customs duties are extremely complicated. Even the appropriate authorities have difficulty in saying exactly what they are. Generally speaking, anything you take home with you does not incur duties if the total value is under £200 or equivalent. However, if you post or send goods by freight, different sets of rules apply. You are well advised to make sure you know what is in force at the time.

Customs duties

Over the £200 limit, carpets taken to the UK are liable to 15 per cent VAT and a variable import duty. In the US they incur 5.1 per cent import tax and must be accompanied by a certificate of origin. Hand-made carpets sent to Australia are liable to 14 per cent tax: be sure to get a certificate stating that they are indeed hand made, as the duty on machine-made carpets is 46 per cent. Australia also imposes a 115 per cent tax on imported leather jackets – make sure you are wearing it! New Zealanders will find themselves paying tax of some 32 per cent on carpets: you need a certificate of origin, as this rate is a special arrangement for Turkey, and it would otherwise be over 50 per cent. Leather jackets technically incur tax of over 50 per cent in New Zealand, but the customs there say that certainly one and possibly two jackets would be considered to be personal effects as long as they were carried in your luggage.

Off the If you wander away from the usual tourist haunts you
beaten track will find all sorts of delights. Cotton furnishing
fabrics with patterns of traditional Turkish motifs are
cheap, as are simple wooden (but alas, plastic too)
kitchen implements. You can also find those bath
towels with a coarse linen nap that dry you rather
than just spreading the water around, which seem to
have disappeared further west.

Attar of roses is produced from the great fields
of roses on the plains to the north of İsparta. Rose
water, used in cooking and as a perfume, is a
by-product of the distillation and can be bought from
apothecaries in the bazaar.

Prescription spectacles are good value and well
made. If you take your own prescription they can be
made up in a few hours; if you break your glasses any
optician will arrange an eye-test by an oculist and
have a new pair made up within half a day.

A Turkish man will rarely shave himself: instead he
will go to the *berber*, an old fashioned barber-shop,
where his *traş* (shave) will be performed with a
cut-throat razor. For a few hundred lira it is an
exhilarating experience. In the cities the more modern
kuaför, formerly the name for a ladies' hairdresser
only, do the western styles that Turkish youth
demand. Women will find hair-stylists as elsewhere in
Europe, but away from the main cities they are
unlikely to be so up-to-date.

Shoe-shine boys seem to be everywhere, in ranks
or patrolling the streets with their kit of highly
polished brass box, bottles of various coloured leather
lotions and assorted brushes. There is a fixed price of
a few hundred lira, but this does go up for foreigners.
They take great pride in their work, put in protectors
to guard your socks from the polish, and spend a
good five minutes getting a bright shine.

Sport

Turkey has, or is developing, facilities for just about every sport and recreational activity you can imagine – except cricket and rugby – and many you may never have heard of.

Ball games

Football Spectator sport (*spor*) is very popular and young Turks are as fanatical, without quite the crowd problems, about football (*futbol*) as the youth in most western European countries. There is a match (*maç*) in the local sports ground (*stadyum*, usually abbreviated to *stad*) most Saturday or Sunday afternoons during the season, from September to April. The professional League Federation (*Federasyon*) has three divisions, organized on the same system as that in Britain. Foreign players achieve cult status and are limited to two per club. On the Sunday of the Federation Cup final, and the days of the matches for the president's and prime minister's cups, the towns of the competing teams are brought to a standstill by columns of hooting cars packed with scarf- and flag-waving supporters.

Football is not as new to Turkey as might be presumed. The first recorded match was in İzmir in 1895, between teams of English traders. The Black Socks Football Club was formed in Istanbul in 1899, also by Englishmen, and 1905 saw the formation of the celebrated Turkish club Galatasaray: when you see supporters waving red and yellow scarves and shouting Jim Bom Bom, that is the team they are supporting.

Basketball Basketball, and to a lesser extent volleyball, also have keen followings. Most schools, youth clubs, local factories and universities have amateur basketball teams. The dream of most of the players is to join one of the professional teams which compete in a two-division league organized on the same lines as the football league. Foreign players are limited to one in each team.

Traditional sports

The ascendancy of football and other western sporting activities has resulted in the three traditional Turkish sports being reduced almost to the status of quaint displays of old customs put on for visitors.

Wrestling

Wrestling is traditionally the national sport, and, although it is becoming less popular, bouts can be seen in Anatolian villages in the summer.

Thrace is the birthplace of mysteries and orgiastic rites associated with the worship of Dionysus, and is famous for its horses and horsemen and for ecstatic religious rituals. A relic of this can be seen in July in the grease wrestling (*yağlı güreş*) contests that take place at Kirkpina in the north-west of the region. The contestants, wearing leather shorts, are covered in olive oil and grapple in an open meadow to the cheers of their supporters. Kirkpınar, which translates literally as 'forty water sources', has many mythological associations which the local people will happily relate to you.

Turkish jousting

Real *cirit oyunu* can only be seen in the east, and only on rare occasions nowadays. It is a rather dangerous, exhilarating sport which involves galloping horsemen throwing blunted wooden javelins at their mounted opponents. The Erzurum Riding Club (Atlıspor Klübu) can tell you when matches are likely to happen. Displays of *Cirit* are put on for tourists in Konya on summer weekends.

Camel wrestling

In December and January, especially in the vicinity of Selçuk, you may be fortunate enough to find *deve güreşi* (camel wrestling). Cumbersome males are pitted in pairs in a large field; sometimes a female is introduced to make them more aggressive. One beast, in an almost elegant ritual, establishes dominance over the other. The few camels in Turkey these days are highly prized, so they are parted before they can harm each other.

Water sports For many visitors water sports will be the main attraction. Flotilla sailing, for both the novice and the expert, and chartering are well established, as a look at the holiday advertisements in the Sunday papers will show.

For the less enthusiastic sailor there is what for generations of Turks has been known as the Blue Cruise. For this you charter a Bodrum boat – a heavy but luxurious, locally built, wooden boat, often sleeping up to twelve people, with a powerful engine, and sails mainly for decoration. These boats have a local crew and the time is spent exploring, swimming and sunbathing in unspoilt coves and bays.

Sailors' winds In July the *meltem* gets up from the north-east, lasting about twenty days and usually only blowing in the afternoons. It causes choppy seas and makes mooring difficult, but the weather remains fine and the skies clear. In the Aegean region the *imbat*, a stiff summer sea breeze, is the delight of yachtsmen.

The Turkish meteorology office broadcasts a weather bulletin in several languages on the 25 m short-wave band at 08.00, 10.00, 12.00, 14.00 and 19.00 hours.

Water skiing and wind surfing are possible all round the Aegean and Mediterranean coasts. The sea is calm enough, even for novices, for most of the summer. Equipment can be hired at many of the popular tourist beaches. White-water rafting and canoeing are newly discovered activities on the Çorum River near Bayburt in the centre of the Black Sea region.

Diving Scuba diving was prohibited until recently, to protect the many ancient wrecks that lie off the coasts. Now that the controls have been eased, enthusiasts report that the diving is superb and conditions are very good. The water is still, shallow and clear with the right amount of rock to make for interesting dives;

first-timers underwater can snorkel among colourful fish, and with an aqualung you can discover ancient amphoras lying on the bottom. However, it must be remembered that the penalties are severe for anyone caught in possession of antiquities taken from wrecks.

Diving is still only permitted by recognized parties, who must have an accredited Turkish diver to accompany them. There are diving schools and clubs at some of the major tourist hotels. In the case of serious expeditions, permissions have to be obtained in advance, and they can take a long time. Bodrum Castle, where there is now a museum of marine archaeology, is the centre of an American-led expedition researching and recording wrecks. Istanbul, Ankara and Bodrum have diving equipment shops where gear and advice can be obtained.

Sea fishing as a sport has not really caught on yet. The *Fishing* fish are there for the catching and it is surely only a matter of time. Commercial fishing by foreigners carries a heavy penalty and amateur equipment with non-commercial multi-hooked lines should be used. Certain zones are prohibited to protect the important local fishing industry, and there are limits on the numbers of fish that may be landed. The Fisheries Department at Kumkapı, Istanbul, can provide further information. Fish caught, and eaten, include anchovies, mackeral, sardines, blue fish, bonito, squid and octopus. In August crabs can be caught in the lagoons by hanging in the water a piece of meat tied to a string. The curious crabs are then lazily hoisted out of the water and straight into a pot. They are delectable.

Fresh water fishing is similarly as yet undeveloped, although in the National Park areas fishing rods can be hired. In the more than 100,000 miles (160,000 km) of rivers and 1,000 square miles (250,000 hectares) of lakes are carp, mullet, trout and crawfish, all of which can be seen in fishmongers' and restaurants.

Bathing is idyllic all round the coast away from the **Swimming** cities, though sea pollution is becoming something of a problem near crowded urban areas. Showers with lukewarm water heated naturally by the sun will be found on many of the popular beaches, and changing rooms and beach huts can be hired. At some beaches there is a charge for entry and use of the facilities, but these tend to be dirtier than elsewhere owing to constant use.

Game hunting   Hunting and shooting are extremely popular with Turks and organized parties of foreigners can be arranged. The season starts in mid-December with rabbits, stock dove and quail. These give way later in the season to wood pigeon, and duck and wild boar can be hunted from November through to March. Information as to exact seasons and prohibited species can be obtained from the Turkish Hunting Club (see p. 262). The authorities are naturally concerned about firearms being brought into the country and anybody planning a trip with their own guns should contact the Turkish Embassy at a very early stage.

Mountain and hill sports

Skiing   Turkey is not yet recognized for its winter sports, but international interest is increasing as facilities and access are opened up. There are four main ski resorts.

Uludag   This is in the National Park, 22 miles (35 km) south of Bursa by road. There is a cable-car up to the pistes. The season here, in the most sophisticated and accessible of the resorts, is from January to April and the slopes lie at an altitude of some 6,500 feet (2,000 m). There are three ski-lifts, and slalom courses and beginners' slopes of varying degrees of difficulty. Equipment can be hired at the hotels, and much of the accommodation is in Swiss-style chalets.

Saklıkent   North of Antalya in the Beydağı Mountains, this resort has a season from January to April and is at 8,200 feet (2,500 m). In March and April you can ski in the morning and swim in the Mediterranean in the afternoon. Accommodation is in pensions and chalets.

Kartalkaya This fine all-round winter resort on Köroğlu Dağ is at 6,500 feet (2,000 m) above the Istanbul–Ankara road, 30 miles (50 km) from Bolu. The slopes are surrounded by pine woods and there is a good hotel, with swimming pool, where equipment can be hired and instruction arranged. In the evening try to get one of the locals to tell you the legend of Köroğlu, who was born on Bolu in the sixteenth century – he is the same figure as Robin Hood.

Sarıkamış Rather inaccessible in the eastern highlands near Kars on the USSR border, 7,400 feet (2,250 m), Sarıkamış has good courses and ideal snow conditions from January to March. Skiers can stay in Kars and go up daily, or there is a centrally heated ski-lodge at the foot of the ski-lifts. Instructors are on hand most of the time.

Serious skiers may like to consider the long and difficult courses at Erciyes, 15 miles (24 km) from Kayseri, or Palandöken, 4 miles (6 km) along a reasonably good road from Erzurum. Permission is needed from the General Directorate of Physical Training, through the Kayak Federasyonu (Ski club – see p. 262). Enthusiasts maintain the best snow conditions in Turkey are to be found here. In the long season from November to May on the eastern face of Mont Erciyes at the Tekir Yaylası (plateau), the 120-bed lodge is often full. For Palandöken, with slopes up to 10,100 feet (3,100 m), skiers stay in Erzurum or at the ski-lodge at the foot of the lift to the runs. The season is from December to April. Equipment and instruction are available at both centres.

Mountaineering as a sport is also in its infancy. Information is available from the Dağcılık Federasyonu (Turkish Mountaineering Club) at the same address and phone number as the Ski Federation. It is advisable to tell them of any planned trips and they

Mountain climbing

can inform the relevant authorities. Permission, which they can also obtain, is needed to climb in the Ağrı Dağı (Mount Ararat) and Cilo-Sat ranges. Some tourist offices may have a list of mountain excursions for beginners and experts, and more detailed information can be obtained from the main towns in the regions concerned.

Hill walking   For novices, once the snows have melted in the ski area on Erciyes Dağı, the extinct volcano south of Kayseri becomes a good starting point for climbing. From the plateau Tekir Yaylasi the ten-hour climb up the north face is a pleasant, if energetic, day's walk. The other route over the Sutdonduran glacier is only for experienced climbers with picks and ropes.

The Kackar range, which runs for about 18 miles (29 km) between Rize and Hopa in the Black sea region, has peaks up to 13,000 feet (4,000 m). With its glaciers, lakes, waterfalls, forests and numerous hot springs, it is an extremely pleasant area for climbing and mountain walking in summer.

The starting point for climbing in any of the three groups in the range is usually Ardeşen, a small town east of Rize. Many climbers set up a base camp on the Upper Kavrun at about 9,000 feet (2,750 m), from where it is possible to climb Kaçkar peak at 12,900 feet (3,932 m) and return in about eight hours. From the same base camp, Varos at 11,350 feet (3,458 m), or the Versembek Peak at 12,150 feet (3,709 m) can be conquered in about seven hours. For less strenuous activity a good starting point is the village of Çat, reached via Çamlıhemsin, from where the lower slopes can be reached.

Gentle rambling, as well as serious mountain climbing, can be found in the Cilo-Sat mountains once the necessary permission has been obtained, and the best season is from June to September. The starting point is usually the high plateau of Mercan, which can be reached by minibus or dolmus. There you will find the glacial lake Bey Gölü (literally translated as 'Mr Lake') surrounded by alpine flowers.

For really serious climbers the Aladağlar Mountains
40 miles (65 km) to the south of Nigde in the
Yedigöller (Seven Lakes) National Park are in season
from June to September. Up to and down from the
Demirkazık Peak at 12,300 feet (3,756 m) the
Kızılkaya at 12,200 feet (3,723 m) or the Direktas at
11,400 feet (3,470 m) takes about ten hours.

Organized climbing

The Turasan Mountains are a continuation of the
Aladağlar Range. The second highest peak in Anatolia
is there, *Suphan Dağ* at 14,550 feet (4,434 m), with its
crater lake; it can be reached in about two days from
Adilcevaz.

Mount Ararat – supposed landing place of Noah's
Ark – at 16,950 feet (5,165 m) is ice capped the whole
year round. From June to September authorized
parties attempt it with full climbing gear. From base
camp at Doğubayazıt or Aralık, two more camps are
usually made before the final trek to the peak, which
takes about eight hours.

Other sports

Another activity still in its infancy, but for which
there is enormous potential, is caving. For those into
caves, contact is best made with the Caving Club (see
p. 262). It can give information about, and sometimes
arrange visits to, Turkey's numerous and often
spectacularly beautiful caves.

Caving

Flying and parachuting are organized by THK, the
Turkish Aviation Institution (see p. 262) who can
arrange use of the parachute tower on Hipodrom
Street, Ankara, and flying lessons at the airfield at
Etimesğut. Groups of UK youngsters in the Air
Training Corps report very successful exchange visits
making use of these facilities.

Air sports

Entertainment

Music

The music of the court Formal courtly music has been popular in Turkey from Ottoman times, and musical influences from both western and eastern traditions and scales have, over the years, brought about an indigenous style that draws upon both. Simultaneously Turkey's own native style has had no small influence on what is known in the west as 'classical' music.

Suleyman the Magnificent brought musicians from the west to play at his court, though the influence was not lasting and music continued along the lines of the eastern tradition. This was itself taken to Europe by the *Mehter takımı* of the Ottoman armies – huge sixty-six-piece military bands, with drums so enormous they were carted round on their own waggons, making grand and glorious music intended to dishearten the defenders of besieged towns. They introduced the idea of military bands to western Europe via Austria, and the influence was strongest in Vienna. It can be heard in Haydn's Military Symphony, and in Mozart's Turkish March, Turkish Violin Concerto, *The Abduction from the Seraglio*, and *Ziade*.

Janissary bands If you are fortunate you may see a band of *mehter takımı* marching down the street. Modern revivals of the band of *yeniçeri* (janissary) of the sultan's guard, they sometimes perform on national holidays. The upturned waxed moustaches are stuck on these days, but the music still has a wonderfully dramatic, stirring and at the same time romantic quality.

Western classical music In 1826 Sultan Mahmut II, in an attempt to modernize the army, organized bands similar to those found in the British and French forces. Two years later the Italian conductor Giuseppe Donizetti was invited to Istanbul to form the Imperial Orchestra, performing mainly

French and Italian operas. Today a great deal of western classical music is performed in Istanbul, İzmir and Ankara – and each city has its own conservatory of music.

Performances

The name of the Imperial Orchestra has been changed to the Presidential Symphony Orchestra. Their concerts every Friday night from October to May at the Atatürk Cultural Centre in Ankara are very popular; tickets, only from the box office (tel. 311 75 48), need to be booked at least a week ahead. The British Council and American and several other Cultural Centres from time to time promote concerts by visiting performers – the Austrian Cultural Centre in Istanbul is well known to expatriates for its excellent chamber music.

The opera and ballet in Istanbul, İzmir and Ankara frequently invite international guest conductors and artists to perform in the modern culture centres. (Balletomanes may be interested to know that the Turkish National Ballet was established by Dame Ninette de Valois immediately after the war.)

Traditional and folk music

The Turkish people love their traditional classical and folk music, and it seems to pour from loudspeakers all over the country.

The origins of traditional folk music lie in Antioch and Syria, from where it was taken by troubadours to Byzantium and also eastwards into Persia. The scale is different to that of the west, the rhythms are extremely complex, and melody plays a greater part than harmony. It may sound monotonous to western ears – almost plaintive – and if you could but understand the words this is indeed what it is. Social occasions are enlivened by old favourites such as 'Death in Foreign Parts' and 'The Consumptive Girl'. Originally the balladeers made up words appropriate to the occasions, almost invariably dealing with relationships with nature and each other.

Classical traditional music

This includes Ottoman courtly music whose grace, precision and rhythm give it an echo of the plainsong with which it had common origins. Mystic music comes from the Islamic religious retreats of various sects, such as the Mevlevi dervishes. Mosque music takes the form of recitations from the Koran, chants and intoned *salât* (prayer).

Popular music   Western pop elements have inevitably crept in too, and the cheap cassettes found on sale in the bazaar span the whole gamut, from tear-jerkers to the latest European or American hit sung in Turkish. Turkish pop music has developed almost into a genre of its own, as you will not fail to hear.

Live music in   In the cities and the tourist areas there are several sorts
the clubs   of night club. They range from those intended specially for tourists to those that have entertainment on traditional lines for Turks. You will also find belly-dancing – but always specially put on for the tourist. Drinks are ludicrously expensive in all of these establishments: when questioned about it they make the fallacious argument that one would pay more in London or New York.

Discos   The young population of Turkey has taken to discos in a big way. They vary from the open-air dance floor and bar on a beach to the supposedly sophisticated, and expensive, light shows attached to the international hotels. There is usually a house rule that men are not admitted alone; this is presumably because once in they may try to pick up women, which is quite offensive to the Turkish tradition and frowned upon even in the most liberated areas. As a result some ladies may find they are invited to a disco by Turkish lads in the first instance as an admission ticket.

Cultural   The cultural department of the State Planning Office –
preservation   the equivalent of Britain's Arts Council – is determined that despite accelerating westernization, traditional art forms shall not be lost. Talented performers in all fields are given five-year contracts with high salaries, and university departments are encouraged to collect and record traditional folk material.

   The National Theatre has ten resident and forty mobile companies. They are required to ensure that 40 per cent of their work is original Turkish material; thus you can find a repertoire ranging from Shakespeare and Henry Miller in translation to one of the five forms of Turkish traditional theatre outlined below.

In '*Karagöz*', silhouetted figures are projected on to a white cloth with the manipulator providing the voices. The ribald pieces are about the fallibility of the individual and society – the main character, Karagöz, is the wise fool and his foil is Hacivat, the pedantic opportunist. They are surrounded by, amongst others, a janissary with a sword and a bottle of wine, Tuzsus Deli Bekir, the dandy son of a good family, Celibi, the whore Zenna and the dervish Hak. After a series of misadventures Karagöz always has the final word. If you can find one of the rare performances it is well worth a visit, and if you remember the above characters the action becomes pretty self-evident without the need for language.

Kukla (puppet) shows use glove and string puppets and are an adaptation of the *kavurkuc* (doll) theatre used to present the relationship between God and creation after the adoption of Islam. Traditionally they are found in theatres in the Dikiltas area of Istanbul, and in parks in the summer.

A *meddah* is a story-teller who characterizes the parts in the tale. Originally religious stories, they are now parables of modern life.

Orta oyunu (theatre-in-the-round) comprises music and comic turns followed by an improvised play in which the humour revolves around double meanings. The play has traditional characters which are very similar to those in 'Karagöz', together with female impersonation and representation of the various racial groups found within the Ottoman Empire.

Tulûat was the main form of theatre in Istanbul in Ottoman times and has elements of the other four types.

Plays performed by amateurs are found in the villages at festival times. Their traditional form has its roots in pre-Christian rituals.

Village plays and the fringe

There is also a flourishing fringe theatre in the major cities, where you will find not only plays by modern

Turkish playwrights, but translations of world classics
and visits from overseas touring companies.

Cinema and television The cinema has come back into its own as it has come to
terms with television. Open-air cinemas are a feature of
the tourist regions, and there and in the cities films are
often shown in the original English with subtitles.
Watch out for cinemas away from the city centres that
still have 'ladies-only' matinees or a 'ladies'' section
of the auditorium.

Türkiye Radıyo ve Televizyon (TRT) has been available in colour across the whole country since 1982.
State controlled, as a public service organization, it
nevertheless takes some advertising. It broadcasts
some very good cultural and music programmes which
are likely to be of interest to non-Turkish speakers.
Programme schedules are published in the *Turkish
Daily News*, which also produces a weekly programme
distributed to the main hotels.

The original language sound-track of dubbed foreign television films is transmitted on FM radio on 94.7
MHz. It is synchronized with the television transmission.

Entertain- ment listings Theatre, cinema and other entertainments are not as
widely advertised as you may be used to. Friday's
Turkish Daily News and the weekend *Dateline Turkey*
both have a listing page covering cultural events in the
major cities. Monday's arts page in *Cumhuriyet* is very
comprehensive, especially for cinema, and in Istanbul
an arts free-sheet, published on the first and sixteenth
of each month, is available from Pinar supermarkets
and news-stands. In most cases the translations are
self-evident, and original English titles are usually
quoted where appropriate. Dates and times are given in
figures. Libraries in the British Council, American
Cultural Center and elsewhere generally have up-to-
date information on forthcoming activities.

Religion

Religion and religions have played a fundamental part in creating the Turkey we know today. It was to the people of Anatolia that Christianity was taken after its birth in Judaea, and amongst whom it flourished. When Islam came with the Seljuks it too flourished. It was in Anatolia that animus between the two faiths was most evident in the crusades.

Before Christianity arrived, deities ranged from the various Neolithic earth-mother figures (Cybele being the most common) through to the polytheistic Greeks' Zeus, Apollo, Dionysus and Artemis (also called Diana). Many of these had their own shrines and places of worship.

Pagan worship

One of the most fascinating is at Mount Nimrod (*Nemrut daği*), in the province of Adiyaman in the south-east of the country. It was built by the King of Commagene, a small and then rich and fertile state irrigated by the River Euphrates. It was a fiefdom of the Romans for some fifty years before and fifty years after the birth of Christ. The kings were descended from Alexander the Great and the Persian Darius, as is revealed by the inscriptions on the back of statues and on the altar – which can be recognized by the large H painted on it, as it is now used to land VIPs by helicopter.

The conical peak to the mountain was made as the sepulchre of the last King Antiochus, a feat as incredible as the building of the pyramids. As you approach the east terrace you see Antiochus' enormous statue flanked by those of Apollo, the female Tyche, Zeus and Heracles – that the heads have fallen to the ground makes them that much more dramatic. Follow the path to the west terrace to see an identical group in a better state of preservation. Bas-reliefs have survived here, in which the king is seen shaking hands with some of the gods. The kings carried on the Alexandrian practice of synthesizing similar gods from differing cultures, so that Apollo, for example, was a composite which also included Mithra and Helios, and by this means Antioch himself became a deity.

The king of Armenia was converted from paganism by St Gregory and espoused Christianity as the state religion by 330.

Early Christianity   The birth of Christianity may have been in Jerusalem, but its cradle was certainly in Anatolia. Its spread is largely attributable to St Paul, the Apostle of the Gentiles, who was able to take advantage of the excellent Roman road system. The well of the house in which he was supposedly born can be seen in Tarsus, about 24 km (15 miles) from Mersin. All that remains of the old city is a short section of wall on the road to Mersin and a simple gate. That this is known as Cleopatra's Gate has more to do with the tourist appeal of the fact that she met Antony in Tarsus than with historical accuracy.

St Paul's first journey (Acts 13 and 14) took him from Antioch (now Antakya) to Seleucia (Silifke). He then crossed over to Cyprus and returned to Asia Minor at Perge (a superb archaeological site now, 9 miles (15 km) east of Antalya and worth a visit for its amphitheatre alone). He turned inland and up into the mountains to Antioch-in-Pisidia, where he and St Barnabus preached to the Romans – the uncharted remains of the city can be seen just north of Yalvaç and the ruined aqueduct. He went on to preach to the Galatians (see his epistle) at their capital Iconium (Konya), where he also spoke, and made conversions (Acts 14.1), in a synagogue. When they preached in Lystra and Derbe, St Barnabus was addressed by the crowd as Zeus and St Paul as Hermes – they were considered to be gods come down in human form. St Paul then retraced his route to Perge and travelled along the Pamphylian coastal plain to Attaleia (Antalya), then, as now, in the most magnificent setting on the Mediterranean coast.

His second journey took him through Anatolia again, and on through Troas to Greece. On his third journey he returned to Ephesus, where he was to preach for two years. On his arrival the silversmiths who made effigies of Diana rioted at the loss of their livelihood – their successors in tin do a roaring trade today. St Paul says he 'fought with beasts at Ephesus', and although this may be metaphorical, men certainly fought wild animals in the great theatre at the time.

St Paul saw Anatolia once more – when he changed ships at Myra (then a port but now three miles inland, just north of Kale) on his way to be tried in Rome. During his life the extent to which Christianity was tolerated within the Byzantine empire varied according to rulers and officials.

St John the seer died at Ephesus and a church, now in ruins, was built over the supposed place of his tomb. Tradition says he brought the Virgin Mary to spend the last years of her life in a house in the hills above the town; Pope Paul VI visited the chapel built on the foundations of the house, and it is now a place for tourists and pilgrims alike.

It is still possible in Turkey to hear the language spoken by Jesus. The two monks and a few students at the Deyrulzafaran monastery, 5 miles (8 km) up into the hills from the town of Mardin near the Syrian border, use the ancient language of Aramaic. The Syrian Orthodox archbishop in the monastery at Mor Gabriel near Mydia, together with six monks, forty-five students and twelve sisters, is always pleased to welcome visitors.

Constantinople

With the accession of Constantine – the patron saint of the present Anglican church in Istanbul is St Helena, Constantine's mother, who was said to have been born in York – persecution of Christians was officially stopped. His son built the first Church of the Holy Wisdom, St Sophia and by 390 Christianity was the official religion of the empire.

The Emperor Justinian built the present St Sophia, now known as Aya Sophia, on the same site. It was completed in 537, and it became the most important Christian building in the world until St Mark's in

Venice was built. As it is, the plan of St Mark's is based on that of St Sophia, and many of the original treasures from there, looted in the crusades, can be found in St Mark's today.

St Irene, in the shadow of St Sophia, now converted to a museum, has never been used by any religion other than Christianity. It makes an excellent setting for concerts during the Istanbul festival.

The only Byzantine church still being used for orthodox worship is St Mary of the Mongols. It can be found not far from the Greek Orthodox Patriarchate in Istanbul, on Sadrazam Ali Paşa Cad.

The Nicene Creed   The Protestant, Catholic and Orthodox churches all use a version of the statement of beliefs set out by the Council of Nicaea in 325. At Nicaea, now called İznik, there is on the lake-side some brickwork that may well be from one of the royal palaces in which the councils were held. The St Sophia where the second ecumenical council was held in 787 is in a derelict state; it is in the centre of the town, surrounded by rose gardens.

The troglodytes of Cappadocia   The inhabitants of Cappadocia have from time immemorial carved homes into the soft tufa rock which characterizes the area. The Phrygians and the Galatians here found little difficulty in the transition from the worship of their mother goddess to Christianity with its mother figure. The churches in the area, of which there are reckoned to be more than a thousand, are hewn out of rock. Little is visible from the outside, yet inside can be found the finest collection of medieval wall paintings in the world, many representing familiar biblical scenes.

You can also go down into the vast cities tunnelled underground to which people retreated to escape persecution by Romans and, later, Muslim Arabs.

The iconoclasts   The Christian party in the eighth century – by then religion had become politicized in the Byzantine empire – opposed the veneration of icons and pictorial representation. They considered it to be not true devotion and equivalent to image worship, and a great deal of beautiful decoration disappeared under paint and plaster. The date of rock churches can be established by whether they have representation or patterned decoration, since many of the old churches were abandoned and new ones carved.

The essential creed of Islam is monotheism – that there is one god, Allah – and that Mohammed is his prophet. Mohammed was born in Mecca in 570 and the revelations made to him by God are recorded in the Koran; these make up the complex legal and social as well as religious system which is followed by Muslims (sometimes called Mohammedans).   **Islam**

Islam shares a number of beliefs with Christianity and Judaism, and references to Moses and Jesus also appear in the Koran.

There are five 'pillars' of Islam incumbent upon Muslims:

1 The profession of the belief in one God and his prophet Mohammed. This can be seen written in Arabic script above the door of every mosque and in many homes.
2 Prayer in the direction of Mecca at five fixed times during the day. The cries of 'Allah akba' ('God is great') from all the minarets at prayer time call the faithful to worship.
3 The contribution of a certain proportion of wealth and income for charitable purposes.
4 At least one *hadj* pilgrimage to Mecca in a lifetime.
5 Fasting – and that means no food or drink may pass the lips – during the hours between sunrise and sunset for the lunar month of Ramadan.

Before praying a Muslim must wash feet, ankles, hands and arms in running water – there is a fountain (*çeşme*) outside every mosque for men to wash in. If no water is available then the gestures of washing must be made. The head must be covered before praying, which follows a strict ritual and pattern of movements. Women pray at home except on Fridays, when there is a special section of the mosque reserved for them.

You will notice there is no image of God in any of the mosques you visit. Such representations are strictly prohibited, and indeed any form of representation of the human form – photographs, paintings and sculptures – is forbidden by strict Muslims. It follows that you should exercise great care and discretion with a camera where people are praying, as it could well cause offence. In more remote areas older people, especially women, may take exception to being photographed for the same reason.

There is no formally organized church or priesthood and the imams are teachers and spiritual leaders based in the mosque. *Caliphs*, abolished by Atatürk, were heads of state in all religious matters. The *medrese* or school attached to the mosque used to have a central function, but it has declined with secularization.

In some Muslim countries non-believers are not admitted to the mosque. In Turkey you will be made extremely welcome in most places, providing you respect the fact that you are in a place of worship. You must be respectably dressed, remove your shoes on going in, and women must cover their heads and should also cover their arms and legs. Shorts will almost invariably be unacceptable. You should not enter the mosque whilst a service is in progress, and you may come across a few particularly orthodox mosques where non-muslims are not welcomed.

Sunni Muslims Muslims are divided into two sects, which differ in matters of doctrine. Most of the Turkish population is Sunni, the majority sect in the Islamic world. They are strictly orthodox in their obedience to the strictures of the Koran, and in the emphasis they place on following the deeds and utterances of the Prophet Muhammad.

Shiites Shiites, who broke away from the main stream, believe that Ali, the fourth Caliph, is the only legitimate successor to the Prophet Mohammed. To them all imams, who have absolute authority in

secular and religious matters, are descended from him. Shiites also still embrace the concept of *jihad* or holy war, which gives them the reputation of being more ruthless in the pursuit of their religious objectives. There are very few Shiites in Turkey, and most of those are immigrants from Iran and other Shiite countries.

Recently historians have suggested that the avowed motive for the crusades – to put down the spread of Islam – was to some extent a front for looting and territorial aggrandizement. Three of the seven crusades were waged mainly in Anatolia.

The crusades

The first crusade, under the auspices of the pope, lasted from 1095 to 1099. After camping under the walls of Constantinople, crusaders went on to take Nicaea (Iznik) in a bloody battle, which can well be imagined as you look at the formidable walls with a hundred towers still standing. Another group took Caesarea, now Kayseri, and eventually reached Antioch (Antakya). This had from earliest times been the centre of Christendom in the region. In the Acts of the Apostles it says that believers in Christ were first called Christians there. There is a cave 2 miles (3 km) above the town – the crusaders built the present facade and entrance in the thirteenth century – with mosaics and a secret passage down which persecuted Christians could flee, which could have been seen by St Peter.

The third crusade was led by Richard the Lionheart and the Holy Roman Emperor Frederick Barbarossa. The latter drowned while swimming in the Calcadnus (Göksu) River at Silifke where the crusaders' castle still stands on a rocky spur above the town. The fourth crusade, which started from Venice, sacked Constantinople in 1204.

The Knights of St John The Knights of St John were originally formed, about the time of the first crusade, to defend the pilgrim routes to Jerusalem, and the remains of their defensive castles can be seen at strategic sites throughout Anatolia. The best preserved of these is at Bodrum, where many artefacts of English origin can be seen. Eventually they made their headquarters at Rhodes, from where they were driven by the Turks in 1522.

Religion today The religions coexist in harmony today – but they are inhibited from any form of proselytizing, which is an arrestable offence. Christians have been tried very recently under a law that prohibits the use of religion for personal or political purposes. The fundamental difficulty is that a secular state in an Islamic environment is something of a contradiction in terms. Islam makes no distinction between earthly kingdoms and the kingdom of heaven, and by implication it requires control of the state, as indeed it does in all other Muslim countries.

The Orthodox church came into being when the church in the east and the west split in the doctrinal schism of 1054. The ecumenical patriarch of Constantinople still has his headquarters in Istanbul.

The Eastern Orthodox church

The Orthodox church still follows the old Julian calendar, which is now some thirteen days behind our own Gregorian; as a result Easter, their principal feast, seems to go on for ever in the Galatasaray district of Istanbul where many Christian churches are centred.

To slip in the back of an Orthodox church while a service is going on is to step back many hundreds of years. Beauty is central to the act of worship, and the service is heavy with symbolism which is deeply rooted in doctrine and ritual. As in Islam, the invocation of saints is not permitted.

The difference between the Orthodox religion and the other Christian communions is that Orthodoxy relies on emotional rather than rational appeal. Worship takes place in front of a screen which represents the separation between heaven and earth. The liturgy, which dramatizes scriptural events in Christ's life, is in the form of questions and responses between the celebrant and the congregation. You will see the celebrant break pieces from the altar bread which represent the apostles, and this is followed by the singing of the cherubic hymn which is the most significant part of the service. Candles are lit to symbolize that Christ is the light of the world.

The Anglican church is led by the Archdeacon of the Aegean, based in İzmir. The archdiocese stretches from Vienna to the Mediterranean – more or less the area of the old Ottoman empire. It does a great deal of pastoral work with travellers and expatriates, and people who find themselves in difficulty (tel. 21 27 74).

The Anglican church

The table gives details of Christian and Jewish services.

Christian and Jewish services

Place	Anglican	Catholic	Jewish	Orthodox
Ankara	St Nicholas (Embassy chapel: tel. 136 25 56) 10 a.m.	St Paul (Italian Embassy: tel. 126 65 18) 10 a.m. (Latin)		
Istanbul	St Helena (Consulate Chapel: tel. 127 43 10) 10 a.m.	St Antoine (İstiklâl Cad. 325: tel. 144 09 35) 10 a.m. (English)	Neve Shalom (Büyük Heldek Cad. 67: tel. 144 15 76) 8 a.m. (Saturdays)	Panaghia (İstiklâl Olive Cilma 26: tel. 144 11 84) 9 a.m.
Moda	All Saints, monthly (enquire)			
İzmir	St John (Consulate chapel: tel. 21 27 74) 9.30 a.m.	St Polycarp (Necatibey Sok. 2: tel. 14 84 36) 11 a.m. (French)		
Bornova	St Mary, monthly (enquire)	St Marie convent (enquire: tel. 18 11 77) 12.15 a.m.		

For other Jewish and orthodox services, enquire at the phone numbers given above.

Customs

Despite the secular state and in spite of the secular nature of contemporary society, it must be remembered that much of the Turkish way of life has its roots in the principles and teachings of Islam. This should hardly be surprising since the same can be said about western societies and Christianity – only in Turkey the influence has not weakened very much, at least not yet. Perhaps fortunately for its visitors, traditions and customs that pre-date the religion have enriched the Muslim way of life in a fashion that enables it to be more in harmony with the twentieth century than is the case in some other Islamic countries.

Hospitality

Turkish hospitality is legendary (see p. 11). It seems to come from an innate natural response to travellers, stemming from the nomadic origins of the people coupled with tenets found in the Koran. Even the poorest family feels an obligation to entertain its guests, to the extent that there is sometimes a surfeit of food and drink. You may well be embarrassed by the fact that in relative terms the feast will have cost your hosts many hundreds of times what it might have cost you. There is nothing to be done about it except enjoy it: both to refuse the hospitality and, even worse, to offer to pay cause great offence.

There has, however, been a noticeable change in this attitude in the cities over the last ten years or so, as western attitudes and contacts have developed. Even though you are the guest abroad, these days you are more likely to be allowed to reciprocate hospitality.

An interesting facet of the welcome in Turkey is a determination on the part of the hosts to communicate with their guests. If you go to a home where you have no common language whatsoever, it is likely you will come away amazed at how much you have learned about your hosts – simply by the use of gestures and signs. And many a laborious conversation has been conducted word by word from the dictionary. Turkish people, who seem to have a natural flair for languages, will go through their stock of foreign words irrespective of the language in an attempt to get through.

The family Turkish family life – we might be inclined to call it traditional – has many similarities to that of the extended family once common in western society. It is strictly hierarchical with a male head (*baba*) who is accorded enormous respect and deference. The eldest son is usually not referred to by his given name but addressed as *abi*, in accordance with his position as deputy to his father. Mother (*ana*) is responsible for running the home with the help of the daughters. This pattern is found even in middle-class or westernized families, but it is strongest in rural areas.

The hierarchy within the extended family is much more closely defined than that we are used to. Grandparents have different names depending on whether they come from the father's or mother's side of the family – the former, *büyük baba* and *büyük ana* (literally 'big father' and 'big mother') take precedence over the latter, *ana baba* and *ana ana*. This is continued to uncles and aunts – *amca* and *hala*, the father's brother and sister, are much higher up the pecking order than *dayı* and *teyze*, the mother's. There is also a special relationship between the husbands of sisters (*bacanak*).

Listen to a comedian on television and it will not be long before you catch the word *kaynana* – the mother-in-law – who is the butt of jokes in Turkey as elsewhere. The typical caricature has her incessantly gossiping, with the added refinement that the husband's mother in particular is supposed to be jealous of his wife.

Traditional ceremonies associated with birth, childhood, adolescence, marriage and death are common, the extent of their importance depending on area and circumstance. Usually the extended family all come together for celebrations of these landmarks in family life, and the gatherings are assuming a new importance as migration to the cities causes families to become more fragmented.

Marriage

In rural areas arranged marriages are still commonplace, but the practice is much less followed in the cities. Girls may legally marry at fifteen, boys at seventeen.

A party is held in the house of the bride on the day before the wedding. Traditionally her supporters rub the bride's hand with henna. The groom and his supporters go to the bride's family house to collect the bride. Formerly they would have taken the bride-price with them; nowadays this may be simply a token, depending on the arrangements that have been made between the families. You will see the processions of hooting cars, often on a Sunday, with well-dressed young men cheering and shouting – if they are on the way back the bride, in a red veil, can be seen with them. There are two ceremonies, one at the town hall which is a legal requirement and one at the mosque which is optional.

After the formal part there is a *düğün* (party), usually in a public hall, to which whole villages will often be invited and which goes on well into the night as the bride and groom go off to consummate the marriage. If you are asked to go along to the party, even if you have never met the bride and groom, the invitation is quite genuine and you will be made very welcome. Be prepared for the collection of money which is intended to give the couple a good start in life.

Babies

The birth of babies, especially the first-born, is also celebrated with family parties. Usually a dinner will be given at the house of the new parents, when presents, often gold, are given to the child. There is no equivalent to Christian baptism; the names of the baby are registered at the local registry office.

Customarily the father will have whispered the name into the baby's ear shortly after birth.

It is still important to your status that you produce offspring, and preferably a male heir (*abi*). One of the first questions you will be asked by a new acquaintance is how many children you have. This will be followed by all sorts of questions that might be considered personal in the west, but which are a normal part of social intercourse for the Turks. You will find all forms of questioning much more forthright than you may be used to, with less of the subtlety conventional in English-speaking societies.

Circumcision A boy comes of age when he moves into adolescence with his *sünnet* (circumcision) ceremony, which has both social and religious significance. This is again a time for celebration and festivities (*düğün*). Traditionally the youth, mounted on a pony and wearing a spangled jerkin and peaked cap, leads a procession of his male relatives and friends round the community. This part of the ceremony you may see, although cars rather than ponies are becoming common nowadays.

It is still usual for rich fathers to include boys from poor families in their celebrations as an act of charity. For families too poor to afford surgeons fees, mass circumcisions are regularly arranged by the local authorities, but an unfortunate stigma attaches to those whose *sünnet* is performed this way.

Funerals Muslim funerals are less processional and more discreet than the Christian equivalent. Prayers are not usually said over the deceased at the mosque, and the obligatory ablutions and burial are the important parts of the ceremony.

Away from the cities In the traditional way of life the society revolves around the men: women are seldom seen in public places, and never alone. If you want to find out what is going on, and assuming you understand Turkish, go to the *çay evi* (tea houses), which are the centre of the community. Gossip is exchanged and local affairs discussed over tea or coffee. The local *muhtan* (village

headman) or *başkan* (town mayor) is often to be
found here, almost holding court.

Sadly, the background noise in the tea house these
days is likely to be a dubbed film on the television set
in the corner. However, the rattle of dice can still be
heard, and people get very intense over the *tavla*
board. If you can play backgammon you should have
no difficulty with *tavla* since the differences in the
rules are quickly picked up. However, *tavla* is played
extremely quickly – if you must stop and think before
each move local players will get irritated.

Backgammon and the water-pipe

The air may well be thick with smoke from
hookahs (*nargile*) – water-pipes with strong tobacco.
You will rarely, if at all, find one with opium these
days. Hubble-bubble pipes are stoked up at the
counter with charcoal and tobacco, and rented for as
long as they take to smoke.

The clicks of worry beads being skilfully flicked
through the fingers, and of dominoes snapped onto
the table, complete the background effects.

Women and children are completely excluded from
the tea house, although a courteous exception seems
to be made for foreigners in most places. In every
town you will find the *aile çay bahçesi* (family tea
gardens), often attached to the tea house, where you
will politely be asked to leave if you are obviously not
in family company. The same applies to a family
room (*aile salonu*) in a restaurant.

Family tea-gardens

Even today men prefer to think of their women – and
that includes daughters as well as wives – safely at
home. This reflects both women's traditional subservient role, and the moral code in which modesty is
their most important virtue. In the countryside the
majority of the women are veiled when outside the
home, or in the company of strangers. It is becoming
unusual to see veiled women in the cities – usually it is
an indication that they have come in from an outlying
district – although there has been a recent upsurge in
the number of female students re-adopting the veil.
This trend is reckoned to be either a result of a rise in

The role of women

the numbers turning back to religion, or possibly an indication of an increasing interest in Islamic fundamentalism.

However, since the proclamation that women had equal status to men, made when Islamic law was dropped on the formation of the republic, great strides have been taken in that direction. Women work equally alongside men in the universities and the professions, and female lawyers, doctors, dentists and so on are quite common. That there have never been more than six women members of parliament means that the proportion of men to women in parliament has remained approximately the same as that in most fully developed countries – although there has been one woman Minister of Labour. The charter of the International Labour Organization, demanding 'equal wages for both sexes for work of an equivalent nature', was ratified by Turkey as far back as 1966, and the UN charter on sexual discrimination was ratified by parliament in 1985.

The role of every woman ultimately depends upon the feeling within her family – but it must be remembered, as every emancipated Turkish woman will tell you, the debate begins from a position of male supremacy.

Divorce Secular divorce has been legal for some time, and in fact nearly 30 per cent of Turkish marriages end in this way. Under Islamic law a man has only to tell his wife three times that he divorces her, and he is free – which is one reason the requirement for a civil marriage was introduced on the formation of the republic. Under the secular law it is easier for a woman to divorce a man than vice versa; and if the woman refuses her consent, divorce becomes virtually impossible.

Social codes and attitudes

Begging Giving alms to the poor is a fundamental part of the Islamic code. Outside the mosques, especially on

Fridays, *dilenci* can be seen with their hands out-stretched. The nearest English equivalent to *dilenci* is 'beggar', but this is imprecise because in the Turkish culture there is not the derogatory connotation – 'someone who seeks alms' better expresses the sense.

The strict moral code, stemming initially from Islam and imparted by the family upbringing, means that people walking the streets are relatively safe, and certainly more so than in many westernized cities. Turkish people rarely lock their houses or their cars, except in Istanbul. If a person leaves the house or shop unattended, a token physical barrier is placed in the doorway: a chair or a thin piece of string across the opening is universally respected, and a Turkish person would not presume to cross the barrier. *Law and order*

'An old friend never becomes an enemy', is one of the many maxims that pepper Turkish conversation. The English language and English-speaking societies are rather inadequate in the realm of relationships, and in Turkey the concepts are more Latin than Anglo-Saxon. It is no coincidence that *kardaş* and *arkadaş* (brother and friend) are so similar in sound. Once you have been accorded the status of *arkadaş*, you are almost as a brother. But you will find you quickly become *arkadaş* and the friendship is not completely exclusive. However, Turkish people are by nature protective, almost jealous, both of their friends and their friendship – and this becomes more apparent if you are accorded the status of *dost*. *Dostluk* is much more than friendship, and children are taught at an early age the unquestioning loyalty that must be accorded to *dost*. *Friendship*

It clearly follows from this, and from the status afforded to travellers, that it is extremely difficult for a foreigner to arouse the enmity of a Turk. Once aroused, though, it is explosive.

A factor that sometimes disconcerts visitors is a lack of privacy. Not only is this a general trait found in Islamic countries, it is compounded by the gregarious nature and the sociability of the Turks. It is thought a *Privacy* little unusual for someone to want to do something on their own, and a person travelling alone is considered mildly eccentric. The whole group in its widest sense (*hep beraber*) is always included in any invitation. If you are unsure whether or not you have been invited to something, it will be fairly certain you have. In the home the idea of separate and private rooms within the family is also slightly unusual.

Body language It is quite usual for men to walk around holding hands. This is no more than a normal extension of the attitude to friendship and there is no sexual connotation.

There is a big difference in gestures from those common in western Europe. 'Come here', for example, is indicated with the palm down, and 'no' can be conveyed with a tut while raising the eyes heavenwards. A most useful gesture, especially after a surfeit of tea, is to place the arm and palm flat on the chest. This means 'it is most kind of you to offer, but no', and also acts as a fairly adamant refusal.

Shaking the head in our own 'no' gesture means 'I don't understand', which can result in some amusing encounters until you learn to control what is for us a spontaneous piece of body language. The length of something is indicated by holding out your right arm and indicating the distance from your fingertips with the flat of your left palm.

A great mark of respect shown by children taking leave of their elders is kissing the proffered hand and pressing it to the forehead. It may also be used by subservient people to those in authority but there is a risk that it will be seen as obsequious – and it is often used humorously in television soap operas.

It is quite likely that when you speak to people you look them in the eye, turning away as they begin to speak. In Turkey you will find the Middle Eastern custom prevails, which is exactly the reverse.

Tipping The giving of *bahşiş* (a tip or gift) is rooted in the culture, and the unwary can easily cause offence. If

someone looks after you more than the call of duty
you may be inclined to offer money. The person will
almost certainly need it but convention calls for at
least two refusals. Offer *bahşiş* three times, but no
more – if it is refused the third time the help has been
in the spirit of friendship and hospitality, and further
offers of payment become insulting. If you have some
small gift, especially something from your own
country, this is often appreciated.

Certain tipping is obligatory; cinema and theatre
ushers, and lavatory attendants, should all be given
500 lira. If you are given slippers when you take off
your shoes to enter a mosque, a tip of a few hundred
lira is required. The sleeping car attendant on a train
or the cabin attendant on a boat will come round at
the end of the trip for his 10 per cent service, for
which he will give you an official receipt – and he will
also expect about 5 per cent on top of that. In Turkish
baths the staff often line up as you pay your bill on
leaving. You should leave about 30 per cent of the
total bill between them, more if the service has been
very good. Alternatively you can tip the masseur
separately. Turkish people, for whom going to the
hamam is for many as commonplace as our going to
the bathroom, only tip the masseur and for special
services.

In other situations the western practice of tipping is
creeping in. Some restaurant bills have *servis ücreti*
(service charge) at 10 or 15 per cent. This rarely goes
to the staff and it is usual to leave about 5 per cent on
top. If the bill is *servis dahil* (included) it is becoming
the norm to leave about 10 per cent, except in the
most basic local restaurants.

In international style hotels the staff have come to
expect international style tips. In four- to two-star
establishments it is the convention to give relatively
small tips with larger amounts for special service. It is
as well to remember that the boy who carries your
bags probably earns about £45 or $75 US a month –
from that you can work out how much a tip is
appreciated, and also how easy it is to give a fortune.

For taxis, see p. 89.

Traditional establishments

The 'open house'

Every town has its licensed brothel. The Turkish word *genelev* (literally meaning 'open house') is offensive, causes embarrassment if used in public and is never, repeat never, used in front of women. The euphemism *mektep* (school) is used by, for example, a man asking directions. Traditionally a boy was often taken to the brothel by his male relatives to establish his manhood. They are bawdy places, reminiscent of an earlier age, and the similarity to the harem of old is more than passing; to pay a visit to look at the women in their cages – a visit for men only, of course – is to see another side of Turkey. The women there are medically tested once a week, for all possible diseases, but it would be an unwise man tempted to dalliance who did not take the current precautions. Turkish men have to hand over their identity card to the policeman at the gate, foreigners are asked to show a passport or similar.

The Turkish bath

The *hamam* is the direct successor to the Roman bath, although the latter's four rooms have given way to two important ones. You enter a vestibule surrounded by cubicles; these are for changing and have a couch for relaxing and taking tea after the bath. The next room is usually little more than a passage to the main steam room with the toilets leading off.

In the centre of the main room is a large stone slab, heated from underneath, where you may lounge and on which massages are done. Sometimes there are cubicles round the slab, sometimes smaller rooms opening off, but always stone or marble basins at floor level with hot and cold taps for you to perform your ablutions.

You will be given towels; the long lightweight one should be tied round the waist as a sarong. Men should never expose themselves totally in the *hamam* as this is considered rebarbative by people from a Muslim background. Where there are cubicles a towel should be hung over the opening for privacy when washing. It is reported that women are less concerned about nudity than men.

Most *hamam* have separate days or sessions for men and women, though a few of the larger ones have separate buildings. A notice outside will tell you when you can go in. In Ottoman times a visit to the *hamam* was, for women, one of the few escapes from the house; it became something of a social event with chatting, eating and even dancing on occasions.

You should not be shy of going into the *hamam*, although the first experience can be daunting. You will invariably be made welcome, and there is always somebody there who will show you the ropes. Some of the *hamam* date from the twelfth century and most are several hundred years old, so a visit is well worth while if only to see the traditional architecture: the walls of many are covered with ancient tiles and the domed roofs have thick bottle-glass lights to concentrate the sunlight. With half-closed eyes, you can imagine Saracens lounging on the marble slab before going off to fight the crusaders.

Soap, shampoo and various other toiletries can be picked up at the reception desk as you go in, or you can take your own. The basic charge is not high and a massage or someone to wash you are extra.

If you decide to be washed by an attendant, he uses a *kese*, a rough mitten that peels off the top layers of skin with the dirt. You will surely come away feeling refreshed, if a little raw. Should you decide upon a massage – and be warned that the masseurs are extremely forceful – you lie on the central stone with a wooden block under your neck while they work first on one side then on the other. They manipulate the joints as well as the muscles, and you should indicate in advance if you have any particular weaknesses.

Other customs

Many Turks are genuinely sickened at the thought of eating pork, although they will rarely prevent foreigners from so doing. Habit rather than Islam

Fasting and food restrictions

makes shellfish and snails equally revolting to some,
although there is not the lack of interest in fish found
in stricter Muslim societies. Orthodox shiite Muslims
do not eat hare. The prohibition on alcohol is
disregarded by many people.

Even those who are not particularly religious may
well observe the fast on certain days in Ramadan.

Feasting Most people observe the feast of Şeker Bayramı
which lasts for three and a half days after the
Ramadan fast. Children are given sweets and relations
are visited. It is a bad time to travel on public
transport, which is always very crowded then, as it is
during the Kurban Bayramı, a four-and-a-half-day
festival two months and ten days later.

Sacrifices At the beginning of Kurban Bayramı sheep are
traditionally sacrificed. Their throats are cut in the
street by the heads of more orthodox families, or
alternatively someone can be paid to do it more
discreetly on their behalf. Some of the meat is eaten
by the family and some given to the poor. The skins
are often donated to a charity which sells them to
leather factories.

This festival is in remembrance of Abraham's
near-sacrifice of his son, called Ishmael in the Koran
(Sura 37), but whom you may recognize as Isaac
(Genesis 22).

Sacrifices are not at all uncommon – they can be
seen, for example, at the launching of a boat or the
inauguration of a new train service, when the blood is
smeared on the front of the vehicle to ensure safe
travels. A sheep will always be killed to celebrate the
arrival of a visiting politician.

The whirling Islam allows for no saints but the thirteenth-century
dervishes mystic Celaleddin Rumi, given the title *mevlana*
(meaning 'our guide'), who founded the order of
dervishes, has come pretty close to achieving rever-
ence. The dervish orders exercised a great deal of
influence in Ottoman times, in such a xenophobic,
monarchic and conservative direction that Atatürk

outlawed them. Their hermitages were converted to museums.

Several of the orders have survived as religious fraternities without influence. Walk down İstiklâl Cad. away from Istanbul's Taksim Square, and just past the Four Seasons restaurant and the *tünel* (funicular) entrance, you will find a discreet iron gateway just on Galip Dede Cad. Inside is a haven of courtyards and gardens, with monastic novices who are ostensibly there as librarians of the Museum of Dervish Literature (closes 5 p.m.).

The ritualistic *senna*, the whirling dervishes' trance-like dance, can be seen in the middle of December in Konya, on the anniversary of the death of the Mevlana. It embodies his principles of the abandonment of self; the dervishes' high hats symbolize their own gravestones. As they shed their jackets they are shedding their souls, and the spinning dancers simultaneously reflect the movements of stars in the cosmos and the soul's search for God.

Music and dance

Folk instruments

You will certainly hear the *saz* somewhere while you are in Turkey. They are stringed instruments of the lute family and you are most likely to come across the *bozuk* or the smaller, three-stringed *bağlama*. If you are fortunate in a home, a restaurant or even a public park some successor to the troubadours will pick up an instrument and spontaneously start to play and sing ballads. He may be accompanied by a large drum and a shrill pipe in central Anatolia, by the wooden spoons common round Silifke and Konya, or by a small violin-like instrument on the Black Sea coast.

Folk dances

Just as the instruments have regional variations, so do the dances that often accompany them. Altogether there are reckoned to be around a thousand different regional folk dances, but nowadays most of them are only performed as an attraction for both Turkish and foreign tourists.

Near the Black Sea there is the *horon*, in which the men, wearing black and silver jackets, link arms and quiver.

Around Bursa the sword and shield dance is a representation of the Ottoman conquest of the city. Men wearing military costumes strut around to the rhythm only of clashing swords and shields.

In the Aegean region colourfully dressed men dance the *zeybek* with arms outstretched, in movements popularly associated with Zorba and Greece (with which they do indeed have common origins).

The *kaşik oyunu* (the spoon dance), in which the rhythm is kept up on the castanet-like instruments, is performed by men and women together.

Party dances What we might call old-fashioned formal dancing is very common at weddings and large family gatherings. The bride and groom or the chief guests often lead off with a waltz or a quickstep, but the rhythm gets faster and faster and before long the music has almost imperceptibly changed to a traditional tune. Then improvised folk dancing of that particular region will surely take over. Someone may be playing the zither-like *cura*, whose origins can be traced back to the Hittites, or if it is a large gathering there may be a *kanun* – a seventy-eight stringed dulcimer – and nowadays a clarinet or accordion.

If women get up to dance alone it will be *çiftetelli*, the belly dance, which they accompany on castanets while the men snap their fingers. This happens only within the family – if you see it, it will be professional dancers performing.

Folklore Folklore – and the English word has been used since the stories and verbal traditions started to be recorded in Turkey at the turn of the century – has become an academic study in an attempt to preserve and record the customs, legends and myths that were the cornerstone of life before modern communications. Traditional law is also being studied, whereby disputes in the village were settled locally without recourse to any central authority. It is believed these practices still continue in the extreme remote areas, but a visitor would be unlikely to come across them.

Turkish people are very generous and fond of giving presents. In return something associated with your own country is always appreciated. Few Turkish people will go anywhere without a *mavi boncuk* (a blue glass bead) tucked away somewhere. Traditionally it is woven into a child's hair or a horse's mane to ward off the evil eye. And when a new business opens the first money taken (*siftah*) is kept as a lucky charm for continued good fortune.

Gifts and charms

Historical Highlights

Turkey can claim to be one of the cradles of civilization. The present inhabitants are relative new-comers, and they have in the recent past tended to take little interest in the peoples that preceded their arrival; the quest for national origins as part of the development of national consciousness came to them much later than, say, to the Armenians, Greeks and Slavs, all of whom they ruled at one time or another. There is now a growing awareness that they are heirs to several great cultures which, it is now accepted, contributed to their own Turkish culture.

The pre-Hittite period Relatively little is known of the earliest history of Asia Minor prior to 3000 BC, and much of what has been discovered is displayed in the Museum of Anatolian Cultures at Ankara. If you are planning a visit and happen to see a guidebook in English anywhere, be sure to get it as one is not always available on the premises. Dates this far back are always imprecise, and there is not always a clear delineation between one culture or civilization ending and another rising to prominence. A point that often confuses people is that Anatolia was never really a cohesive unit, but was occupied in different regions at differing times by various tribes and civilizations, some of which were ruled from outside the area. Even in the Ottoman period 'Anadolu' took in only the western half, and the eastern part was usually associated with Syria.

The Palaeolithic period Very few objects exist from the palaeolithic period (prior to 7000 BC) and the greater part of those were found in a cave at Karain some 16 miles (25 km) north-west of Antalya. They are now displayed in the first gallery of the Ankara Museum; the exhibits are arranged chronologically. They include the skull of a Neanderthal man and fragments of wall paintings, some of the earliest in existence. A cave has recently been unearthed west of Istanbul – the exact location is being kept secret for security reasons – with the oldest paintings ever discovered, which are now being studied by academics.

The remains of the earliest known urban culture, Catal Huyuk near Konya, covered some 30 acres (12 hectares) at its height. It is believed to have been a matriarchal society and clay representations of what has become known as the Anatolian Earth Mother, a figure with disproportionately enormous breasts, thighs and buttocks, were found near the house which has been reconstructed in the second gallery of the Ankara museum. Hand-made pottery and wall paintings were also discovered. These have representations of hunters stalking a bull, and also abstract designs that are reminiscent of those still used on *kilim* from this region today.

The Neolithic period

The Hittites and Troy

The Hatti were the original Bronze Age population of central Anatolia. Around 2000 BC they were overrun by European Nessians, who adopted the name Hittites, and who eventually moved their capital from Kanesh to the old Hatti capital of Hattusas where their state archives were found in 1909. Little was previously known of them save the reference in the Old Testament to the Hittite tribes inhabiting the promised land. Then, when cuneiform inscriptions were deciphered, it was discovered that these were the same peoples: they controlled an empire which spread into the Holy Land and beyond, and was in competition with Egypt for the control of the Middle East. It is believed that hieroglyphic script from this period found in south-east Anatolia was invented by the Hittites.

Hatti and Hittite peoples (2500– 1100 BC)

They were a feudal aristocracy and the kings, who chose their own successors, ruled with a council of elders. The kingship gradually became hereditary and by the fourteenth century BC had become almost sacred. Their road system linked Hattusas with the Aegean near Sardis, and with the Mediterranean and Syria via the Cilician Gates (*Gülek Boğazı*): the road still goes through this pass near the town of Pozantı. The pass was widened by Ibrahim Pasha of Egypt who came as an invader in the 1830's – in Hittite times it was a narrow gorge the width of a camel's load.

The Hittites have really caught the Turkish popular imagination. Their exploits are often referred to on television and you will see many a 'Hitit' Restaurant and Carpet Shop. In the 1930s, Nationalist theory made the Turks the direct descendants of the Hittites, which is physically impossible.

Troy A related group of peoples, the Luvians, had simultaneously established themselves at Troy, which had already been rebuilt several times. Not only did that settlement command the Dardanelles and the trade route to the Black Sea, but recent research has suggested that it was a port for the export of Bronze Age products to the west.

The city was destroyed by an earthquake in the thirteenth century BC, and a new city was built on the site. This was the Troy of King Priam, who in Homer's *Iliad* has seen the death of many of his fifty sons, pleads with Achilles for the body of his son Hector, who has been killed by Achilles, and is himself killed at the altar of Zeus.

The Trojan war of the *Iliad* is traditionally reckoned to have been caused by the abduction of Helen by Paris and Aphrodite; more recently historians have suggested that control of sea trade was responsible. The Greeks, led by Agamemnon and Odysseus, eventually captured the city in about 1250 BC with the legendary wooden horse containing warriors that the Trojans took in, believing it to be a gift to Athena.

The dark period Simultaneously with Troy falling to the Greeks the Hittites of central Anatolia were overrun by unknown invaders from the West. The whole of Anatolia entered into a dark age.

After the Hittites

That these people, progenitors of the Armenians, managed to establish an empire in the climatic extremes of eastern Anatolia is remarkable. They gave their name to Mount Ararat, and any name starting with 'ur' or 'er', such as Erzurum, has Armenian origins. They are particularly known for the quality of their metal-work and stone reliefs, of which large quantities have recently been discovered at a number of sites round Lake Van. The irrigation canals they built near their capital at Tushpa Van are still in use.

Urartu peoples (900–600 BC)

The Carians lived in the coastal region from modern Milâs to Fethiye and inland as far as Aydun. The Lycians had the next section of coast to Antalya and the mountains behind. Their warrior reputation and the remoteness of the region kept them isolated, although they were allied with the Trojans for the war with Greece.

Lycians and Carians (c.1500–550 BC)

These were a hedonistic people, who took over the ruins of the Hittite empire. They established their capital at Gordium – named after their king whose knot, binding the yoke and beam of his chariot, was said by the oracles to be so complicated that whoever could untie it would rule Asia. It was eventually, legend has it, cut with a single stroke of his sword by Alexander the Great.

Phrygians (900–650 BC)

Another of their kings, Midas, is familiar to us from writings of Greeks in some awe of his fabulous wealth. He, it is said, was a spendthrift who appealed to the gods for the power to turn all that he touched to gold – hence 'the Midas touch'. On the point of starvation, since even his food became gold, he broke the curse by bathing in the river Pactolus, known today as *Sarp Çayı* and famous for the golden sands along its banks. Midas is also thought to have coined the first money, which was used by the Phrygians

in their export trade in wool and cloth to the
Greeks.

When they were defeated by the marauding nomadic Cimmerians and then the Lydians, the Phrygians
retreated to the mountains between Eskişehir and
Afyon where they built strange facades on the
hillsides. They adopted the mother goddess of the
Hittites, calling her Cybele, and accepted her orgiastic rites; she was later to be taken up by the Greeks as
Artemis and by the Romans as Diana.

Lydians (700–
546 BC)

Like the Phrygians whom they eventually overran,
the Lydians probably came to Anatolia from Thrace.
At first they settled in an area bounded by the coasts
of the Marmara Sea and the Aegean down to Kuşadası
and inland to Afyon. By the seventh century their
influential kingdom, centred on Sardis, had subdued
the Greek coastal city-states: Greeks were employed
as mercenaries, craftsmen and builders and they took
back with them the Lydian's love of perfumes, indoor
games and the seven-stringed lyre.

The Lydians panned and mined gold and are
reckoned to have minted the world's first coins. At
the height of their powers their territory covered
much of the western half of modern Turkey with the
exception of the Lycian kingdom, centred around
what is modern Antalya. When their last king,
Croesus, tried to push even further east he came up
against the Persian Cyrus the Great who retaliated by
conquering the whole Lydian kingdom. Nevertheless
the Lydian King's wealth was fabled even in his own
time, resulting in the expression 'richer than
Croesus'.

The Greeks
and Persians

Anatolian
Greek
settlements
(1100–550
BC)

During the whole of this time there had been small
independent Greek coastal settlements, organized
into three loose confederations. The Aeolian league
north of Smyrna (birth place of Homer, the present
day İzmir) and the Dorian league south of Halicarnassus (now Bodrum) are of little consequence.

However, the Ionian league centred on Miletus (now Milas) became the centre of Greek sea-trade, art and culture. This city exceeded Plato's ideal size of 5,040 citizens, a category excluding slaves, foreigners, women and children, and probably held more than 30,000 people at its height. They moved from kingship to rule by assembly of the citizens and a senate, and classical philosophy and architecture flourished.

Cyrus II had gradually moved the Persian sphere of influence through western Anatolia, and after they defeated the Lydians, the Persians were able to install their own satraps or governors throughout the region. The Ionian states tried tentatively to break free but were soon put down. The most important uprising was the attempt by Mausolus at Halicarnassus to form a unified Greek state, but he died young and was buried in his 'mausoleum'. The Persians had little effect on the architecture but they did build the Royal Road from Sardis to Susa in Iran, following the line of the old Hittite road.

The Persians (585–334 BC)

A pupil of Aristotle, King Alexander of Macedon and later Greece conquered a great deal of Anatolia on his way to Persia and then India. He appointed his subject people to posts of responsibility in kingdoms that recognizably determined the provinces of later Roman and Byzantine times; the then satrapies of Cappadocia and Armenia are recognizable today. On his orders new cities were started, and building continued in typical Hellenistic style for many years.

Alexander the Great

Amongst the other waves of invaders who set up city-states were the Gauls, who established the kingdom of Galatia with a capital at Ancyra (now Ankara), where their red-haired descendants can still be seen.

These times are noted for the spread of Greek culture from the west and religion from the east. New towns at Pergamum and Antioch became great trading centres. Although Anatolia became the centre of western civilization and noted for its prosperity, the

Hellenistic period (334–133 BC)

period was marked by quarrelling between the successors to Alexander's generals, until a ruling caste of Macedonians, Greeks and Hellenic Anatolians evolved.

With Roman help, the Gauls and many of the city-states were eventually defeated in 275 BC by the Hellenized kings of Pergamum. Under Roman patronage they established a cultivated polity whose libraries and medicine were the envy of the civilized world.

Rome and Byzantium

The Roman Empire (133 BC–330 AD) The Romans took Anatolia province by province, bringing with them two hundred years of peace, and a prosperity hitherto unknown. They conquered western Anatolia at Magnesis (now Manisa) but gave the land to their allies at Pergamum. The last king of Pergamum, Attalus, left his province to the Romans, who named it 'Asia', with Ephesus as its capital.

Before Augustus, great-nephew and adopted son of Julius Caesar, could bring the Pax Romana and complete the grandeur of the Roman Empire, he had to defeat Antony and Cleopatra in Anatolia. Plutarch describes them raising support at Tarsus: under the auspices of the mother goddess, Cleopatra dressed as Venus goes out to meet Antony dressed as Bacchus. And if Cleopatra had swum from all beaches named after her she could have been a champion at the games then held in Olympia.

In the second century AD it was so peaceful that Hadrian was able to progress round the outposts of the Roman Empire for pleasure. Cities that had been built on high ground for security were moved to the plains and new ones were built. Ephesus, Smyrna (now İzmir) and Antioch (now Antakya) flourished, as trade moved by sea and across new Roman roads. Roman citizenship was extended to all free men and women.

By the middle of the third century all this had changed; the Roman Empire was under attack from all sides and in a state of civil unrest. In an attempt to control the situation the Emperor Diocletian divided the empire into East and West, each ruled by an emperor and an associate. He himself took the capital of the eastern half of Nicodemia (now İzmit) with Galerius.

After a series of civil wars the Emperor Constantine, who helped establish Christianity (although he was not baptized until he was on his deathbed), took the legendary city of Byzantium – the present Istanbul. In 330 AD, when his wall from the Golden Horn to the Sea of Marmara had been built, he renamed it New Rome and moved the headquarters of the empire. It was not long before it was acclaimed as Constantinople.

This Later or Eastern Roman Empire is more commonly if somewhat confusingly known as the Byzantine Empire, in spite of the change of name of its capital. It inherited all the traditions of Rome, with a centralized government and a large bureaucracy, but these were eroded towards the end by the growing power of a hereditary nobility. Orthodox Christianity became the state religion and church and state were closely linked. However, as the power of the state diminished so the church gained in prestige and power. When Constantine's successor Theodosius destroyed all the pagan temples and banned the hitherto tolerated paganism, he sealed the supremacy of religion that was to typify the Byzantine period.

The Byzantine Empire (330–1071)

Constantinople became the focus of the empire, and the various provinces and declining towns in Anatolia served only to provide labour, raw materials and estates for the nobility. The rule of the emperor became so absolute that, by 527, Justinian was able to pass a law legalizing marriage to a prostitute so that he could bring his ex-prostitute wife Theodora to the throne as associate emperor.

In the eighth century AD destructive raids by the early Muslims, Arabs from the east, devastated the cities in central and western Anatolia, and Constantinople itself was besieged. During this period all trade ceased; the prosperous merchants and cultivated people gravitated to Constantinople, and the rest of the population gradually returned to the soil.

From Byzantium to the Ottomans

The Armenians   The feudal Armenian state in eastern Anatolia had coexisted with the Byzantine empire, acting as a buffer against Iranian Persia and the Arabs. The Armenians had embraced Christianity in the third century, but their rite was regarded heretical by the Byzantines. They handled much of the empire's commerce as well as filling important posts as individuals, for which they had to renounce their religion. From the start of the ninth century they had something of a cultural renaissance, and a great deal of the resulting architecture can still be seen in their capital or Ani and around the shores of Lake Van.

The Georgians   In the mountainous north-east of Anatolia, and stretching beyond the borders of the present USSR, the feudal state of Georgia had less contact with Byzantium than the Armenians. Their folklore relates that they were converted to Christianity by a lady, St Nino, at the same time as Constantinople was founded, although as a remote and fairly insular people they had little contact over the centuries with the great empires. A good many of their churches have survived and can still be seen in very inaccessible parts of north-east Turkey.

The Seljuks (1071–1243)   How Anatolia came to be Turkefied and Islamicized is still an area of considerable historical debate. Certainly the Oguz, a nomadic Turkic people, embraced Islam in Turkestan in about 988 AD – at about the same time as the Russians accepted Christianity. A group of the Oguz under their chieftain Seljuk migrated to the Jand area east of the Khyber Pass in present Pakistan, and eventually extended their territory to cover most of present-day Iran and Iraq.

In the confused times that followed the dissolution

of the Byzantine Empire, the Seljuks made forays into Anatolia and a good number of people were converted to Islam. However, in 1071 under their leader Alp Arslan they captured the Byzantine Emperor Diogenes at Manzikert, just above Lake Van. He ceded part of Anatolia, and the Seljuks set up a state which they called the Sultanate of Rum, centred on Konya. This quickly became one of the strongest, and at the same time most cultivated, states in the region, based on Persian models. A flourishing trade with Italian city-states brought prosperity. Their architecture reached its apogee under Alaeddin Keykubad and their stone bridges and caravanserais are still to be seen. It was their poet Celaleddin Rumi who founded the Order of Whirling Dervishes (see pp. 180–1).

Raiding Turkomans, barely under the control of the Seljuks, led an expansion to the Aegean and Marmara Seas. At first they occupied the countryside, making communication between Byzantine cities difficult, and wrecking their administration. They were not unwelcome to the Greeks, who were unhappy with Byzantine taxes.

The Seljuks themselves were under constant threat from their own people. The Assassins (the name in Arabic means 'hashish eaters'), an Ismaili sect of Shiite Muslims, harried the Seljuks and carried off many of their leaders. The Seljuks split into two groups: the tribes of the Rum Seljuks in Anatolia quarrelled amongst themselves, while the Great Seljuks in Syria and Iraq were fighting the crusaders. The Sultanate of Rum lasted until 1243, when a Mongol tribe defeated them at the Battle of Kosedag. The Byzantines, who were quite barbarously driven out of Constantinople by the fourth crusade in 1204, retreated to Nicaea (now İznik). They retook Constantinople in 1261, and were able to exist as a city-state behind is impregnable walls.

As Anatolia lapsed once again into lawnessness, more and more Turkoman tribes moved in and organized themselves into small emirates. From the very beginning some were warriors, administrators and crafts-

The Ottoman Empire (1300–1922)

men in the towns, while others led a nomadic life outside.

Legend has it that a band of horsemen from an obscure emirate was riding across the Anatolian plains when they came across a battle. In a spirit of chivalry and sportsmanship they joined with the losing side and tipped the balance – to discover they had allied themselves to the Seljuks, who rewarded them with lands in western Anatolia. In reality it is more likely that this emirate, ruled by one Osman and centred on Sogut just north of the modern Eskişehir, laid claim to the remnants of the Sultanate of Rum. They raided westwards towards Constantinople, taking territory that was to be the basis of the Islamic empire named after their leader. Osman was the founder of the Osmanlı dynasty (known as 'Ottoman' in English) that was to last until the twentieth century.

Expansion

At first expansion was slow. Osman's son Orhan captured Bursa in 1326 and made it his capital; he married a Byzantine princess to consolidate his position. After a few years Nicaea and Nicodemia (now İzmit) were added quickly followed by Thrace. Orhan's son Murat went on to annex Bulgaria, Albania and Serbia, from his new capital at Edirne and the fortified base he established in Gallipoli.

One of the worst outbreaks of the Black Death began in the Crimea in 1347 and swept in an arc round Europe for the next five years. Constantinople was affected, but the Turks were for some reason by-passed, which aided their conquests. They were also helped by the longevity of their rulers, which made for stability.

Slaves, both captured and bought, were trained as the corps of foot-soldiers known as Janissaries. Later a more organized conscription was put into effect under the *devşirme* system (literally meaning 'collecting'). This was looked upon as head-tax: boys excluding the first-born were taken from Christian families and trained in Islam and warfare. Some were also sent to the Topkapı Palace school where, alongside the children of the sultan, they studied philosophy, mathematics, history and the arts. These schools were well ahead of their time – educated Muslims had studied Pythagoras while the rest of Europe was still in the dark ages. It came as no surprise to them that the world was round. *Devşirme* boys could, and sometimes did, rise through the administrative ranks to become *vizir*, the ministers responsible for the organization of the royal household. The idea of racism was then completely unheard of – a quality that lives on today in Turkey.

The ultimate goal of Constantinople was not to be realized until 1453 under the rule of Mehmet. A remarkable sultan, this one: he spoke six languages and had his portrait painted by Gentille Bellini, contrary to the tenet of Islam that forbids likenesses. (One of these portraits can be seen in London's National Gallery, no. 3099).

The fall of Constantinople

Mehmet the Conqueror sent a thousand stonemasons to the narrowest point of the Bosphorus and built the siege castle whose ruins, now known as Rumeli Hisar, are still a spectacular sight. The siege lasted two months, and ten Christian galleys held the iron boom that closed the mouth of the Golden Horn. The Pope sent three galleys of food and armaments which managed to get through to the city. The Turks, however, built massive wheeled trucks on to which they floated their galleys and which they hauled with teams of oxen over a new road they had built to a point upstream on the Golden Horn. They bypassed the boom and entered the city by an undefended gate which stood somewhere near the present Spice Market.

Mehmet gave orders that in the three days' pillage that was the usual reward for a successful conquest, all the buildings were to be spared. He went himself to St Sophia, at last in command of that potent symbol of empire, where the population had, the night before, said the last mass that was ever to be heard there.

It is as well to remember that where we speak of the fall of Constantinople, Turks refer to the conquest of Istanbul.

*The zenith
and the nadir* From moving into the Topkapı Palace in the now
renamed Istanbul, the empire flourished and declined
according to the calibre of the sultans. A cruel system
of fratricide was practised: on the accession of a
sultan all his brothers were strangled with a silken
cord, the justification being that a few controlled
deaths were preferable to the havoc that might be
caused if the brothers were to lead a revolt.

Sultans were usually given epithets by the Europeans – Beyazit II, for example, who rarely left his
books, was known as 'the Mystic'. Selim, his successor, is known to the Turks as *Yavuz* (meaning 'the
formidable') but he is usually referred to as Selim the
Grim, from his contemplated massacre of Shiite
muslims and from his regular beheading of his grand
viziers. He extended the empire into Egypt and Syria.

The apogee, both in territorial conquests and in art
and culture, was reached under Suleyman the Magnificent. Sultan from 1520 to 1566, the empire he
controlled from the Topkapı Palace in Istanbul ruled
half the civilized world. When he brought his
favourite wife Roxelana, and the rest of the harem
attended by their eunuchs, into the palace itself, he set
in train the palace intrigues that would eventually
undermine the regime.

He was succeeded by such figures as Selim the Sot
and Ibrahim the Mad, and when the line nearly died
out the policy of fratricide and succession was
changed. The crown now went to the oldest surviving
male and the brothers were kept in a *kafes* (cage)
where they led an idle and mentally debilitating life.
They were permitted concubines but any children
were left to die at birth – only the sultan was allowed
to father children.

In the seventeenth century, effective power passed
from the sultans to the grand vizier. The *divan* – the
council held four days a week to which any subject
could bring grievances – came to be held more and
more frequently at the vizier's official residence. This
overlooked the gate through which only the sultan
could enter on horseback and which became known
as Pasha's Gate or Bab i Ali. It was referred to as the
Sublime Porte by the Europeans, and in time the

name came to refer to the whole regime. The actual gate can be seen in the walls of the Topkapı Palace in Istanbul, near the entrance to Gulhane Park.

The Ottomans were involved in many conflicts in the nineteenth century. The Serbians (1804), the Egyptians (1811), the Greeks (1821) and the Bulgarians (1876) broke free from the empire; attempts by the Armenians to gain independence resulted in massacres. The Russians declared war on the Ottomans in a succession of attempts to take over the Balkan territories. This precipitated the Crimean War in 1853, when the British and French allied with the Turks against the Tzarist armies. During a year-long siege of Sebastapol Florence Nightingale was sent out to inspect hospital conditions. Her office at Scutari on the Asian side of Istanbul remains just as she left it, but as it is within a military complex special permission is needed to visit it.

The Eastern question

Westernization had begun in the eighteenth century and the Sublime Porte in Istanbul tended to take its cultural ideas from Europe and especially from France, rather than from its Anatolian territories. In Victorian times Sultan Abdul Hamid allowed European ambassadors to dictate economic policy from their palatial embassies in the Pera district of Istanbul. Consulates-general now, they are still as palatial.

Frustrated by the empire's role as the sick man of Europe, the Committee for Union and Progress – popularly known as the Young Turks – deposed the sultan in 1909 and installed a triumvirate under Enver Pasha.

The emergence of the modern republic

Many reforms followed; the press was made more free, political parties and a parliament were established, religious discussion and debate were allowed and, most importantly for what had hitherto been a strictly Islamic society, women were admitted to public life. In 1913 an ardent feminist even bombarded the population with suffragette literature from a small plane.

But the First World War intervened. Enver Pasha could not resist allying his country against the old enemy Russia, in spite of the fact that most of the country wanted neutrality. The Turks fought on six fronts and only in Gallipoli (Gelibolu) did they distinguish themselves, where one of their divisions was led by a Colonel Mustafa Kemal. Thousands of Australian and New Zealand troops were lost on the beaches in the Anzac landings.

Today, if you cross the thousand metres of water that separate Europe and Asia at Canakkale, you will find the Turkish War Memorial at Abide and the British and Commonwealth War Memorial at Cape Helles. Since the Peloponnesian Wars, when Sparta beat the Athenians, this has been a strategic battle-ground. The carefully tended war graves with evocative names – Twelve Tree Copse, Pink Farm, Lancashire Landings, The Redoubt and many more – have few visitors these days. There are three commonwealth-owned lodges there, overlooking the sea: one is the home of the custodian of the war graves, and another is available to rent at a very reasonable rate. Arrangements can be made with the custodian.

After the Armistice, Sultan Mehmet VI was installed. He signed the peace treaty which left the Dardanelles and the Bosphorus under an international commission with the brief to ensure free passage for ships. Anatolia came into the French and Italian spheres of influence, and the area round Smyrna (İzmir) was left to the Greeks.

Immediately following the Greek landings, Mustafa Kemal secured an appointment as military inspector for eastern Anatolia and on 10 May – a day now marked as Youth and Sports Day – he landed at Samsun. He went on to organize a guerilla movement for national independence as a counter to the Greek attempt to reconstitute the Byzantine empire. In the bitter struggle that followed, Mustafa Kemal's army cleared all foreign troops from Turkish soil. In 1920 he had set up a grand national assembly in Ankara, and for two years the nationalist government there and the sultanate in Istanbul were at loggerheads.

As the original peace treaty was now *de facto* obsolete, the great powers called another conference at Lausanne, inviting both governments. The Ankara assembly pre-empted this by voting to abolish the sultanate, and Mehmet VI fled. He was smuggled from the Yıldız Sarayı (Palace) in a British ambulance, and taken to Malta and then to exile in San Remo on a gunboat. A month after his departure one of his eunuchs returned to Istanbul to arrange for the transfer of his wives and family. The news of this brought a telegram to the British Embassy from an American impresario: 'Hippodrome New York could use wives of ex-Sultan kindly put me in touch with party who could procure them'.

The Lausanne conference confirmed the boundaries of the new Turkey more or less as the Assembly wanted; the initial proposals for states of Armenia and Kurdistan were dropped, but the Assembly had to accept two losses – Mosul was ceded to Iraq by a League of Nations award, and the area round Iskenderum remained in Syria. The rights of passage in the Bosphorus were controlled by an international commission.

More controversially, the Lausanne Conference arranged for the wholesale exchange of Greek and Turkish populations. Only the Greeks in Istanbul and the Turks in Thrace were excepted. Whilst this caused a great deal of human suffering at the time, it did ensure that the question of minority groups was later less of a problem than it might otherwise have been.

The National Assembly declared Turkey a republic in 1923 and Mustafa Kemal was elected the first president, with the sobriquet '*Atatürk*' – father of the Turks. He, and they, then set about transforming the new nation (see p.13) into a modern state.

Archaeology

That we have in the past accorded the accolade of the birthplace of civilization to Egypt, Italy or Greece can be explained by the fact that archaeologists got to those places first.

There is such a wealth of archaeological sites in Turkey it would be quite impossible to see them all in a short visit. There is space to refer here only to some of the historically more important sites and to point you in the direction of a few of the lesser known ones. At present Turkish experts are excavating over fifty sites, and the museum authorities are staging rescue operations in another forty-five areas. Foreign organizations are working on a further twenty-seven sites – German archaeological teams account for nine of these, and the United States, under the auspices of the American Research Institute in Turkey, for five. Britain has only one, a dig at Tille Hoyuk not far from Kahta in Adiyaman province, which is filling in some important gaps in Bronze Age knowledge. It is being run by the British Institute of Archaeology.

Some terms In guidebooks you may well come across references to the following terms.

Pediment Pediments are typical of Hellenistic and Greek architecture, and can also be seen in Lycian and Lydian rock tombs. They became a classical feature of the British country house, and can be seen in a great deal of colonial architecture and many New England mansions.

Column The column was developed to such an extent by the Greeks and the Romans that the proportions between its constituent parts frequently determined the proportions of the whole building. If you think you have

THE DORIC ORDER | THE IONIC ORDER | THE CORINTHIAN ORDER | CARYATID

seen many of the orders (types) before, then perhaps your local town hall was built in the classical revival in the Victorian period.

The Ionic order was actually developed in Anatolia, in the cities of the Ionian league centred on Milâs. The others were taken there from Greece and Rome.

The Greeks preferred to build on hills, and the *Acropolis* acropolis (literally meaning 'city at the top') was the citadel on the summit which contained the principal temples and treasure houses. Those of later periods are often referred to as citadels, the literal meaning of which is any fortress or stronghold that commands or guards a city.

Agora or forum A central feature of the Greek town plan was the agora, whose primary function was as a market-place. However, it also became the main social and political meeting place. Later, in Roman towns, it was known as the forum and the main civic buildings and temples were grouped round it.

Vault An arched covering in stone or brick over any building is known as a vault. It does not have to be underground, as the popular use of the word would suggest.

Theatre and amphitheatre The area has a wealth of Greek and Roman theatres and amphitheatres, whose shape and conventions evolved with time. Greek theatres were built in natural bowls in the hillside. The Romans, where they did not develop an existing Greek theatre, built theirs on flat ground. The *orchestra*, the Greeks' circular central playing area, became in Roman times a smaller, semicircular area, equivalent to the amphitheatre's *arena*, so called from the Latin word for the sand with which it was strewn to absorb the blood of combatants.

Skene, proskenion and pulpitum The *skene* where the actors in the theatre dressed, which provided a backdrop to plays, and the *proskenion*, a row of columns in front of the *skene* supporting a platform that came to be used as a stage, were temporary structures in Greek times. In the Roman theatre they became elaborately decorated buildings, with permanent substructures under the roofed *pulpitum* (stage), which was backed by the *scaena frons*, a wall ornamented with columns.

Odeon Smaller theatres known as *odeons* were used for musical competitions. Some were built on the same plan as the theatres, some were just roofed halls.

Theatron and cavea Classical theatres had tiers of seats, usually stone benches, for the audience – the Great Theatre at

Ephesus can hold nearly 25,000 people. This auditorium area was called a *theatron* by the Greeks and a
cavea by the Romans.

The all-purpose building in Greek towns was the
stoa, a long, open colonnade that, like the agora, was
a place for social and political meetings, with the
advantage that it also gave shelter from the weather.
The Roman equivalent is the portico.

*Stoa and
portico*

Hittite sites

If necessary the remains of the Hatti and Hittite
capital Hattusas can be seen in a long day trip from
Ankara. Alternatively the Hitit Moteli in Sungurlu,
on the Ankara to Samsun road, has beautiful land-
scaping where nightingales sing in the evening, and
the basic but comfortable Touristik Motel at Boğazköy is very near the ruins.

Hattusas

Boğazköy is a pretty, prosperous, farming village,
and the ruins, mainly dating from the fourteenth
century BC, are scattered over a site of some 2 square
miles (500 hectares). As you walk up the hill from the
village you first come across the Great Temple of the
Weather God. It was built of mud brick reinforced by
a timber frame, on the stone foundation and lower
storey which you see today. You get an immediate
impression of its vastness – originally it had seventy-
eight storerooms for treasure and archives, surrounding the central open space which was the temple itself.

High above the temple is the citadel which contained the royal palace. The southern part of the walls
are the best preserved, and there you come first to the
Kings' Gate with the pointed arch that is so character-
istically Hittite. Further on, where the hill is less
steep, is the Sphinx Gate. One of the carved Sphinxes
that once guarded the portal is in the Istanbul
Museum of the Orient; the other is in the State
Museum in East Berlin.

Follow the signposted road about 1½ miles (2.5 km)
to Yazılıkaya, and you reach the Hittites' holiest
shrine. It consisted of two galleries in an outcrop of

Yazılıkaya

rock enclosing a temple of which only the foundations remain.

However, the galleries have representations of some seventy of the Hittites' thousand gods. They are carved in low relief in profile. The best time to see them is as they are caught in the light of the midday sun.

Alaca Hüyük About 18 miles (29 km) further on down a minor track is Alaca Hüyük. Archaeologically this is the most exciting city of the group, as it was inhabited from around 4000 BC to Ottoman times. It was here that much of the metal-work, jewellery and art seen in the Ankara Museum was found. Two rather worn sphinxes still guard the remains of the city gate and there is an eerie carving of a double-headed eagle with two hares in its talons. On the site is a small museum displaying a few of the lesser finds, and copies of some of the metal pieces.

Lycian sites Fethye, virtually wiped out in an earthquake in 1958 save for the rock tombs dating from about 400 BC (when the town was called Telmessos), is a good base from which to explore Lycian sites. Try the Otel Dedeoglu next to the tourist office for comfortable rooms with a sea view.

The most important Lycian site is at Xanthos. However, before going there, those for whom it is possible should consider a visit to the British Museum in London where many of the most important finds can be seen. The Nereid Monument, brought from Xanthos by Sir Charles Fellowes in 1842, is stunningly displayed there in Room 7. It is in the form of an Ionic temple which stood on a tall base. One interpretation of the figures between the columns, from which the building gets its name, is that they are Nereids – daughters of the Old Man of the Sea. They are meant to be visualized skimming over the surface of waves and the various sea-creatures below them.

A road from the village of Kınık leads up to the site, which has been cleared so that the layout is clear. As you walk to the small theatre in the centre the sage and mint are pungent underfoot. The *cavea* is almost intact and nearby are the foundations of a Roman agora. Beside this is – the Nereid Monument. It is a reproduction on the original base and is known to the locals as the Harpies' Tomb from their identification of the figures.

The sheer drop to the river at the northern end of the city, once a valuable part of the defence system, is an impressive sight today.

Phrygian sites

Midas Şehri

Phrygian remains in the region between Kütahya and Ankara are well preserved and as yet little documented by archaeologists. Here is a chance for some real exploration; the locals can often be persuaded to take you to remote ruins of which nothing is known.

The best base for this area is the town of Eskişehir. The Has Otel Termal and the Sultan Termal Hotel both have thermal baths which are very relaxing after a day spent trudging round lonely and remote sites.

The name of the best-known Phrygian town is unknown. It is set on a long, steeply sided hill beside the village of Yazılıkaya. At the end of the acropolis is a striking facade, some 60 feet (18 m) high and carved into the rock. It is thought not to be a tomb, and may have been connected with the worship of Cybele – originally it may have had a statue of the goddess attended by two lions in the niche at the base. From material found in the holes and depressions in the ground in front of the facade, it is now thought that this might, alternatively, even have been a metal foundry. The pediment looks something like roof-beams resting on a central roof-pole and it is possible that this is a representation of nearby wooden buildings that have long disappeared.

When the site was visited by the British traveller Captain Leake in 1814, he announced to the world that he had found the tomb of the legendary King Midas, and this site is wrongly known as Midas City (Midas Şehri). In fact he had incorrectly translated the inscription that can be seen on the facade.

The smaller facade, carved into the north face of the hill, was never finished. It has an interesting frieze with an acanthus leaf design, in a style usually associated with the Greeks.

In the west of the town are two staircases cut into the rock, which eventually lead underground to wells. Originally there were also tunnels, leading under the walls of which little remains. It is easy to spend a whole day rambling round this site, stumbling on niches, altars perhaps, tombs and pieces of inscriptions amongst the detritus of a forgotten people.

King Midas Archaeologists now believe that the Phrygians introduced the tumulus or mound form of burial to central Anatolia. King Midas' tomb is thought in fact to be one of the ninety earth mounds near the village of Yassıhöyük 60 miles (95 km) south-west of Ankara and not far from the site of the city of Gordium. So far one third of the tombs have been excavated and the largest – which has a wooden frame and is thus probably the oldest surviving wood structure – has fluctuations in humidity that are as yet inexplicable, while the temperature remains constant. The phenomenon is being investigated by a team of archaeologists from the US University of Pennsylvania Museum. The remains of wooden tables and inlaid wooden screens were found in the tomb, probably Midas', all dating from the seventh century BC.

A skeleton, presumed to be that of King Midas, was unearthed in 1957. Most of it was lost but the skull lay forgotten in a box in the Ankara museum. From it experts from the University of Manchester have recently been invited to make a reconstruction of Midas' head, and it is now on display in the Manchester Museum.

Termessos Well preserved although little excavated, the city of Termessos is one of the most attractive sites in Anatolia. It is 20 miles (32 km) up into the mountains behind Antalya.

Leave by the dual carriageway towards Burdur and, after climbing 7 miles (11 km) through the pine forests, take the left turn signposted Korkuteli. Turn left into Termessos Milli Park (National Park) where there is a small museum. The ruins are a further 5 miles (8 km) up a rough track which passes through several gates in the original city walls. The agora is the only flat space in the site, and from there exploration must be on foot.

In summer the best time to go is in the early morning. Then you may well have the site almost to yourselves with the mist swirling round the craggy mountains above and below. But only almost, because deer, wild boar, eagles and falcons live here, in close harmony with the family of bears which has moved in.

The inhabitants of the city referred to themselves as Solymian, and the *Iliad* tells us that Bellerophon, when he fought and conquered them, thought it the worst battle he had ever been in. Other than that they were never defeated; Alexander the Great abandoned a siege here and although the city was Hellenized there were no Greek settlers. They were friends and allies of Rome, but never part of the empire. The ruins date from the Hellenistic and Roman periods.

North of the agora, the Street of the Kings turns into a colonnaded street of shops, once lined with statues. The inscriptions remain and show that many were of wrestling champions – there still are many wrestlers from this area. East of the agora is a small, well-preserved, second-century BC theatre built in the Greek style. The adjacent *odeon* is believed, unusually for its time, to have seated over 600 people under cover. To the south of the bases of columns, and the doorway, are the remains of a Temple of Artemis. Close by can be seen the foundations of two other temples.

Away from the centre you must watch your step as there are many unfenced underground cisterns, once used to store olive oil as well as water. The nearest group of five is still plastered and if you peer down into the darkness you can see the projecting stones that marked the level.

The whole of the hillside is a vast necropolis, but the tombs are split open and damaged. The inscriptions on many tell of the fines payable by robbers or anyone attempting to reuse them, and of the amount payable to anyone giving information on offenders. The deterrent seems not to have worked.

Ephesus   Known locally as Efes, this must rank as one of the world's most stupendous archaeological excavations and reconstructions. It has a magical quality about it. Walking along the paved streets it takes but little imagination to see togad inhabitants going about their civic business.

Ephesus can be reached in about an hour and a half by road from İzmir, as can Sardis and Pergamon. Kuşadası with its burgeoning tourist hotels is where many people base themselves, and from there Priene, Miletus and Didyma can also be easily reached. However, the sleepy little town of Selçuk, which now has storks nesting on the chimneys and which grew up 4 miles (6 km) away when the harbour at Ephesus finally completely silted up, should not be disregarded. The basic but comfortable Kale Han Guest House, on Kalealti Sok (tel. 5451 154) is in a restored stone *han*, and the Tusan Efes Moteli (tel. 5451 1060) is ten minutes' walk from the entrance to the ruins on the Selçuk–Kuşadası road. In any case the Efes Museum at Selçuk (closed Mondays) has some very important discoveries and is well worth a visit.

Even those not keen on ruins and archaeology should not miss Ephesus. It is so well restored that it immediately comes to life, and in such a beautiful setting that it can almost be taken as a country walk. It gets very hot at midday in high summer, and the best time to visit is early morning. People are always amazed by the sheer amount of carving and relics lying around – far more than the guidebooks could ever chronicle.

The area divides into four quite distinct sections, including the House of the Virgin Mary which is 5 miles (8 km) up in the hills. When there, do not miss the waters from the stream running through the foundations: they are supposed to have special properties and have been piped to three taps for convenience. From left to right they are for health, wealth and love.

As you approach Selçuk from Kuşadası there is a swampy open space down on the left. This was the site of one of the seven wonders of the ancient world, the Temple of Artemis or Diana. Little remains now save a single reinstated column, and the main discoveries can be seen in the British Museum. Not far from here is the Basilica where St John is said to be buried, and just below the church stands one of the masterpieces of Seljuk architecture, the Isa Bey Mosque, built in 1375

In the hills above the main site are all sorts of unrecorded and unmarked finds. Amongst them are an impressive early Christian cemetery surrounding a church, and the remains of the Grotto of the Seven Sleepers (in fact a Byzantine necropolis).

The seven sleepers are a common theme in Christian and Turkish folklore. In this case seven young men of Ephesus fled third-century persecution and hid in a cave, but they were discovered and the entrance was sealed. Two hundred years later an earthquake broke open the cave and woke the young men. They found the city had become Christian and, not surprisingly, that all their friends were dead. They were eventually buried in the cave and a church was built on top.

The site of the main archaeological reconstruction is fairly well signposted, but a guidebook is recommended to appreciate it to the full. Of the two entrances it is preferable to use that off the Kuşadası–Selçuk road, as the contours of the town cause it to unfold more dramatically from this side.

To the right of the car park is the silted harbour. The buildings there have not yet been fully excavated although work is now under way on reconstruction of much of the church of the Holy Virgin.

Walk down the cypress-lined avenue, leaving the Harbour Gymnasium on the right, until you come to the marble-paved Arcadian Way. This was the grandest promenade in the city. Once it was lined with shops, and some of the triumphal columns and statues have been reinstated. It led from the harbour to the theatre and must have been a grand sight when the colonnades were illuminated at night.

From the highest tier of the 24,000-seat theatre, carved into Mount Pion, is a wonderful view of the city. It was originally built in the Hellenistic period and was remodelled by the Romans. In classical Greece all the action took place in the *orchestra*, but in Hellenistic times a small stage was set above the *orchestra* which was relegated to become the chorus. In Roman times fashion had moved all the action to the stage, and that at Ephesus was particularly noted for its grandeur. Built on three levels with an ornate facade, it was adorned by statues, columns and niches. To demonstrate the acoustics, try whispering from the stage to a companion in the highest seats.

The Arcadian Way turns right at the theatre and leads eventually to the restored Library of Celsus. It faces east, so letting the morning light into its high windows. Inside can be seen the niches for books and scrolls. Beneath the niche in the back wall is the tomb and marble sarcophagus containing the lead casket with the undisturbed bones of Caius Julius Celsus Polemaeanus, in whose honour the library was built by his son.

The road turns left here and becomes the Street of Curetes – the down-town part of the city. Here is the building that has long been identified as the brothel: it is thought to have been connected to the library by a tunnel. Opposite are the public lavatories, whose function is unmistakable, showing how little their design has changed over the years. Set on the hillside above are the terraced houses, some of which have been restored. Their simplicity is a reflection of the fact that the accommodation was only for sleeping and dressing. All other functions, from business to bathing, were carried out in the appropriate public places.

Marine archaeology   Turkey has more than just land-found artefacts. Marine archaeologists have excavated a ship that went down in about 1200 BC off Cape Gelidonya on the southern coast. Some of its copper and tin ingots, probably being transported from the Levant – the western Mediterranean coast now comprising Syria and Lebanon – are on display at the crusaders' castle at Bodrum, where there is a large number of marine artefacts.

Do not take any archaeological material out of the country, or even have it in your possession. Not only are the Turkish authorities concerned that their heritage should remain intact, but they do not like putting their guests in prison. They take an extremely strong line on this and the penalties are very severe indeed for anyone caught with unauthorized objects.

A plea from the authorities

Architecture

There is a variety of architectural styles which may be unfamiliar to western eyes. They are, however, quite distinctive, and with a little practice it is easy to see buildings in their context. The various waves of migration have brought influences from the orient, from Arabia and from Christian Europe, resulting in an eclectic urban environment that is unique to Anatolia.

The Byzantines

Architecture was one of the highest art forms in the Byzantine empire, evolving in a style of its own that was quite distinct from its Roman origins. Sadly most of the masterpieces of civic buildings have been lost and now come into the realm of archaeology, but many of the churches remain, and it is for these that Byzantine architecture is renowned.

Construction

Byzantine building techniques fall into two broad types. The first is ashlar masonry – square-hewn stones, often with carved vertical surfaces and timber roofs, found where the materials were to hand.

The other form, and typical of Constantinople, has a double skin of brick and stone filled with rubble. This could be formed into the arches, vaults and domes that are so typical of the period. Usually each course (layer) of stone is relieved by a line of brick which goes right through the building, giving added strength.

Byzantine buildings can be recognized by brick-work and mortar of equal thickness: later Turkish architecture has thicker bricks and less mortar. Doors and windows are usually spanned by semicircular arches, and the windows are often arranged in tiers. Mouldings were little used, and the interiors can seem rather plain, as much of the original marble and mosaic facing has been lost.

There is little left in Turkey in the way of wholly Byzantine houses – the practice of adapting existing buildings has seen to that. However, from time to time you will come across a recognizably Byzantine wall or familiar style of window in an otherwise unremarkable building.

Domestic building

   In Istanbul can be seen one of the most noteworthy examples of architectural salvage, carried out by the Byzantines in 532 AD. The Basilica Cistern (Yerebatan) was built underground to store water brought by viaduct from the Belgrade Forest. The vaulted roof is supported on 336 columns in a variety of styles: these columns were either salvaged from older buildings or had been made in bulk and were surplus to requirements. Recently cleaned out, the cistern has walkways and a restaurant and is one of the wonders of the tourist world.

Churches which are distinctively Byzantine can be seen not only in Anatolia, but throughout Greece and as far apart as Italy and Russia. The style and form was used for over a thousand years, long after the fall of Constantinople and the collapse of the Byzantine empire.

Ecclesiastical architecture

   There are two basic shapes; the basilica and the central plan. The usual form of the basilica is a rectangle twice as long as its width, with two or four rows of columns dividing it into a central nave and side aisles. Its origin lies in the halls of justice and commerce of old Rome. The columns became stylized and they were eventually considered to be an important adjunct to the building irrespective of their function of supporting the roof. Entry is through an entrance vestibule (often referred to as the narthex) outside which there is usually a courtyard or atrium. The altar was in a semicircular apse at the end of the nave, in a form recognizable to us today.

   From the sixth century a central dome came to be considered essential to the basilica, as it was by then technically possible. To get it to stay up it was often.

necessary to add side arms (transepts) to the plan, and the cruciform church became common. Before long the transepts came to dominate the nave, giving the church the shape of a Greek cross.

The central plan is seen more often in tombs or smaller churches. With its simple circular walls supporting a central dome, it is instantly recognizable. Sometimes there are cloisters, or the walls may be multi-faceted, but the basic simplicity remains.

Decoration The walls of many Byzantine churches were gloriously decorated, with either paintings or mosaics. Frequently these took the form of what we would consider to be scenes from the Bible, but in their time they were representations of events related by word of mouth. A great deal of this rich decoration remains, much of it *in situ*.

The Byzantine style of church building spread into Cappadocia where the population, although they had embraced Christianity, were not part of the empire. There, in the wonderfully decorated churches cut into the rock, are pillars that are purely decorative and with no load-bearing function whatsoever.

The Seljuks The Seljuks brought a quite distinctively Islamic, essentially Persian style with them. However, the contrast between their architecture and the Byzantines' is not all that great, since they tried to harmonize their buildings with the environment and used local craftsmen who adapted the old styles.

Brick was the common building material and Seljuk arches are much more pointed, with a slight oriental feel about them. These can be seen particularly clearly in mosques, but also in bridges, of which many are in use today. Window openings were often formed of distinctive honeycomb-patterned brickwork.

Konya is the home of Seljuk architecture and a great deal of sensitive restoration has been carried out there. On the harbour shore at Alanya is one of Turkey's oldest buildings. The Kızıl Kule (Red Tower) dates from the fortifications built in the thirteenth century and was very skilfully restored in the 1950s.

Many mosques are Byzantine churches which were *Mosques*
taken over by the Seljuks. Others were built using the
adopted basilica layout, and columns salvaged from
demolished churches were often used.

Decoration is elaborate, especially on gates and
doorways; there is often a *mihrap* or prayer niche at
the entrance. As calligraphy became an art form in its
own right, so the decoration became even more
elaborate.

Attached to many mosques was a *medrese*, a place
of study for men who would eventually become
religious and social leaders. Often these take the form
of cloistered cells round a central court.

One day's journey apart on the routes radiating from *Caravanserais*
Konya are found the *han*, also known as caravanser-
ais, which translates as caravan palace. Resting places
for caravan trains, these buildings are very elaborately
decorated, especially on the entrances. There is often
a mosque in the centre of the complex.

They were defended by a thick outside wall within
which there is a courtyard with bedrooms,
storerooms and workshops opening off a colonnaded
walk. At the opposite end of the complex from the
entrance is a vaulted hall, often with a domed roof.

Since the Ottomans took so many towns by con- **The**
quest, a great deal of rebuilding had of necessity to **Ottomans**
take place. Starting at Bursa, then at Edirne and
eventually in Istanbul itself, they created new capitals.
Stone was used more widely than hitherto for
mosques, and a great deal of wood was used for
domestic buildings.

Ottoman architecture is often distinguishable from
Seljuk by the increased amount of decoration
employed. Interiors are frequently tiled in the distinctive blues and reds of the İznik potteries. Wooden
exteriors are often elaborately carved in the later
period of the empire.

The Ottomans continued with the practice of using
caravanserais on commercial journeys, but also built
hans in the cities for commercial activities. The *han*
were built round a courtyard in a similar manner to

the caravanserais, but rarely had stabling. The restored Hasan Paşa Han at Diyarbakır, built in about 1580, is a typical example.

Whereas the Seljuks held markets and fairs on open sites wherever there were goods and produce to sell, the Ottomans developed bazaars (çarşı in Turkish) wherever they established cities. That at Istanbul (see p. 56) is a typical, although much restored and rebuilt, example. The *bedesten* is the inner chamber of an Ottoman bazaar, built to keep safe the merchants' valuables.

Religious building Ottoman mosques are squarer and more compact, and the Byzantine-style narthex or entrance vestibule reappears. The minarets are thinner, taller and plainer, and part of an external composition in their relation to the dominant feature of the central dome. Arches are rounder and portals less elaborate.

Mimar Sinan The finest and most important architect of Ottoman Turkey, if not the whole Islamic world, Mimar Sinan was a *devşirme* conscripted as a Janissary (see p. 194) in the sultanate of Suleyman the Magnificent. He spent many years building roads and bridges for the army. He was a genius at solving engineering problems, such as the bridge still in use today at Küçükçekmece between Edirne and Istanbul, which is constructed on five artificial islands.

Eventually, as Royal Chief Architect, he was responsible for hundreds of projects – roads, water supplies, baths, tombs and mosques. Like the contemporary cathedrals in Europe, the mosque was then the main symbol of spiritual and political power. It was in mosque building that Sinan Bey is renowned, to the extent that he was given the soubriquet '*mimar*', meaning architect.

In his first commission from the Sultan himself he placed acoustic dishes in the Şehzade Mehmet Mosque in Istanbul. He went on to solve the classic architectural dilemma of how to reconcile a large dome with a square foundation. All Islamic architecture followed the tradition of St Sophia in the importance of the dome. But the Islamic requirement was for a vast space below, unencumbered by pillars. Sinan's solution was to place a half dome on each of four sides of the main dome. Not only did that ease the structural problems and free the large central area of pillars, it achieved *dajami* – the Islamic principal of bringing the whole congregation together under one dome. Cast your eyes heavenwards in any of thousands of mosques and you will see the efficacy of his ideas.

Ottoman houses tended to be made of wood, often with a projecting upper storey. These were relatively safe in earthquakes but large areas were often destroyed by fire. In central Anatolia houses were built, as they still are, of baked mud brick. Then as now they had a roof made of packed mud, which can be tamped down after rains.

Domestic buildings

In the declining period of the Ottoman Empire the palaces and houses of the rich tended to follow western European fashions. The Europeans who settled in the Pera district of Istanbul (usually known as Galatasaray or Beyoğlu these days) built wonderfully grand and ornate *fin de siècle* mansions. They are still there, but how sad and dilapidated they seem now. To be transported back to the days of decadence and intrigue, lift your eyes above the modern shop-fronts.

Late nineteenth and twentieth century

Most Turkish towns, save the three main cities, escaped the worst of ubiquitous 1960s' building, but the present tourism development is transforming the face of coastal areas. Whilst some modern architecture is excellent and draws on the whole of Anatolia's cultural tradition, there is too much going up that could equally well be in Spain or Greece.

A delightful architectural oddity, looking rather forlorn and unloved these days as the buildings all around it have been cleared away, is the church of St Stephen of the Bulgars. It stands on the Byzantine side of the Golden Horn between the two bridges. Pre-fabricated in cast iron in Vienna, it was floated down the Danube and assembled in 1871.

Conservation The concern for buildings of historic or architectural interest that we more or less now take for granted has only just reached Turkey. The one exception has been the Turkish Touring Club, whose secretary general started almost a one-man crusade in the early 1970s. There are as a result, in the most unlikely places, old buildings restored, put to new uses and operated by the Touring Club.

The authorities have now recognized the importance of their architectural heritage, especially in relation to tourist development, and some good conservation projects are getting under way.

Doing Business

There is an accelerating increase in the number of foreign firms operating in Turkey. The government now operates a deliberate policy of welcoming well-run, financially sound businesses and investment – and the new technology and off-shore finance that come with them. Companies coming to Turkey are able to take advantage of a large local market with a gross national product of $50 billion US, a good raw material base and a geographical location which is well placed for the additional markets of the Middle East. They will also find labour costs which, in relative terms, are low. One indicator of the level a developing country has reached is the quality of locally made machine-tools. Whilst in Turkey they are not made to the highest level of precision, most people seem to agree that they work quite acceptably well.

Companies from the developed world should not move in with the expectation that everything will be the same as in the rest of Europe. In successful cases there is always a certain amount of give and take, and adaptation to the Turkish way of doing business. For its part the country is working hard at updating the economy and business methods. Turkish business-men often remark that when they meet their counter-parts from the west for the first time, they feel they should wear baggy trousers and fez instead of the extremely smart business suits that are *de rigeur*, just so the visitors do not have their illusions shattered too suddenly.

Working times

A lot of people, especially if they have been working *Weekends* in other countries with an Islamic tradition, arrive expecting the weekend to include Friday. The western weekend of Saturday and Sunday, however, was adopted as part of Atatürk's reforms. Employees who wish to go to the mosque on Friday must be given the time off, but this is rarely disruptive of the normal forty-five-hour week – which many employers reduce in any case.

Normal business hours Business hours tend to be fairly flexible, but generally they are 9 a.m. to 12 p.m. and 1 p.m. to 5 or 6 p.m., Monday to Friday. Quite a few offices are open on Saturday mornings but appointments are often difficult to arrange then, especially in summer and in August in particular. This is the most popular holiday month, when businessmen tend to go to the coast to join their families, who have moved to the second home.

Some companies allow staff to work slightly shorter hours during the month of Ramadan and it can be difficult then to get hold of the person you need. Ramadan is about eleven days earlier each year (see p. 270).

The three-and-a-half day Şeker Bayramı holiday comes at the end of Ramadan. The four-and-a-half day Kurban Bayramı is two months and ten days after that (see p. 270). Everything is shut down and anyone planning a visit likely to coincide with these dates should check the availability of their contacts.

Offices are also closed 1 January, 23 April, 30 August, and 29 and 30 October, for statutory public holidays.

Business ownership It is not possible for non-resident foreigners to own a business: theoretically and under certain circumstances, anyone with a residence permit can. There are one or two examples of British and American individuals and couples running small hotels, and one Britisher has built a tourist hotel at Dalyan. For the moment they are exceptions and it is established companies that are coming to Turkey.

In companies with a substantial foreign ownership a limitation is often put on the number of shareholders, which makes it a closely held company – a concept familiar in western business circles too.

There are two types of company, with the abbreviations 'AS' and 'TLS'. They are roughly equivalent to the 'PLC' and 'Ltd' public and private limited companies found in Britain, in which the liability of the shareholders is limited to the nominal value of the shares. A company with AS (Anonim Şirket) after the name has the right to offer shares to the public and is usually relatively large. A TLS (Türk Limited Şirketi) company does not have this right and is usually quite small. There is familiar ring to the names seen on many advertising hoardings since companies in this latter group often use the abbreviation 'Ltd'. *Types of company*

From buying fruit at a roadside stall to hiring a small boat from a quayside office for a sea or river trip, you are likely to come across a *kooperatif* somewhere. Often these are based on a loose federation of small or individual enterprises. The extent to which they work together can range from a mutual marketing operation to actual profit sharing. *Cooperatives*

In principle at least, all legal forms of doing business are open to foreign investment – but with permission. Turkey is unique in that permission is needed to invest in the country. **Investment and finance**

The most important licensing authority is the Federal Investment Department, which comes under the Department of Finance and Foreign Trade. It is responsible for actively encouraging overseas investment and can help in locating possible Turkish partners and projects. It must also be noted that every investment move or change needs this department's permission. Theoretically all decisions are announced, one way or another, in ten days, but sometimes this ambitious time-scale slips a little in practice.

Overseas business visitors find themselves working closely with the Central Bank – more or less equivalent nowadays to the Bank of England or the

Federal Reserve Bank – in their foreign exchange transfers and capital structuring of new operations.

Incentives Tourism, electronics, defence, textiles and energy are considered important to the local economy. Companies in these fields can expect considerable help from the authorities, and most favourable consideration for incentives.

Almost all new investments qualify for some or all of a wide range of incentives. These can take five forms: exemption from customs and other duties on the import of machinery; subsidized domestic and foreign credits; tax exemptions; tax benefits, especially in the form of deductions of start-up expenditure; and permission to import second-hand plant and equipment – normally not allowed under any circumstances.

In budgeting for incentives, four cautionary factors should be taken into account: the small print can be quite constrictive; the rules can change quite suddenly and during the course of negotiation; bureaucratic procedures can seem endless; and if the annual budget has run out, then it is necessary to wait until next year.

Specialist agents exist to handle incentive applications and it is strongly recommended that one is used.

Build/ operate/ transfer system For major infrastructure projects there is what is known as the BOT (build/operate/transfer) system. This is a scheme to encourage foreign companies to become involved in large-scale capital projects such as power stations. The theory is that a consortium builds the plant, operates it and sells the output to the appropriate authority at the prevailing price. Once the operating costs and the builder's profits have been recovered, the plant is handed over to the government.

Free trade zones Free trade zones are in operation at Mersin and Antalya, and two more are opening at Adana and İzmir. Companies operating in these zones are absolved from many normal limitations, and in particular come outside customs restrictions.

The principal taxes are corporation tax, income tax, customs duties and a few special taxes on the sale of certain goods and services. All goods are liable to KDV (VAT) at variable rates. Over 60 per cent of total tax revenue comes from direct sources. All businesses are required to display prominently a certificate of the revenue for the previous year and the amount of tax paid.

Taxes

Setting up

Businesses just starting operating in Turkey often find a problem in getting things, especially electronic office equipment, into the country. It seems that the bureaucracy of the customs department has not caught up with administrative changes – and changes in attitude – to foreign imports. There are also twenty-one items, including fax and other telecommunications equipment, which are on a restricted list and for which permission is needed. When permission is given the company is required to provide spare parts and service facilities for the next five years, in the case of electronic equipment; for construction machinery that requirement is increased to ten years. Those who have been through these procedures report that, although it is not a strict requirement, if you do not have the purchase receipt for the equipment it gets held up at customs. Again, it is often advisable to get a specialist agent to help things along.

Office and operating equipment

Most enterprises begin with the appointment of a Turkish agent – in fact the great bulk of foreign trade is done through intermediaries. It is important that the standing and any possible conflict of interests of prospective agents is checked out well in advance. The British Overseas Trade Board and the US Department of Commerce will supply lists of authorized agents on request. Since the market and foreign trade and exchange regulations are subject to quite rapid change, regular visits by representatives of the principal companies are vital.

Agents

Trade fairs and missions A useful way to initiate contact with the market is through trade missions to and from Turkey. The British Overseas Trade Board takes the view that specialized trade fairs are particularly useful, and they can give a great deal of assistance in this direction.

People visiting Turkey on business are invited to telephone their appropriate embassy or consulate on arrival to discuss any help that can be given. If you contact the Department of Trade and Industry in London or the Department of Commerce in Washington before leaving, and let them know the object of your visit, the people in Turkey can be prepared in advance.

Business visitors and missions are recommended to make contact with the British Chamber of Commerce of Turkey and the US Business Council on arrival. It is also useful to give fifteen days' notice of any proposed trade visit to the Istanbul Chamber of Commerce. They can arrange accreditation and set up meetings with Turkish businesses likely to be interested.

The International Trade Fair held each August in İzmir has over two million visitors – but these are mainly ordinary members of the public. Privately organized specialist trade fairs are a common form of marketing in Turkey, and are usually held in Istanbul.

Promotions Information about forthcoming British promotions can be obtained from the Department of Trade and Industry or the Department of Commerce. They can help too with lists of useful contacts, but appreciate about a month's notice for this.

The BBC World Service has a lot of coverage of British industry, science and technology, and often features new products and processes, mentioning the name of the firm concerned. Any enquiries received as a result of the broadcasts are passed on.

Advertising British exporters can seek advice from the Overseas Press and Media Association.

The Turkish national press, mainly based in Istanbul, is amenable to public relations handouts, but these need, of course, to be in Turkish. The Ankara-based *Turkish Daily News* often features foreign promotions, and the weekly *Dateline Turkey* covers important trade events. There is a growing number of trade press publications. Those dealing with computers and the construction industry are fairly well established; others tend to come and go.

Radio has short advertising slots. Television carries advertisements which are similar in style to those found anywhere else in the world, although in many cases they are deliberately kept simple and are less flashy. Cinemas carry slides and advertising shorts between the programmes, and this is considered an important medium by the Turkish business community.

Anyone contemplating public relations or advertising campaigns should seek advice from someone who is familiar with what goes on.

Tendering, funding and presentation

Tenders

Most prices are negotiated by tender and should be quoted in sterling or US dollars. Although this is a diminishing proportion, about half the industrial output still comes from the state sector. State-run organizations are very bureaucratic, adhere rigidly to tendering conditions and are extremely unlikely to be able to come to any arrangement for a variation in their specifications.

Allowance should be made for the 0.5 to 0.7 per cent of the total contract price which is the charge for compulsory certification of local contracts by notaries public.

Funding

It is advisable for foreign companies to try to retain the final say in sources of funding, even if Turkish partners have equal access to credit and grants. World Bank money or credits from Britain's Overseas Development Ministry are irrevocable once committed; funds from Turkish sources have been known to dry up and cause delays in projects.

Presentations In making a proposal it is important to establish at what level final decisions can be taken, and to try to see the right person. To get a quick answer it is advisable to have the crucial figures set out concisely on one sheet of paper. A detailed presentation is necessary for consideration lower down the line, either before or after decisions have been taken; but in the crucial discussions it is the summary with essential totals that is required.

Languages and translation Any weights and measures should be quoted in the metric system, in both contracts and all literature. It is quite acceptable for correspondence to be conducted in English, and trade catalogues need not be translated. However, the specification of technical goods, instruction leaflets and sales catalogues must be provided in Turkish.

English has become the lingua franca, after Turkish, in business circles. French is the second language of some older people and German is known by many technicians. These days there is usually somebody nearby who can help in translation of basic needs, but for formal meetings it is worthwhile checking in advance what languages are spoken and what arrangements you should make. Diplomatic missions can give information about translation and interpretation agencies and services, and can also be extremely helpful with the provision of any urgently needed facilities when companies are testing the market.

Business conventions It is important that anyone planning to enter into any discussions or negotiations is aware of the fundamental cultural differences that exist between Turkish and English-speaking people. The Turks will, hospitable and liberal people that they are, accept all the foibles of people coming from another culture without question. However, if you pay them the courtesy of meeting them half way they appreciate it, and objectives are likely to be that much more quickly realized. There are some minor differences in methods of doing business that are of great importance.

The Turkish way of conducting a meeting is to spend some time at the beginning with courtesies. Thus visitors will be asked about their health and that of their family, even if the hosts have never met the family. Tea and coffee will be offered, and should not be refused – ask for water, as Turkish people often do, if you cannot face any more tea or coffee – then honour is satisfied.

Meetings and courtesies

If you are meeting a very senior person you may have been allocated a fixed period of time. In that case it is prudent to try to find out how long you have got – at this level his secretary will be at least bi- and probably trilingual – and make sure you have time to achieve your objectives after the courtesies.

Timing

At lower levels, meeting times are more flexible than you may be used to. Appointment times are not so rigid and meetings may be cancelled at short notice. Meetings can go on for quite a while, so do not arrange appointments too close together.

There may be all sorts of people sitting in that you might not have expected to see. The convention seems to be that it is better to have everyone there who might possibly have an interest rather than leave someone out. Do not be surprised if in the course of a meeting you are asked to go and sit elsewhere while something unconnected is discussed. You will not, however, be asked to leave the room as privacy is not considered as important as it is in the west.

Privacy

Visiting cards are important. They are usually exchanged at the start of a meeting, and staff at all levels are likely to have them. It is usual for the host to open the meeting, irrespective of who requested it, and where there is no written agenda (as there rarely will be) the host should be allowed to set the heads of discussion. A note sent in advance listing any important points to be covered is often appreciated, especially if you have gone to the trouble of getting it translated.

Cards and agenda

You may find your host has gone to considerable lengths to prepare what almost amounts to a paper on what he thinks you will want to hear. Turkish people also love statistics; you will be bombarded with them, and if you reciprocate your status is likely to increase.

Entertaining Most business entertaining is done in hotels. Only at the most senior level will businessmen entertain in their homes.

Mutual under- standing There are certain factors, accidents of history, that are important in understanding the Turkish approach to expatriates. In Ottoman times, and for a good proportion of the republican period, Turks were very introspective and mistrustful of foreigners. Sad though it is to relate, quite a number of foreigners maintain that this has never completely disappeared – that the very evident superficial charm cannot disguise an instinctive xenophobia. That this is the case should hardly cause any great surprise, since this is an attitude common throughout the Middle East; and as Turkey moves closer to the rest of Europe it is something that is changing rapidly.

Influence Another concept with which it is necessary to become familiar is *torpil* – literally it is 'torpedo', but in Ottoman times it was the slang for 'a friend at court'. In reality it still means just that, and if you hear two businessmen discussing a project one may say to the other *'Torpil var?'*, meaning 'Do you have any influence?' The response could be anything from a relation on the board to a useful friendship.

Status In doing business the status you project is all-important. Not only neatness and appropriateness of dress, but the car you use, whether or not you have a driver, and how you entertain are all factors likely to colour the perception of Turkish associates.

'The desk makes the man' is a Turkish aphorism often used, especially in respect of petty officials. Respect the desire for status and cooperation increases.

Corruption Bribery is not as endemic to the system as it is in many developing countries, and the government is very keen to root out any examples that come to light. The area of business where it is most likely to be come across is at a fairly low level of bureaucracy, where some sort of *bahşiş* is needed to smooth through some changes. It can take the form of a brown envelope but quite often a perhaps otherwise unobtainable piece of office machinery is what is required.

In this very sensitive area, all those who have had dealings are adamant that should any negotiations take place they must be conducted by a Turkish employee who understands the conventions.

Staff

The employment of foreigners is restricted to occupations for which local staff are not available, and in general work permits are extremely hard to come by. Applications should be made well in advance to the Foreign Investment Department and permission is normally given for key personnel, especially during the initial stages of an operation. There are also special provisions made for the tourist industry.

Local staff

There is a considerable differential between the wage rates of expatriates, local skilled and local unskilled staffs. This seems to cause no resentment. The Turkish work-force is on the whole reasonably well trained and enjoy working for foreign enterprises, although most managers seem to be in agreement that local employees need, and expect, firm discipline and a strict regime. Generally speaking, it is not difficult to find good skilled and semi-skilled manual workers. However, you should be aware of a fundamental difference of loyalty in the Turkish culture: the family comes first, Turkey comes second and loyalty to the company takes third place.

On the engineering side, there are graduates of the Middle East Technical University in Ankara whose education is in English and who are reckoned in many fields to be as good as will be found anywhere.

It is fundamental to the Turkish approach to foreigners that they only like to tell you what they think you want to hear; they cannot bear to be the bearer of bad news to a guest of their country. Nor do they like to say they do not know something as this represents a failure in their duty to a visitor. This has unfortunate ramifications for management in that senior overseas personnel are often the last people to learn of any problems, or the information they are given is inaccurate.

Employment regulations
Contracts of employment are little different from those found in western Europe. Statutory holidays are twelve days on one year's service, rising to twenty-four days after fifteen years. Employers pay a percentage of workers' salaries for accident, health, maternity and retirement benefits, to which employees make a small contribution. There is also now a compulsory savings scheme. Most employers pay more than the fixed minimum wage.

Tourist development areas
Special provisions are made to encourage foreign tourist development, and the British have been second only to the Germans in taking advantage of these. The brochure *Tourism Opportunities for Investors*, available from overseas offices of the Ministry of Tourism, is interesting even to people not directly involved in business or tourism. Large areas – whole stretches of coastline in many cases – have been designated tourist development areas, and here assistance is given in putting together large sites and planning procedures are speeded up and considered under special rules.

The general policy is for the government to provide the main infrastructure – roads, water supplies, electricity and telephone lines, but not waste disposal – while private companies provide the rest. The Ministry of Tourism can in some cases grant a long lease on government-owned lands to tourist operators, who then install their own services and recover the cost by means of a rent-free period. The Ministry can also, slightly contentiously, assist in assembling complete sites by compulsory purchase. All government funding in relation to tourism development is channelled through the Tourist Development Bank (Turbank), which plays a crucial role in the whole process.

The procedures prior to starting building have in theory been reduced to the most amazing simplicity for so bureaucratic a society, and companies and individuals who have been through it report it is almost equally painless in practice. Pre-printed forms and drafts in English are provided for all the stages. It is later in the project that bureaucratic difficulties seem to arise.

Once the operators have decided on their site they submit a letter of intent. The Tourist Ministry then researches land ownership and proposed future developments in the area.

Based on this the operators prepare a land-use plan setting out in detail the proposed services, including the provision of waste disposal. The government is extremely concerned to prevent the pollution found in some of the other countries that have had rapid tourist development. Theoretically, new developments are continuously monitored to ensure that pollution controls are in operation.

Detailed plans must then be sent to the Ministry, and while they are being considered a Turkish company must be formed. When an investment certificate has been issued, the operators can apply for subsidized start-up loans from the Tourist Development Bank. These are intended as pump-priming funding to get tourist projects off the ground and are not a substitute for hard currency investment. From this point, the Tourist Development Bank acts as consultant to the project. The operators must obtain a construction licence from all and any relevant local or municipal authorities. The signatures on these need to be obtained in the correct order, which can be a frustrating process.

When the project is completed the Ministry issues an operating licence, on receipt of a notice from the local authority that the building is habitable. Theoretically it is the continued renewal of this licence that ensures standards are maintained, and here too some help may be needed to ease the procedures.

Information sources

There is a great deal of information available to anyone contemplating doing business with Turkey, and much of it is regularly updated to cope with constantly changing legislation and economic circumstances.

The British Overseas Trade Board produces a very good preliminary briefing booklet. The Department of Trade and Industry issues a range of handouts on Turkish markets, legislation and procedures. It also has a Statistics and Market Intelligence Library open to the public, and produces the weekly *British Business Journal* for exporters, at £75 for a one-year subscription. International Business Services in Istanbul, in association with Business International in London, have brought out *Doing Business in Turkey* in loose-leaf form. It is regularly updated and covers investing, licensing and trading.

The Turkish–British Chamber of Commerce in London provides commercial research and trade information to its members. The international banks operating in Turkey produce useful and regularly updated economic reports. Accountancy firms such as Price Waterhouse and Arthur Anderson publish well-researched booklets on business, taxation and accountancy procedures.

Asking for information

In Turkey the attitude to information is different from what you may be used to. Whereas in the west the tendency is to disseminate information continuously and let the recipient choose to use it or bin it, in Turkey you have to ask for everything. The difficulty this poses is in knowing what is available where, and whom to ask. Many a western business man has thrown up his hands in horror and asked why he was not told something before. The answer is invariably 'You did not ask!'

Libraries

The embassies moved to Ankara when the capital was moved and all political activities are conducted from there, but the consulates-general in Istanbul remain the important commercial centres. The British, American and most European consulates have libraries and research facilities which can be used by bona fide business people. The British Council and American Cultural Center libraries may be used with permission. The British Chamber of Commerce has a research department. The new publication *Who's Who in Turkey* (PROFESYONEL, 1988) (written in Turkish) can provide useful background information on your contacts.

Business organizations

YASED is the Turkish-run guild of foreign capital companies operating in Turkey. They act as a pressure group for foreign invested companies and have close contact with politicians and bureaucrats. They produce some useful publications and bulletins of interest to intending investors, and the organization is highly regarded by both the expatriate and the local communities.

YASED

An independent lobby of some 250 invited members, TUSIAD is the equivalent of the British CBI and the American AIB. It acts as a high-powered pressure group and liaises with similar institutions in other countries.

TUSIAD

Every business community is obliged by law to join a chamber of commerce, of which the doyen is undoubtedly that in Istanbul, which has more than 100,000 members. Founded over a hundred years ago, it is the oldest commercial institution in Turkey, and its main aims are concerned with fostering the spirit of free enterprise – a vital role in the past when statism was the orthodoxy. Many of the staff are English speaking and their Department of Foreign Trade can be extremely helpful to people on a business visit, especially in providing contacts and background information. They are a quite separate organization from the British Chamber of Commerce and contact should be made with both independently.

Chambers of commerce

The Union of Chambers of Commerce, based in Ankara, is important for its semi-official role as economic adviser to the government. It organizes Turkish trade fairs overseas and coordinates the activities of individual chambers.

Settling In

In Turkey there is a welcoming expatriate community of all nationalities. As the demand for foreign expertise has increased, so the growing number of expats has tended to group together into smaller social units. These are usually not on national lines but by multinational interest group, and are small enough for gossip to be endemic – or so they say.

The hospitality and *joie de vivre* of the host country seem to rub off on the visitors and it is rare to find people not enjoying their stay in the country, although wives without children sometimes feel a little lost. The wide variety of outside activities means there is plenty to do, and someone spending even several years in the country would not have seen all it has to offer.

The life-style depends very much on where you are living – clearly the social life in Istanbul is more active than in, say, one of the smaller towns. Anyone living overseas for the first time must allow at least a couple of months to settle in. Old hands at expatriate life will find Turkey one of the easiest postings they have had.

Residence and work permits

A residence permit, which must be carried at all times, is required from the municipality in which it is planned to live. To obtain one, foreigners must be able to demonstrate they can support themselves. If that financial support is from employment in Turkey then the employer needs a work permit from the Federal Investment Department. Residence permits are annual and renewable, and should not be regarded as unlimited even for those purchasing property.

Permits can be obtained in Turkey by people who have entered on a border visa, but it involves a trip to Ankara and visits to a succession of offices. The easiest method is to get a multiple entry work visa from the Turkish consulate before leaving home. Four photographs are required and for people who are going to provide special technical expertise, or teachers, the visa can be arranged in forty-eight hours – although it is prudent to allow longer. A multiple entry business visa can take up to four weeks to come through. On arrival find an expert 'gofer' who will take you, and another four photographs, round all the necessary offices in the municipality in which you plan to live to get a residence document.

In practice most people on business go, at least in the first instance, on a normal border entry stamp (see p. 3).

Personnel who are working for a non-Turkish company whilst setting up or negotiating new businesses can do so on the normal three-month border visa. However, the high fines for overstaying, even by a matter of hours, are strictly enforced. Some companies who regularly have staff on these visas make special arrangements at the Komotini post on the Greek border, so that people can go out and come in again, avoiding the queues.

Accommod-ation

Although there are plenty of long-term rented flats and apartments on the market, they are quite difficult to find. Drive around and look for a handwritten sign reading *kiralık* with a phone number. Word of mouth is the best means of finding accommodation. Failing that, agencies (*emlâkci*) and individuals advertise in the English-language papers.

Furnished flats are more expensive than unfurnished, but as in most cases the furniture is not worth having it's better to go for the latter. Most companies arrange accommodation, at least on a temporary basis, on arrival.

Rents are low relative to the rest of Europe. However, landlords often want paying in hard currencies, and usually insist on six months' rent, plus a bond, in advance.

Services

Responsibility for electricity and water is usually taken on by the tenant. The respective authorities require a deposit and the quarterly bills can be paid at any bank. The electricity supply is 220 volts 50 cycles, not 60 cycles as found in the US, so some American equipment is not compatible. Any electrical equipment that works in Britain will also work in Turkey, except for televisions (see below). Plugs and sockets are the two-round-pin type, as found in France.

Television is transmitted on the SECAM system so a set from the UK will not work in Turkey, but Turkish sets are multi-system, so video can be compatible. The VHS system has ousted Betamax.

There are limited piped gas services in the cities but most people use bottled gas for cooking. Landlords usually provide the phone number for replacement canisters. Natural gas is expected to be on stream by 1992.

It can take a long time to get a telephone installed if there is not one already there. Employers can often help, and the appropriate ministry may be able to put pressure on the telephone authorities if yours is considered a critical post.

The table gives some useful telephone numbers.

Number	Service
021	Telephone faults
026	Post office (PTT) information
068	Water emergencies
031	Intercity operator ⎫ Becoming less frequently
032	International operator ⎭ used as calls are dialled direct
061	To complain that the call you booked on 031 has not come through
062	To complain that your international call has not yet been connected
033	Message service (Turkish only)
041	Telegrams (Turkish only)
091	Express intercity connections – relatively very expensive
066	Children's story – in Turkish, and good for language practice

The first Yellow Pages, from the same company that produces them in the rest of Europe, are forecast for the end of 1989.

Buying property

In recent years there has been some confusion and doubt over the legal position of foreigners buying property in Turkey. The common practice has been to buy a long lease and register it in Turkey, or to have a Turkish partner and respective deeds of trust. Quite a few foreigners occupy property on this basis. Another method is to form a company just to hold the property, and quite a few people have bought by this means. However, under Turkish law a company with overseas shareholding is counted as being Turkish.

Strictly speaking Turkish law says that a foreigner may buy property if there is a reciprocal arrangement for Turks to buy in their country. This is subject to exceptions that the property must be within a municipal area and cannot be in a village. It is likely that anyone wanting to buy property on his or her own account would need permission from the Foreign Ministry in Ankara, and would certainly be wise to obtain it.

One of the main difficulties is establishing title to the land. Each municipality has the responsibility for preparing a land registry. Where this has been completed fewer problems will be encountered, as a registered title is considered to be absolute. Where land has not been registered the title passes with the deed (the *tapu*) and this can cause problems. Under the old Islamic law a deceased estate was divided into portions according to strict rules. At any time subsequently, heirs to these subdivisions may come forward and lay claim to their portion of the land.

A local lawyer, recommended by someone aware of the pitfalls, is very necessary if property purchase is contemplated. It should also be remembered that any subsequent sale is likely to be as difficult as the purchase, if not more so.

A firm of estate agents specializing in Turkish property has recently opened in London. Turkish Properties and Rentals are arranging sales and the hire of villas and they can find special properties to order. They can also provide accommodation for business clients.

Social life   The British Embassy and Consulate-General have social clubs which are quite extensively used by Commonwealth expatriates. Because of the security requirements, membership is by introduction and strictly controlled.

In Istanbul, international business people meet regularly at the Sheraton Hotel under the aegis of the United States-run Propeller Club. The Hilton hotel hosts international business lunches on the first Monday of every month. These are all useful forums for expatriate business people, especially new arrivals. The International Women's Association hold regular meetings under the auspices of the US Consulate-General, and there is a morning coffee at 10.30 every Wednesday for British women at the consulate-general. The British Community Council provides valuable and necessary helps for elderly long-term British residents. Hash House Harriers, the world-wide expatriate running and social group, meet regularly in Ankara and Istanbul. Details can be obtained from your consulate-general.

Marriage   Mixed marriages are becoming more and more common as visitors travel to Turkey. Turkish women marrying British, Australian, Canadian, New Zealand and American partners are entitled to carry two passports, and dual nationality is permitted under Turkish law. The same does not apply for men who marry Turkish women.

Not many years ago it was the case that a foreign girl, who had to convert to Islam on marrying a Turkish man, became a Turk both in popular estimation and in the eyes of the secular authorities. Away from the more sophisticated middle-class families there is a wish that this was still the case, even though the conversion is no longer necessary in law. A Turkish man who marries outside the faith is still considered by older members to be letting down the family, but television is proving the great leveller.

Other areas

Foreign nationals are liable to income tax of 30 per *Taxation*
cent deducted at source. All payments from Turkish
sources are liable to withholding taxes at varying
rates. There is a small annual property tax that UK
residents will recognize as almost identical to their
own (disappearing) rates.

Whilst the postal delivery system is fairly good, many *PO boxes*
people living in towns find it more convenient to hire
a private post box. Arrangements are made at the
main PTT.

Privately owned cars can be brought into the country *Cars*
for the use of foreign residents. A special registration
form should be obtained from the licensing authorities or, more easily, from the Turkish Touring Club.
A blue licence plate will be issued. The car may not be
sold or scrapped within Turkey and problems can
arise if it is stolen. It is technically possible to bring a
car in on a border visa and transfer it to overseas
registration once it is in the country.

Cars on foreign resident registration can only be
transferred between foreigners, so it is possible to buy
second-hand cars whilst in the country. They are
advertised in the English-language newspapers and
there are agencies and dealers working solely with
this sort of vehicle.

Foreigners working for Turkish registered companies often drive locally purchased and registered
cars, which they are also free to take abroad if they
wish.

Schooling in English is not a particular problem for *Schools*
those living in the main cities, but it is expensive and
needs to be planned in advance. In Istanbul, the
International Community School and the British
Embassy Study Centre in Ankara both have good
reputations. In Adana and İzmir there are schools
restricted to US service personnel.

Robert College, on the Asian side of the Bosphorus
in Istanbul, was for some time restricted to Turkish

pupils after it was nationalized. It now runs parallel classes for foreign children, and its high international reputation is returning.

In all cases the schools only take pupils to the age of thirteen or fourteen (ninth grade in the American system), and alternative arrangements outside Turkey have to be made from then on. Bosphorus University has a very high reputation and teaching is in English. Expatriate offspring rarely go there, which is unfortunate.

Competition is fierce for the English-medium schools and it is necessary to make early arrangements. There are also Austrian, French and German schools in Istanbul and Ankara, which have a very high standard, and admission to these is easier as long as the appropriate language is spoken.

Reading material English literature can be found in bookshops in the three main cities, but because of the import taxes it is very expensive. Second-hand bookshops often have a shelf of books in English and some good bargains can be found in out-of-the-way places. There is also an excellent second-hand book bazaar attached to Istanbul University.

The British Council and the American Cultural Center have lending libraries in Ankara and Istanbul, which are not restricted to their own nationals.

Pets Animals are not subject to quarantine isolation on entering the country, and quite a few people bring their own dogs. However, rabies is prevalent so it is unwise to adopt, or even to stroke, stray dogs. Cats are very popular with Turkish people and there are also any number of feral and stray animals around. Many expatriates adopt strays, which tend to be passed on as people return home.

Charcoal Once settled in you may want to have barbecues. Some supermarkets sell expensive packets of charcoal, but much more interesting is to find the site of the local charcoal burners (*kömürcü*). There is one on the outskirts of every town, where charcoal is sold by the kilo. Charcoal is a word that has many regional variations, *odun* or *kümür* being the most common. Add the two words to your 'pidgin' vocabulary and it should be possible to track down the yard.

The Language

Turkish is possibly one of the least studied of all languages, probably because the country was never colonized and because it was a relatively closed society until recently.

This section gives you a basic introduction to the structure of the language – many people arrive knowing nothing whatsoever about it. For those staying on in Turkey language lessons are readily available, and it is not particularly difficult to learn. There are no genders and it is regular and logical.

If you start by learning the numbers and a few of the common phrases, you will find simple communication comes very quickly. In fact there is a sort of basic, almost pidgin, Turkish adopted by resident foreigners. This consists mainly of stringing together a sequence of nouns punctuated by gestures.

Background   Before Atatürk's 1928 reforms, the sultanate and the elite spoke Osmanlıca, or Ottoman Turkish. This was an amalgam of Persian and Arabic words with Old Turkish, which had been spoken from the eighth to the thirteenth centuries. The vernacular was *kaba Türkçe*, which translates as 'crude Turkish'.

Atatürk set out to eliminate the gap between the two, and simultaneously changed the script from Arabic to Roman. The Turkish Linguistic Society, which still exists today, produced long lists of words that were 'pure Turkish' replacements for the Arabic and Persian words so beloved by the court. Where indigenous words did not exist they were invented, as were replacements for non-Turkish grammatical constructions. Atatürk himself went round the country with a blackboard and easel teaching groups of people in parks the rudiments of the changes. They were effected in six months.

Since then the language has continued to evolve, losing quite a few of its poetic qualities en route. A young diplomat in the sixties learnt fluent Turkish, and on recently returning to Ankara as a very senior ambassador he found the language quickly came back to him. However, his Turkish friends remark how delightfully quaint and old-fashioned are some of the phrases he uses.

In spite of the efforts of the Linguistic Society, the growth of travel and tourism has resulted in another assault on the purity of the language in the form of the introduction of French and English words. Seemingly following the nineteenth-century diplomatic convention, the French is preferred where a choice exists. Thus *detercan* (pronounced 'deterjan') is used, and not *detercent* (which would be pronounced 'detergent').

Some basics

Turkish has no Latin root. In European languages quite a few words are recognizable to the English speaker, but in Turkish you start from scratch except for the latest adoptions (which include *televizyon*, *telefon* and *radyo*).

You may also have to learn a few changes in pronunciation, and, most importantly, to stress words in a different way.

The centuries-old tradition, almost obligation, of hospitality to *misafir* (travellers) means that communication with strangers is practically a normal part of everyday Turkish life. Any attempt, however inaccurate or halting, to speak their language, which it is appreciated is not universally known, results in Turkish people displaying an even greater welcome than usual. Once you can cope with the difference in pronunciation and stress you can join in the fun.

Pronun-ciation

The script is virtually phonetic – that is to say, each letter has a fixed and unchanging sound. The consonants are almost the same as the English sounds and the vowels like Italian.

There are, however, nine different letters or accented letters (shown in the table) which have to be learned. Six of these have equivalent sounds in English, but three of them have only German or French equivalents.

Capital letter	Lower case	English sound		Example
C	c	j	as in	*j*ug
Ç	ç	ch	as in	*ch*urn
Ğ	ğ	y	as in	*y*et This can also lengthen some preceding vowels. It is not used initially.
I	ı	second vowel sound in soci*a*l		
İ	i	i	as in	b*i*t
J	j	s	as in	mea*s*ure or French *j*e
Ö	ö	eu	as in	a long French f*eu* or German w*ö*hn
Ş	ş	sh	as in	*sh*ift
Ü	ü	no English equivalent		German *ü*ber or French r*u*sse

Once these sounds have been mastered, signs and place names can be read with ease. But remember that every letter is pronounced as it is seen, and watch out for 'sh' and 'th' – they do not form new sounds. So *meshetmek* (to wipe) is pronounced 'mes-het-mek', and *itham* (an accusation) is 'it-ham'.

Stress   There is one fundamental difference between Turkish and English that must always be remembered when you are speaking: Turkish has no syllable stress. All parts of a word have equal weight save a slight accentuation at the end. It is the failure to understand this, above all else, that makes English-speaking novices incomprehensible.

Structure   You could start with the greeting *Merhaba* (mehr-hah-bah), meaning 'hello', which will probably evoke a similar response. (Students and trendies use the greeting *Selâm*, a contraction of *Selamünaleyküm*, which is the formal greeting of Muslims and literally means 'peace be on you'.) Should you respond with *Türkçeyi bilmiyorum* (Turkchey beel-me-yorum) – 'I don't speak Turkish' – you will be employing another important difference between English and Turkish, and that which makes the language similar to Finnish and Hungarian, agglutination. This is the process of adding suffix to suffix, and it can result in huge words. In English one rare example is 'care/*less*/*ness*', but in Turkish one word frequently carries the meaning contained in a whole English phrase or sentence. The word order is nothing like English whatsoever.

So: | *ev* | means | a house |
|---|---|---|
| *evde* | means | at home |
| *evdem* | means | from home |
| *evinden* | means | from his/her/its home |

A look at the sentence *Türkçe bilmiyorum* gives a useful insight into this aspect of the language. While the first word is self-evident, you will need to recognize the root of the verb *bilmek* (to know). This verb is used colloquially in various contexts, so *Istanbulu bilmiyorum* translates as 'I don't know Istanbul', and *Ahmeti bilmiyorum* as 'I don't know Ahmet', while *bilmiyorum* on its own is 'I don't know'.

Verbs are completely regular, with one exception, so the endings, or suffixes, have only to be learned once. It is useful to learn the basic endings at an early stage. Forget the exception *etmek* (to do) for the time being.

You should be aware that there are two infinitive types – those ending in *mek* and those ending in *mak*. Which of these a verb ends in depends on the preceding vowel – that is, the last vowel in the stem. There is a reason for this: it is one of the odd rules that apply to Turkish and is concerned with the actual position of the mouth at which the vowel sound is made. Take the example *bilmek* (to know). If you make the *i* and *e* vowel sounds you can feel that they are made at the back of the mouth. Now try saying *bulmak* (to find). Make the *u* and *a* sounds and you find they are made at the front of the mouth. Thus the important principle of vowel agreement is that wherever the first vowel in the word is made in the mouth, subsequent vowels will be made in that position. Those who go on to study the language in detail with discover that there are two refinements to this, but they are both still related to the position in the mouth in which the sound is made.

The two verbs, *bilmek* and *bulmak*, are conjugated here – this also brings in the use of the pronouns.

Türkçe biliyor **um**	**I** know Turkish
Türkçe biliyor **sun**	**You** know Turkish
Türkçe biliyor (*dur*)	**He/she/it** knows Turkish
Türkçe biliyor **uz**	**We** know Turkish
Türkçe biliyor **sunuz**	**You** know Turkish
Türkçe biliyor (*dur*) **lar**	**They** know Turkish
Türkçe zor buluyor **um**	**I** am finding Turkish difficult
Türkçe zor buluyor **sun**	**You** are finding Turkish difficult
Türkçe zor buluyor (*dur*)	**He/she/it** is finding Turkish difficult
Türkçe zor buluyor **uz**	**We** are finding Turkish difficult
Türkçe zor buluyor **sunuz**	**You** are finding Turkish difficult
Türkçe zor buluyor (*dur*) **lar**	**They** are finding Turkish difficult

Clearly, *zor* is difficult and the sentence reads 'I am finding Turkish difficult', 'You are finding Turkish difficult', and so on. (The *dur* in the third person singular and plural is not used in colloquial speech. It is found only in very formal speech or in written Turkish.)

Negatives Now consider the negative suffix. We have seen that the infinitive of the verb is *bilmek* (to know). The negative infinitive – 'to not know' – is *bilmemek*.

Here we again see the vowel sounds agreeing. The basic negative suffix is **me**, but the actual vowel changes according to the strict rule mentioned above, depending on the preceding vowel. The negation is **me** here because there is an *i* sound preceding it, and Turkish avoids changes of types of vowel sound whenever possible. In the table below the negative **mi** can be seen in the second syllable. (In this particular verb only the **m** provides the negation in practice: 'I don't know' is thus *bilmiyorum*, 'you don't know' *bilmiyorsun* and so on.)

As a rough guide, if you hear an 'm' sound in the middle of a verb it is fairly safe to assume it is negative. So we can look at the negatives of *bilmek* and *bulmak*

Türkçe bilmiyor **um**	**I** don't know Turkish
Türkçe bilmiyor **sun**	**You** don't know Turkish
Türkçe bilmiyor (*dur*)	**He/she/it** doesn't know Turkish
Türkçe bilmiyor **uz**	**We** don't know Turkish
Türkçe bilmiyor **sunuz**	**You** don't know Turkish
Türkçe bilmiyor (*dur*) **lar**	**They** don't know Turkish

bulmuyor **um**	**I** don't find
bulmuyor **sun**	**You** don't find
bulmuyor (*dur*)	**He/she/it** doesn't find
bulmuyor **uz**	**We** don't find
bulmuyor **sunuz**	**You** don't find
bulmuyor (*dur*) **lar**	**They** don't find

In using the two verbs *bilmek* and *bulmak* as examples we can also see how small variations of sound in Turkish can alter the whole meaning. This is particularly difficult for English-speaking people.

'Pidgin' words

Pronouns which are a literal translation of our own are generally used only for emphasis in Turkish, with the added complication that they decline; but that need only concern those who go on to study the language. In practice, however, English-speaking visitors striving for basic communication in Turkish will almost certainly find themselves using them. In their simplest forms they are:

I	*ben*	mine	*benim*
you	*sen*	yours	*senim* (very informal)
	or *siz*		or *sizin* (polite forms equivalent to French *vous*)
he/she/it	*o*	his/hers/its	*onun*
we	*biz*	ours	*bizim*
you	*siz*	yours	*sizin*
they	*onlar*	theirs	*onlarin*

Noun endings Nouns are as regular as verbs, so once again the endings have to be learned only once. Probably the most important noun suffix for the novice is the modifying *i*, which also appears as *ı*, *ü* and *u*. Its most important function is to indicate the possessive. Thus:

(*ev* = house)	*Ahmetin evi*	Ahmet's house
(*gül* = rose)	*gülü*	his/her/its rose
(*sabun* = soap)	*sabunu*	his/her/its soap
(*çay* = tea)	*çayı*	his/her/its tea

However, this suffix also, confusingly, appears on nouns modified by other nouns or pronouns, when it does not have any translatable meaning.

The plural is formed by adding *ler* and *lar* to the noun. Thus:

ev	house	*evler*	houses
gül	rose	*güller*	roses
sabun	soap	*sabunlar*	soaps
çay	tea	*çaylar*	teas

In forming all the noun endings you find 's' and 'y' put in the most unlikely places for no apparent reason.

'Yok' The first word that will be perceived by the new arrival is *yok*. Literally meaning 'I have none', colloquially it means 'no' in virtually any context. Its seeming frequency is perhaps because of the oddness of the sound to the English speaker.

There is no strict difference in Turkish between 'too much' (*çok fazla*) and 'a lot' (*çok*) – the simple *çok* is commonly used for both. Thus the taxi driver who picks you up from your hotel with the greeting, in his limited English, 'you drink too much last night', is not making a rude comment but repeating the staff gossip about your capacity.

'Too much'

Turkish people cannot immediately hear the difference between 'soap' and 'soup', 'suit' and 'sweet', and 'sheep' and 'ship'. 'Sheet' also causes problems which can result in some confusing cross-purpose conversations.
    English speakers have difficulty distinguishing between *efendi*, meaning 'sir', and *efendim*, meaning 'I beg your pardon' (see p. 77).

'Soap'

It is impossible to translate Turkish literally and colloquially to or from English. This is mainly because Turkish is a very flowery language – it translates more easily into French. It also has a limited number of adjectives. Take for example the overworked *güzel*. It can mean 'good', 'nice', 'beautiful', 'pretty' and more besides, depending on the context.
    There is no difference between 'month' and 'moon': *ay* is used for both. So if you tell people you will not return for several months (*bir kaç ay sonra*) you are in reality saying you will not be back for many moons. Should you be a poet or find yourself in a romantic situation, however, you would use the word *mehtab*, which can variously mean 'full moon' or 'moonlight'.

Literal translation

In Ottoman times etiquette was extremely important and stylized, and each encounter had its own ritual. Whilst the ritual has been dropped as the people have adopted western cultural values, the language remains – certain phrases are automatically used at the

Phrases and forms

appropriate time and if you use a few of the ones in the table, people will love it.

Phrase	Pronounced	Literal meaning	Use
afiyet olsun	af-i-e-tol-soon	may it contribute to your health	in the sense of '*bon appetit*'
canınız sağ olsun	jah-nu-nuz-saah-ol-soon	may your soul be safe from harm	said after an accident such as spilling coffee
saatler olsun	sart-ler-ol-soon	may it be so for many hours	said to someone emerging from the *hamam* or barber's
şerefinize	sher-if-een-eez-eh	this is in your honour	a formal salutation
Geçmiş olsun	gech-meesh-ol-soon	may it be in your past	said to someone who is sick, injured or otherwise distressed.

For forms of address, see p. 77.

Schools and lessons   TOMER, the Ankara University Turkish Teaching Centre, runs extremely good classes for foreigners at basic, intermediate and advanced levels. It can also arrange individual and group tuition for expatriates with special needs. It also has centres in Istanbul, İzmir, and in the summer it runs courses in Marmaris, Bodrum, Side, Trabzon, Alanya and Fethiye. Tuition fees are $1 an hour.

The Turko-British and Turko-American Associations also arrange classes in the main cities.

Many private language schools have Turkish classes and some expatriates engage individual tutors. Personal recommendation is the best way to find tuition, but there are plenty of advertisements in the English-language newspapers.

**Useful words
and phrases**

English	Turkish	Pronunciation
Hullo	merhaba	mehr-ha-bah
Hullo (= peace be with you)	selamünaleyküm	selah-maleyikum
good morning	günaydın	goo-nigh-din
good-day	iyi günler	eeye goon-lar
good evening	iyi akşamlar	eeye aksham-lar
good bye (= keep smiling) – (said only by person not leaving)	güle güle	gule-gule
how are you?	nasılsın	nahsil-sin?
very well, thank you	iyiyim sağolun	ee-yee-yeem sa-olun
yes	evet	e-vet
no	hayır	hahyer
I have none	yok	yok
please	lûtfen	lewt-fen
thank you	teşekkür ederim	te-shek-kur ehd-eareem
thank you very much	merci	(as in French)
	çok merci	chok mer-sie
OK	tamam	ta-mam
naturally	tâbii	ta-bee
very	çok	chok
beautiful/nice	güzel	gew-zell
big	büyük	be-yewk
small	küçük	kew-chewk
slow/hang on	yavaş	ya-waash
good	iyi	eeye
bad	kötü	kur-tew
open	açık	acherk
shut	kapalı	kap-ahl-le

English	Turkish	Pronunciation
hot	sicak	si-jack
cold	soğuk	so-ook
Where is a/the . . .?	. . . nerede?	. . . neh-reh-deh
the toilet?	Tuvalet nerede?	too-vahl-et neh-reh-deh
the bus station?	Otobüs durağı nerede?	otobews doorayi neh-reh-deh
the post office?	Postane nerede?	pos-tan-ney neh-reh-deh
Do you know English?	Ingilizce biliyor musunuz?	eengyil-eez-jeh beeleeyor moo-soo-nooz
I don't speak Turkish.	Türkçeyi bilmi-yorum	turk-chey beel-me-yorum
a person's home district	memleket	mem-lek-et
Where are you from?	memleket nerede?	mem-lek-et neh-reh-de
I want/would like	. . . istiyorum	eest-ee-yorum
a room.	Bir oda istiyorum.	beer odah eest-ee-yorum
to eat.	Yemek istiyorum.	ye-meck eest-ee-yorum
some fruit.	Biraz meyve istiyorum.	beeras mey-veh eest-ee-yorum
a ticket.	Bir bilet istiyorum.	beer beelet eest-ee-yorum
How much/many?	ne kadar/kaç tane?	neh kadah/catch tahneh
How many liras?	Kaç lira?	catch leera
How much water?	Ne kadar su?	neh kadar soo
When?	Ne zaman?	neh zahmahn
How many minutes?	Kaç dakika	catch dakeekah
How many hours?	Kaç saat	catch sahrt
morning	sabah	sa-ba
evening	akşam	ak-sham
yesterday	dün	dewn
today	bugün	boo-gewn
tomorrow	yarın	yah-rin
before	önce	urn-jeh
after	sonra	son-rah

English	Turkish	Pronunciation
day	gün	gyewn
week	hafta	hahf-tah
month	ay	I
Anatolia	Anadolu	Anna-do-lu
Greece	Yunan	Yu-narn
Black Sea	Karadeniz	Kara-deneez
Mediterranean (White) Sea	Akdeniz	Ak-deneez
mosque	camii	jarmy
church	kilise	ker-leese
old	eski	esky
new	yeni	yeyny
the same as (similar)	aynı	I-ner
one	bir	beer
two	iki	icky
three	üç	ooch
four	dört	dirt
five	beş	besh
six	altı	alter
seven	yedi	yeddy
eight	sekiz	sekeez
nine	dokuz	dokooz
ten	on	on

Words you will recognize – just try saying them
exactly as they are written

> taksi
> duble
> ekspres
> paket
> polis
> büfe (every syllable is always pronounced, including
>   the final 'e')
> tren
> futbol
> parti
> bira
> gazete

Kleenex is similarly known by the name of the company that produce paper handkerchiefs, Sel Pak. And the almost universally acceptable apology, '*pardon*', used if you bump into someone or spill your drink, is also current in Turkey.

A word you will quickly add to your vocabulary is *buyrun*. It comes from the verb *buyrumak*, which has the literal meaning of to order, deign or condescend to do. You will hear it used colloquially all the time, with a variety of different meanings, e.g. as an invitation to sit down, as an indication that a person may not have heard something correctly, and in many other situations where meaning is evident from context.

Hoş geldiniz is something you will see written up in large letters as you enter the country, and said to you (pronounced hosh-geldiniz) on many occasions. It means 'welcome'. The correct response meaning 'it is pleasant to be here', is *hoş bulduk*.

Useful Organizations and Further Reading

The British Museum in London has an extensive collection of artefacts from archaeological digs in Asia Minor.

The British Institute of Archaeology at Ankara arranges lectures during the winter months from their office: c/o British Academy, 20 Cornwall Terrace, London NW1 4QP (tel. 01 388 4518). They might also be able to help with information on the several university extramural evening courses on the subject.

The Metropolitan Museum in New York has a collection of Turkish arts. Most of the pieces are of the highest quality.

The Centre for International Briefing, Farnham Castle, Surrey GU9 OAG (tel. 0252 721194) has regular courses, and includes Turkey on its programme. The courses are designed for company personnel and their spouses, and prepare expatriates for life and work in the country.

The jewels and decorations presented by Sultan Selim III to Lord Keith in 1801, in recognition of his services as commander of the Allied Fleet, are on display at Bowood House, Calne, Wiltshire. There is also a portrait in oils of the sultan.

Falcon Leisure
33 Notting Hill Gate
London W11 3JQ
Tel. 01 221 6298

Horizon
Broadway
Edgebaston Five Ways B15 1BB
Tel. 021 643 2727

Sunquest
9 Aldine Street
London W12 8AW
Tel. 01 749 9911

Turkish   The Anglo-Turkish Society
cultural and   43 Montrose Place
friendship   London SW1X 7DT
organizations Tel. 01 235 8148

This is for Turkophiles who wish to continue their
links with the country. It works closely with the
embassy and British universities, and organizes lectures and social events.

The American Friends of Turkey
6731 Whittier Avenue
Suite A100
McLean
Virginia 22101

This is for Turkophiles who wish to keep in touch,
and is run by a former American Consul-General.
There are many organizations across the US promoting friendly and cross-cultural relations and activities
between the two countries. A list of them, or the
address of the nearest, can be obtained from the
Federation.

Federation of Turkish American Societies
821 United Nations Plaza
New York 10017
Tel. 212 682 8525

The Federation of Canadian Turkish Associations
253 College St
Unit 129
Toronto M5T 1R5

Britain
170 Piccadilly
London W1V 9DD
Tel. 01 734 8681

Denmark
Vesterbrogade 11A
1620 Copenhagen V
Tel. 22 31 00

Germany
Baseler Str. 37
6000 Frankfurt M1
Tel. 23 30 81

USA
821 UN Plaza
New York 10017
Tel. 687 2194

2010 Massachusetts Ave.
Washington 20026
Tel. 833 8411

Information offices

Ferry Information can be obtained from agents:

Turkish Maritime Lines

Britain
c/o Sunquest Holidays
9 Aldine Street
London W12 8AW
Tel. 01 749 9911

Italy
c/o Bassani SPA
Via XXII Marzo 2414
30124 Venezia
Tel. 522 9544

Istanbul
Rihtim Cad.
Karaköy
Istanbul
Tel. 144 02 07

Buying and Turkish Properties and Rentals Ltd
renting 57 Grosvenor Street
property London W1X 9DA
Tel. 01 355 4068

Business Ankara Business Centre
Simon Bolivar 10/4
Çankaya 0692
Ankara
Tel. 140 30 20

This is a British company providing office communication and presentation facilities for businesses
moving into Turkish markets.

British Overseas Trade Board
Ebury Bridge House
Ebury Bridge Road
London SW1W 8OD
  (and regional offices)
Tel. 01 730 9678

Business International
40 Duke Street
London W1A 1DW
Tel. 01 493 6711

Canadian Council for Turkish Trade
55 Metcalfe
Ottawa K1P 6N4

Department of Trade and Industry
Dept OT 4
1 Victoria Street
London SW1H 0ET
Tel. 01 215 7877

International Business Services
Bronz Sok. 1/4,
Maçka 80200
Istanbul
Tel. 131 66 14

International Chamber of Commerce
1319 F Street NW
Washington DC 20004
Tel. 202 347 7201

Istanbul Chamber of Commerce
Eminonu
Istanbul
Tel. 511 41 50

Overseas Press and Media Association
122 Shaftesbury Avenue
London W1V 8HA
Tel. 01 734 3052

The British Chamber of Commerce of Turkey
   (Association)
PO Box 190
Karaköy
Istanbul
Tel. 149 06 58

Turkish-British Chamber of Commerce and Industry
360 Oxford Street,
London W1N 9HA
Tel. 01 491 4636

Turkish Desk Officer
Room 3044
US Department of Finance
Washington DC 20230
Tel. 202 377 3945

TUSIAD
Turkish Industrialist and Businessman's Association
Cumhuriyet Cad.
Koc Amerikan Bankası
Elmadağı
Istanbul
Tel. 146 24 12

Union of Chambers of Commerce
Atatürk Bulvarı 149
Ankara
Tel. 125 56 14

YASED
Association for Foreign Capital Coordination
OTIM-Ihlamur Sergi Sarayı
Beşiktaş
Istanbul
Tel. 172 50 94

Trading Standards Office
TSE Ankara
Necatibey Cad.
Ankara
Tel. 134 19 90

TSE Istanbul Bölge Müdürlüğü
Meşrutiyet Cad. 162/2
Şişhane
Istanbul
Tel. 143 59 24

Turkish   Adakale Sok. 4/1
Touring and   Yenişehir
Automobile   Ankara
Club   Tel. 131 76 48
(Türkiye
Turing ve   Halâskargazi Cad. 364
Otomobil   Şişli
Kurumu)   Istanbul
                 Tel. 131 36 41

Çömleçekçi Yokuşu (opposite the entrance to the harbour)
Trabzon
Tel. 171 56

They have offices at the main road frontiers.

British Council
Kırlangıç Sok 9
Gaziosmanpaşa 06700
Ankara
Tel. 128 31 65

Libraries and
cultural
centres

Turkish-American Association
Cinnah Cad. 20
Çankaya
Ankara
Tel. 126 26 44

British Institute of Archaeology at Ankara
Research Library
Tahran Cad. 24
Kavaklıdere
Ankara
Tel. 127 54 81

The Research library can only be used by prior
arrangement.

British Council
İstiklâl Cad. 251/53
Beyoğlu
Istanbul
Tel. 152 74 74

Turko-British Association
Cumhuriyet Cad.
Adli Han 279/1
Istanbul
Tel. 141 05 18

American Cultural Center
Meşrutiyet Cad. 145
Tepebaşı
Istanbul
Tel. 143 62 09

Turk-American University Association
Rumeli Cad. 60/1
Osmanbey
Istanbul
Tel. 147 21 88

Sport and entertainment

Archaeology
The British Institute of Archaeology at Ankara
Tahran Cad. 24
Kavaklıdere
Ankara
Tel. 127 54 81

American Research Institute in Turkey
Iran Cad. 12A
Ankara
Tel. 126 97 00

Caving
Caving Club at Bosphorus University
Bebek
Istanbul
Tel. 183 15 00 extension 700

Flying and parachuting
THK
Opera Meydanı
Ulus
Ankara
Tel. 310 48 40

Hunting
Türkiye Avcılar ve Atıcılar Klubü
Tuna Cad.
Yenişehir
Ankara

Skiing
Kayak Federasyonu at Ulus İşhanı
A-Blok
Ulus
Ankara
Tel. 211 07 64

Australia
Nene Hatun Cad. 83
Gaziosmanpaşa
Ankara
Tel. 136 12 40

Britain
Sehit Ersan Cad. 46/A
Çankaya
Ankara
Tel. 127 43 10

Meşrutiyet Cad. 34
Galatasaray
Istanbul
Tel. 144 75 40
This also represents Australia.

1442 Sok. 49
Alsancak
İzmir
Tel. 21 17 95
This also represents Australia.

Canada
Nene Hatun Cad. 75
Gaziosmanpaşa
Ankara
Tel. 136 12 75

Denmark
Kırlangıç Sok. 42
Gaziosmanpaşa
Ankara
Tel. 127 53 68

Silahhane Cad. 31/1
Maçka
Istanbul
Tel. 140 42 17

*Embassies
and
Consulates-
General*

Holland
Köroğlu Sok. 16
Gaziosmanpaşa
Ankara
Tel. 136 10 74

İstiklal Cad. 393
Beyoğlu
Istanbul
Tel. 144 90 96

Norway
Kelebek Sok. 20
Gaziosmanpaşa
Ankara
Tel. 127 10 55

Sweden
Katip Çelebi Sok. 7
Kavaklıdere
Ankara
Tel. 128 67 36

İstiklâl Cad. 497
Tünel
Istanbul
Tel. 143 57 70

USA
Atatürk Bulvarı 110
Kavaklıdere
Ankara
Tel. 126 54 70

Meşrutiyet Cad. 104
Galatasaray
Istanbul
Tel. 151 36 02

Atatürk Cad. 92/3
İzmir
Tel. 113 13 69

West Germany
Atatürk Bulvarı 114
Kavaklıdere
Ankara
Tel. 126 54 65

İnönü Cad. 16–18
Ayazpaşa
Istanbul
Tel. 143 72 20

Atatürk Cad. 260
Alsancak
İzmir
Tel. 21 69 15

**Further
reading**

Spot on Istanbul – a fascinating gazetteer packed full   *Istanbul*
of useful information, and absolutely invaluable to
anyone spending any time in the city. Published in
Istanbul by Panorama Productions, who also do *Spot
on Turkish Travel.* Available from bookshops in
Turkey or from the publishers (tel. 155 32 88).

The secretary general of the Turkish Touring Club
has presented his comprehensive collection of guides
and travelogues on Istanbul to a new library, created
in a restored wooden house on Soğukçeşme Sok. near
St Sophia. It is open to scholars and researchers.
Strolling through Istanbul, H.S. Boyd and John
Freely (Redhouse Press 1973)

George Bean was the doyen of writers of guidebooks   *Archaeology*
on Turkish archaeological sites. His four books deal
with the principal southern sites in depth, and in a
very readable style:

Aegean Turkey (John Murray 1984) covers sites on
the coast from Pergamum down to Heracleia.
Turkey's Southern Shore (Ernest Benn 1979) covers
the south coast and the hinterland as far east as
Tarsus.

Lycian Turkey (Ernest Benn 1978) is a more detailed study of the coast from Fethye to Antalya.

Turkey beyond the Meander (Ernest Benn 1979) covers the area from Bodrum to Pamukkale and down to Marmaris.

Ancient Civilizations and Ruins of Turkey, Ekrem Akurgal (Haset: Mobil Oil Turk. AS 1970) is published in Istanbul. Well translated into English, it is a detailed study of sites from prehistoric times to the Romans.

The Land of the Chimera, Sybille Haynes (Chatto 1974) is an account of an archaeological excursion covering the area visited by most package tourists. It would provide a good background for those who did not want to go into great depth.

Eastern Turkey – An Archaeological and Architectural Survey, T.A. Sinclair (London 1987–) is an exhaustive four-volume study covering both major and little-known sites, putting them in their historical context.

History A very readable history of modern Turkey from a British perspective is *Atatürk – The Birth of a Nation*, Lord Kinross (Weidenfeld 1964). Lord Kinross is the former diplomat and journalist Patrick Balfour.

In the Steps of St Paul, H.V. Morton (Rich and Cowan 1936) is a delightful narrative of pre-war journeys in Anatolia.

Turkey, A Short History, R.H. Davison (Eothen Press 1981) is a good, general, narrative history from Ottoman times to the present day.

Everyday Life in Ottoman Turkey, Raphaela Lewis (Batsford 1971) gives a good general background to the society.

The Cross and the Crescent, Malcolm Billings (BBC Publications 1987). Based on the series of the same name, this is a pleasantly readable history of the crusades.

The Venetian Empire, Jan Morris (Faber, 1983) covers in some detail Turkey's relationship with its western neighbours.

Byzantine Architecture, Cyril Mango (Faber 1978) is a definitive work.

If they can be found, Sir William Ramsey's scholarly late nineteenth-century studies of Christianity in Asia Minor are still considered seminal.

Food from the Anatolian Field, Evelyn Lyle Kalcas (Bornova Turkey: Birlik Matbaasi 1980). The author is an Australian journalist long resident in Turkey, and the book, published in Istanbul, is available in Turkish bookshops. This is the only work on the ethnobotany of the edible wild plants in Turkey. The three indexes give English and Turkish names for the plants, as well as the scientific names.
The Flora of Turkey, ed. P.H. Davis (Edinburgh University Press 1972) is the definitive scholarly work, in seven volumes, on the subject.

Flora and fauna

Guide to Eastern Turkey, Diana Dark (Haag 1987)
Companion Guide to Turkey, John Freely (Collins 1984)
Travellers' Guide to Turkey, Dux Schneider (Cape 1975)
Guide to Turkey, Dana Facaros and Michael Pauls (Cadogan 1986)
A Travel Survival Kit, Tom Brosnahan (Lonely, Planet, 1988)

Where to go and what to see

You should be aware of the Redhouse Press. It was an educational foundation set up by the Americans at the end of the Ottoman period. It now publishes guides, dictionaries and books on Turkish culture in English. These are widely available in larger bookshops in Turkey and well worth looking out for.

On the Shores of the Mediterranean, Eric Newby (Picador 1985)
The Towers of Trebizond, Rose Macaulay (Collins 1965)
Innocents Abroad, Mark Twain (Collins 1985)

Travelogue

Two English-Turkish dictionaries published in Istanbul:
Jeans Pocket (Inkilap Yayınevi 1984)
Redhouse (Redhouse Publications 1975)

The language

Langenscheidt's Universal Turkish-English, English-Turkish Dictionary (Hodder and Stoughton 1965)
The Berlitz *Turkish for Travellers* (1974) is usefully divided into sections. The pronunciation guide was written for American rather than English speakers.
Turkish Grammar, Geoffrey Lewis (OUP 1967) is still reckoned to be the best starting point for serious students.

Literature   *Murder on the Orient Express*, Agatha Christie (Collins 1974)
Stamboul Train, Graham Greene (Bodley Head 1974)
The Iliad, Homer, trans. Robert Fitzgerald (Harvill 1986)

Holidays and Festivals

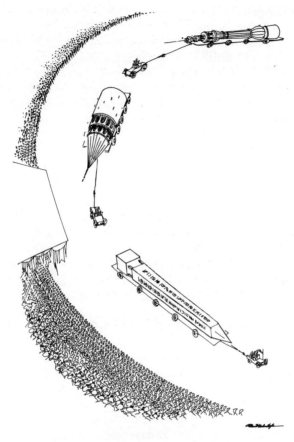

Official Holidays

Date	Purpose	Special celebrations
1 January	New Year's Day	National holiday
23 April	Independence Day	Children's Day
19 May	Atatürk Remembrance Day	Youth and Sports Day
30 August	Victory Day	National holiday
29 October	Republic Day	Street parades

School holidays: all schools close for a long summer
holiday from 15 June to 15 August.
University vacations: the dates of the three-month-
long vacation vary between establishments.

Religious
public
holidays

The Muslim lunar year is about eleven days shorter
than that of the secular Gregorian calendar; thus
religious holidays come some eleven days earlier each
year. The Muslim day is from sundown to sundown,
so, for example, the Friday holy day is considered to
begin on Thursday evening. For important religious
festivals there is also a half-day period of preparation
and on these occasions the shops and banks close at
midday.

Approximate dates	Holiday	Details
8 May 1989 27 April 1990 15 April 1991	Şeker Bayramı	Şeker means sugar and this is the three-and-a-half-day festival, marking the end of Ramadan, when children go from house to house to be given sweets. Adults exchange cards and greetings.
14 July 1989 3 July 1990 22 June 1991	Kurban Bayramı	A four-and-a-half-day festival – for days beforehand you will see sheep being driven through the streets in preparation for the sacrifice.
7 April 1989 27 March 1990 17 March 1991	Ramadan (*Ramazan*)	Because it is a lunar month, i.e. 29 or 30 days, and based on the Islamic *al Hegira* (AH) calendar used in Turkey only for religious matters, it is not possible to state an exact date long in advance. These are predicted dates and it can be seen that Ramadan is about ten or eleven days earlier each year.

Festivals

Month	Day	Place	Activity
January	15,16	Selçuk	Camel wrestling
	Various	Denizli (Aydın)	Camel wrestling
February	Week 2	Birecik	Kel Aynak festival. These pelican-like birds, unique to Turkey, almost became extinct. Now they are carefully guarded and the festival celebrates the first eggs of the season.
March	Week 4	Erzurum	Troubadour festival
		Erzurum	Ski festival
	Week 1 or 2		Mirac Kandili celebrates the Prophet Mohammed's nocturnal journey from Mecca to Jerusalem and thence to heaven astride a winged horse. Mosques are specially illuminated.
	Week 3 or 4		Berat Kandili, a sacred night in the Islamic calendar rather like Hallowe'en
April	Week 2	Manisa	A traditional herbal concoction, *mesir* (usually translated as 'powergum'), is distributed to the people. It is said to restore health, youth and potency after the winter.
	Week 4	Erzurum	Atatürk University folklore and music festival
	Last weekend	Aydın	Sultan Hisar Nyssa festival

	Last week for 2 weeks	Istanbul (centred on suburb of Emirgan)	Tulip festival. *Lâle* (the tulip) is the symbol of Istanbul, and flower parades take place.
May	Every Sat. and Sun. to October	Konya	Cirit, javelin jousting
	First week	Mardin	Snake Friday
		Sinop	Spring festival
		İznik	Spring festival
		Bursa	Spring festival
		Selçuk	Ephesus festival of art and culture. Folk dancing, concerts, exhibitions take place, some in the amphitheatre.
		Manisa	Kırkağaç pine festival
		Gümüşane	Doyduk and Kov Kalesi Festivals
		Eskişehir	Yunus Emre arts and culture week
	Weeks 2 and 3	Ordu	Spring day
		Silifke	Music and folklore festival
		Giresun	Aksu festival
	29	Istanbul	Festival or remembrance for the conquest of the city from the Byzantines
	Last Sunday	Konya	Rose festival
	Last week	Marmaris	British yacht week. Charter yachts based in the Mediterranean are on show to agents.

		Bergama	Festival of Pergamum including drama in the amphitheatre.
June	First week	İzmir	International Mediterranean festival
		Tekirdağ	Cherry festival
		İsparta	Cherry festival
	4 and 5	Konya	Rose growing competition
	Second week	Edirne	Grease wrestling
		Çanakkale	Troy Festival
		Osmaniye	Kastabala arts and culture festival
	Third week	Rize	Tea festival
		Bursa	Keles Kokayala festival
	Last week	Antakya	St Pierre Mass
		Kayseri	Develi Seyrani festival
		Eskişehir	Nasrettin Hoca festival
		Artvin	Kafkasor Bullfighting
June to July		Istanbul	International arts festival Becoming established as a major festival on the international circuit.
July 1			Navy Day, commemorating Turkey's regaining the right to operate her own ships. Under the Ottomans the right of cabotage had been granted by treaty to foreign shipping companies.
	5–10	Akşehir	Nasreddin Hoca celebrations
	7–12	Bursa	International Folk and Music festival

First week	Tekirdağ	Sarkoy wine festival
	İzmit	Yarimca folklore and sports festival
	Arhavi	Tea festival
Mid	Bolu	Chefs' festival
	Kütahaya	Circumcision feast
	Malatya	Apricot festival
	Ordu	Hazelnut festival
	Van	Tourism and culture festival
Last week	Datça	Knidos festival
	(near) Afyon	Derecine and Sultandagi black cherry festival
	Kırklareli	Babaeski agricultural festival
last 2 weeks	Samsun	Folk dance festival
29–31	Foça	Water sports, folklore and music festival
August	First week	İsparta	Veli Baba memorial celebration
	15	Meryemana (Ephesus)	Catholic Archbishop of İzmir celebrates Mass of the Assumption
	15–18	Canakkale	Troy festival
	16	Hacıbektaş (Nevşehir province)	Annual festival of Saint after whom town is named. Alevi Turks come together for weekend of singing and ritual dancing
	26		Armed forces day
	Last week	Burdur	Festival
		Insuyu	Festival

August to September	İzmir	International fair
September 1–9	Bodrum	Culture and art week
2–4	Kırşehir	Ahi Avran handicraft festival
First week	Denizli	Cal wine harvest festival
	Çankırı	Honey festival
	Gölcük	Apple growers competition
	Kuşadası	Tourism festival
	Antalya	Elmali Yesilvayla wrestling
11–12	Çorum	Hittite festival
15–18	Cappadocia	Grape Harvest and Troglodyte festival
Mid	Adana	Arts and culture festival
	Elmadağı	Honey and wool festival
	Germencik	Fig festival
	Aydın	Arts festival
22–30	Konya	Whirling Dervishes perform
26–9	Diyarbakır	Watermelon growing contest judged
Last week	Konya	Culinary contest and pigeon competition
September to October	Mersin	Textile and fashion fair
October 1–9	Anyalya	Film and art festival
	Seben	Apple festival
Mid	Afyon	Suhut Karaddilli wrestling festival
	Surt	Pervari honey festival
21–9	Konya	Troubadours' week

November	First week	Zonguldak	Karaelmas coal festival
December	All month	Aydın province	Camel wrestling
	6–8	Demre	Commemorative ceremonies held in the fourth-century church of St Nicholas – the original Santa Claus
	Mid	Konya	Mevlana festival, celebrating the Whirling Dervishes

Historical Place Names

This list gives the classical or historical equivalent of modern Turkish town names.

Present name	Historical name
Alaşehir	Philadelphia
Ankara	Ankyra, later Angora
Antakya	Antioch
Behramki	Assos
Bergama	Pergamum
Bodrum	Halicarnassus
Bolu	Claudiopolis
Edremit	Adramyttium
Demre	Myra
Edirne	Adrianople
Efes	Ephesus
Foça	Phocea
Gelibolu	Gallipoli
Harbiye	Daphne
Istanbul	Byzantium, later Constantinople
İzmir	Smyrna
İznik	Nicaea
Milâs	Miletus
Pamukkale	Hierapolis
Samsat	Samosata
Sart	Sardis
Trabzon	Trebizond
Zile	Zela (Julius Caesar came here to finish off a war and sent the epigrammatic message back to Rome, 'Veni, vidi, vici.')

Index

TL 13000 = £1.00